Environmental Protection Act 1990

CHAPTER 43

Explanatory Notes are available separately

GRAN*GIS* UK Publishing

Adapted and published by GRANGIS (Grand Register Library).
Online: www.grangis.com
E-mail: contact@grangis.com

In this version:
ISBN: 979-8-88559-018-1

Note: This is the original version (as it was originally enacted). Title, sub-title and the generated date is as marked on the pages.

Environmental Protection Act 1990

CHAPTER 43

ENVIRONMENTAL PROTECTION ACT 1990

PART I

INTEGRATED POLLUTION CONTROL AND AIR POLLUTION CONTROL BY LOCAL AUTHORITIES

Preliminary

Authorisations

Enforcement

Preliminary

General controls

Consents

Inspectors

Enforcement powers and offences

Publicity

Supplementary

PART VII

NATURE CONSERVATION IN GREAT BRITAIN AND COUNTRYSIDE MATTERS IN WALES

New Councils for England, Scotland and Wales

Countryside matters

Nature conservation in Great Britain

Transfer of property, rights and liabilities to new Councils

Employment by new Councils of staff of existing bodies

Dissolution of Nature Conservancy Council

Transitional provisions and savings

PART VIII

MISCELLANEOUS

Other controls on substances, articles or waste

Pollution at sea

Control of Dogs

Preliminary

1 In this Part of this Schedule— "authority" means an existing...

Notice of direction

2 (1) The Secretary of State, before giving any directions to...

Applications for exemption from and representations about directions

3 (1) An authority which has been given notice under paragraph...

Directions

4 (1) A direction may require the authority or authorities to...

Formation and status of companies

5 (1) An authority which has been directed to form a...

Transfer schemes

6 (1) Where an authority has formed a company or companies...

Transfer schemes: supplementary provisions

7 A scheme under paragraph 6 above may define the property,...
8 (1) The provisions of this paragraph apply to the transfer...

Tax and company provisions

9 (1) Any shares in a company which are issued as...

Benefit of certain planning permission

10 (1) This paragraph applies in relation to planning permission deemed...

Right to production of documents of title

11 Where on any transfer by virtue of a transfer scheme...

Proof of title by certificate

12 (1) A joint certificate by or on behalf of the...

Construction of agreements

13 Where any of the rights or liabilities transferred by a...
14 Without prejudice to the generality of the provisions of paragraph...

Third parties affected by vesting provisions

15 (1) Without prejudice to the provisions of paragraphs 13 and...

Transfer of staff

16 (1) The Transfer of Undertakings (Protection of Employment) Regulations 1981...

Retention, return and disposal of trolleys

3 (1) Subject to the following sub-paragraphs, the local authority, as...

Charges

4 (1) The local authority, in fixing the charge to be...

Definitions

5 In this Schedule— "luggage trolley" means a trolley provided by...

SCHEDULE 5 — Further Amendments of the Radioactive Substances Act 1960
Part I — MISCELLANEOUS AND CONSEQUENTIAL AMENDMENTS

Amendments relating to appointment of chief inspector

1 (1) Section 8 of the 1960 Act (requirement for disposal...
2 (1) In section 9 (functions of public and local authorities)...
3 In section 19 (general interpretation), after the definition of "the...

Amendments consequential on the introduction of fees and charges

4 (1) In section 1(2) (applications for registration of users of...
5 In section 19 (interpretation), in the definition of "prescribed" after...

Documents to be sent to local authorities

6 (1) In section 1 of the 1960 Act (registration for...

Mobile radioactive apparatus

7 (1) In section 3 of the 1960 Act (registration of...

Site and disposal records

8 After section 8 of the 1960 Act there shall be...

Hearings in connection with certain authorisations

9 (1) In section 11 of the 1960 Act (procedure in...

Appeals against certain other decisions of the chief inspector

10 After the section 11C of the 1960 Act inserted by...

Period within which applications under Act to be determined

11 (1) In section 1 of the 1960 Act (registration for...

Directions to chief inspector

12 After section 12 of the 1960 Act there shall be...

Inspectors: powers and protection

13 (1) Section 12 of the 1960 Act (rights of entry...

Offences under 1960 Act

14 (1) Section 13 of the 1960 Act (offences) shall be...

Public access to certain information

15 After section 13 (offences) of the 1960 Act there shall...

Expenses and receipts

16 In section 16 of the 1960 Act (expenses and receipts)—...

Meaning of "radioactive material" for purposes of 1960 Act

17 In section 18 of the 1960 Act (meaning of expression...

Part II — AMENDMENTS RELATING TO SCOTLAND AND NORTHERN IRELAND

Scotland

18 In section 20 of the 1960 Act (application of Act...
19 (1) In Schedule 1 to the 1960 Act (enactments, other...

Northern Ireland

20 In section 21 of the 1960 Act (application of Act...

SCHEDULE 6 — The Nature Conservancy Councils for England and Scotland and the Countryside Council for Wales: Constitution.

Preliminary

1 In this Part of this Schedule any reference to the...

Constitution and membership

2 The council shall be a body corporate.
3 (1) The council shall not be regarded as the servant...
4 (1) The Secretary of State shall appoint one of the...
5 A member of the council who ceases to be a...
6 The Secretary of State may remove a member of the...

Remuneration and allowances for members of council

7 (1) The council shall— (a) pay to their members such...

Staff

8 (1) There shall be a chief officer of the council....
9 The council may appoint such number of other employees as...
10 The council shall pay to the chief officer and their...
11 The council shall, in the case of such of their...

Proceedings

12 (1) The council may regulate their own procedure (including making...

Delegation of powers

13 (1) Anything authorised or required by or under any enactment...

Committees

14 (1) The council may appoint persons who are not members...

Documents

15 (1) This paragraph applies in England and Wales only.
16 (1) Sub-paragraphs (2) and (3) below apply in Scotland only;...

Public Records

17 In Schedule 1 to the Public Records Act 1958 (definition...

Land

18 (1) For the purposes of the application of any enactment...

Reports, accounts etc.

19 The council shall— (a) furnish the Secretary of State with...
20 (1) The council shall— (a) as soon as possible after...
21 (1) The council shall keep proper accounts and other records,...

Superannuation Act 1965 (c. 74)

22 In paragraph 7 of section 39(1) of the Superannuation Act...

Parliamentary Commissioner Act 1967 (c. 13)

23 In Schedule 2 to the Parliamentary Commissioner Act 1967 (departments...

House of Commons Disqualification Act 1975 (c. 24)

24 In Part III of Schedule 1 to the House of...

Inheritance Tax Act 1984 (c. 51)

25 In Schedule 3 to the Inheritance Tax Act 1984 (gifts...

SCHEDULE 7 — The Joint Nature Conservation Committee

Preliminary

1 In this Schedule— "chairman" means (except in paragraph 2(1) below)...

Membership

2 (1) The committee shall consist of eleven voting members, namely—...
3 The chairman and the three members appointed by the Secretary...
4 (1) The three members appointed by the Secretary of State...

Remuneration and allowances for members

5 (1) The councils shall— (a) pay to the chairman such...
6 The councils shall pay to the three members appointed by...

Staff etc. and expenses

7 (1) The councils shall provide the committee with such staff,...

Proceedings

8 (1) The committee may regulate their own procedure (including making...

Delegation of functions

9 (1) Anything authorised or required to be done by the...

Annual reports

10 (1) The committee shall— (a) as soon as possible after...

SCHEDULE 8 — Amendment of Enactments relating to Countryside Matters

National Parks and Access to the Countryside Act 1949 (c. 97)

1 (1) The National Parks and Access to the Countryside Act...

The Countryside Act 1968 (c. 41)

2 (1) The Countryside Act 1968 shall be amended as follows....

Local Government Act 1972 (c. 70)

3 In Part I of Schedule 17 to the Local Government...

Local Government Act 1974 (c. 7)

4 In section 7 of the Local Government Act 1974 (supplementary...

Highways Act 1980 (c. 66)

5 (1) The Highways Act 1980 shall be amended as follows....

Wildlife and Countryside Act 1981 (c. 69)

6 (1) The Wildlife and Countryside Act 1981 shall be amended...

The Road Traffic Regulation Act 1984 (c. 27)

7 In section 22 of the Road Traffic Regulation Act 1984...

The Water Act 1989 (c. 15)

8 In section 152 of the Water Act 1989 (restrictions on...

SCHEDULE 9 — Amendment of Enactments conferring Nature Conservancy Functions

National Parks and Access to the Countryside Act 1949 (c. 97)

1 (1) The National Parks and Access to the Countryside Act...

Deer (Scotland) Act 1959 (c. 40)

2 In section 1 of the Deer (Scotland) Act 1959 (constitution...

Deer Act 1963 (c. 36)

3 In section 11 of the Deer Act 1963 (power to...

Countryside Act 1968 (c. 41)

4 (1) The Countryside Act 1968 shall be amended as follows....

Conservation of Seals Act 1970 (c. 30)

5 In section 10 of the Conservation of Seals Act 1970...

Badgers Act 1973 (c. 57)

6 (1) Section 9 of the Badgers Act 1973 (power to...

Import of Live Fish (Scotland) Act 1978 (c. 35)

7 In section 1 of the Import of Live Fish (Scotland)...

Import of Live Fish (England and Wales) Act 1980 (c. 27)

8 In section 1 of the Import of Live Fish (England...

Highways Act 1980 (c. 66)

9 In section 105A of the Highways Act 1980 (environmental assessment...

Animal Health Act 1981 (c. 22)

10 (1) The Animal Health Act 1981 shall be amended as...

Wildlife and Countryside Act 1981 (c. 69)

11 (1) The Wildlife and Countryside Act 1981 shall be amended...

Roads (Scotland) Act 1984 (c. 54)

12 In section 20A of the Roads (Scotland) Act 1984 (environmental...

Agriculture Act 1986 (c. 49)

13 In section 18 of the Agriculture Act 1986 (environmentally sensitive...

Channel Tunnel Act 1987 (c. 53)

14 In paragraph 5 of Schedule 2, and in paragraph 17...

Norfolk and Suffolk Broads Act 1988 (c. 4)

15 In the Norfolk and Suffolk Broads Act 1988, for each...

Electricity Act 1989 (c. 29)

16 In Schedule 9 to the Electricity Act 1989 (preservation of...

Water Act 1989 (c. 15)

17 (1) The Water Act 1989 shall be amended as follows....

SCHEDULE 10 — Transfer Schemes and Staff of Existing Councils
Part I — TRANSFER SCHEMES: NATURE CONSERVANCY COUNCIL

Making and approval of schemes

1 (1) Before such date or dates as the Secretary of...

Modification of schemes

2 (1) If at any time after a transfer scheme has...

Provision of information to Secretary of State

3 It shall be the duty of the Nature Conservancy Council...

Contents of schemes

4 A transfer scheme may— (a) define the property, rights and...
5 For the avoidance of doubt property, rights and liabilities of...
Part II — TRANSFER SCHEMES: THE COUNTRYSIDE COMMISSION

Making and approval of schemes

6 (1) Before such date or dates as the Secretary of...

Modification of schemes

7 (1) If at any time after a transfer scheme has...

Provision of information to Secretary of State

8 It shall be the duty of the Countryside Council for...

Contents of schemes

9 (1) A transfer scheme may— (a) define the property, rights...
Part III — EMPLOYMENT OF STAFF OF EXISTING BODIES

Proposals for staff of Nature Conservancy Council

10 Not later than such date or dates as the Secretary...
11 (1) The Secretary of State may, after consultation with the...

Proposals for certain staff of the Countryside Commission

12 Not later than such date or dates as the Secretary...
13 (1) The Secretary of State may, after consultation with the...

Offers of employment

14 (1) Each new Council shall, before such date as the...

Exclusion of Clean Air Act 1956 for prescribed processes

6 In the Clean Air Act 1956 there shall be inserted,...

Statutory nuisances

7 (1) The following provisions of the Clean Air Act 1956...
8 The Radioactive Substances Act 1960 shall be amended by the...
9 In section 1(1)(g) of the Hovercraft Act 1986 (power to...

Goods vehicle operators' licences: pollution offences

10 (1) The following provisions of of the Transport Act 1968...

National Park Wardens

11 In section 42 of the Countryside Act 1968 (National Park...

Exclusion of Clean Air Act 1968 for prescribed processes

12 In the Clean Air Act 1968 there shall be inserted,...

Sale of electricity: Scotland

13 In section 170A(3) of the Local Government (Scotland) Act 1973...

Workplace emissions into the air

14 Section 5 of the Health and Safety at Work etc....

Water, noise and atmospheric pollution

15 (1) The following provisions of the Control of Pollution Act...
16 (1) The Control of Pollution Act 1974 shall be further...

Exclusion of Part II of Control of Pollution Act 1974 for radioactive substances: Scotland

17 For subsection (6) of section 56 of the Control of...

Statutory nuisances

18 In Section 33(2) of the Land Drainage Act 1976 (restriction...

Refuse Disposal: Scotland

19 (1) Section 1 of the Refuse Disposal (Amenity) Act 1978...

Street cleansing: Scotland

20 In section 25 of the Local Government and Planning (Scotland)...

Byelaws relating to straw or stubble burning

21 Section 43 of the Criminal Justice Act 1982 (creation by...

Functions assignable to London port health authority

22 In section 7(4) of the Public Health (Control of Disease)...

Street cleaning, etc: restriction of traffic

23 (1) Section 14 of the Road Traffic Regulation Act 1984...

Statutory nuisance

24 In section 76(1)(b) and (4)(a) of the Building Act 1984,...

Registers of deposits etc. at sea: Northern Ireland Assembly control of regulations

25 In section 25(3) of the Food and Environment Protection Act...

Constitution of authorities for waste disposal

26 In section 10 of the Local Government Act 1985 (joint...

Meaning of household waste: competition

27 In Schedule 1 to the Local Government Act 1988 (competition:...

Exclusion of Water Act 1989 controls of exercise of trade effluent functions in case of prescribed processes

28 (1) Section 74 of the Water Act 1989 (control by...

Exclusion of Part III of Water Act 1989 for discharges from prescribed processes

29 (1) Section 108 of the Water Act 1989 (no pollution...

Contents of registers of National Rivers Authority

30 In section 117(1) of the Water Act 1989 (registers for...

Carriers of controlled waste

31 (1) The Control of Pollution (Amendment) Act 1989 shall be...

Environmental Protection Act 1990

1990 CHAPTER 43

An Act to make provision for the improved control of pollution arising from certain industrial and other processes; to re-enact the provisions of the Control of Pollution Act 1974 relating to waste on land with modifications as respects the functions of the regulatory and other authorities concerned in the collection and disposal of waste and to make further provision in relation to such waste; to restate the law defining statutory nuisances and improve the summary procedures for dealing with them, to provide for the termination of the existing controls over offensive trades or businesses and to provide for the extension of the Clean Air Acts to prescribed gases; to amend the law relating to litter and make further provision imposing or conferring powers to impose duties to keep public places clear of litter and clean; to make provision conferring powers in relation to trolleys abandoned on land in the open air; to amend the Radioactive Substances Act 1960; to make provision for the control of genetically modified organisms; to make provision for the abolition of the Nature Conservancy Council and for the creation of councils to replace it and discharge the functions of that Council and, as respects Wales, of the Countryside Commission; to make further provision for the control of the importation, exportation, use, supply or storage of prescribed substances and articles and the importation or exportation of prescribed descriptions of waste; to confer powers to obtain information about potentially hazardous substances; to amend the law relating to the control of hazardous substances on, over or under land; to amend section 107(6) of the Water Act 1989 and sections 31(7)(a), 31A(2)(c)(i) and 32(7)(a) of the Control of Pollution Act 1974; to amend the provisions of the Food and Environment Protection Act 1985 as regards the dumping of waste at sea; to make further provision as respects the prevention of oil pollution from ships; to make provision for and in connection with the identification and control of dogs; to confer powers to control the burning of crop residues; to make provision in relation to financial or other assistance for purposes connected with the environment; to make provision as respects superannuation of employees of the Groundwork Foundation and for remunerating the chairman of the Inland Waterways Amenity Advisory Council; and for purposes connected with those purposes. [1st November 1990]

Be it enacted by the Queen's most Excellent Majesty, by and with the advice and consent of the Lords Spiritual and Temporal, and Commons, in this present Parliament assembled, and by the authority of the same, as follows:—

PART I

INTEGRATED POLLUTION CONTROL AND AIR POLLUTION CONTROL BY LOCAL AUTHORITIES

Preliminary

1 Preliminary

(1) The following provisions have effect for the interpretation of this Part.

(2) The "environment" consists of all, or any, of the following media, namely, the air, water and land; and the medium of air includes the air within buildings and the air within other natural or man-made structures above or below ground.

(3) "Pollution of the environment" means pollution of the environment due to the release (into any environmental medium) from any process of substances which are capable of causing harm to man or any other living organisms supported by the environment.

(4) "Harm" means harm to the health of living organisms or other interference with the ecological systems of which they form part and, in the case of man, includes offence caused to any of his senses or harm to his property; and "harmless" has a corresponding meaning.

(5) "Process" means any activities carried on in Great Britain, whether on premises or by means of mobile plant, which are capable of causing pollution of the environment and "prescribed process" means a process prescribed under section 2(1) below.

(6) For the purposes of subsection (5) above—

"activities" means industrial or commercial activities or activities of any other nature whatsoever (including, with or without other activities, the keeping of a substance);

"Great Britain" includes so much of the adjacent territorial sea as is, or is treated as, relevant territorial waters for the purposes of Chapter 1 of Part III of the Water Act 1989 or, as respects Scotland, Part II of the Control of Pollution Act 1974; and

"mobile plant" means plant which is designed to move or to be moved whether on roads or otherwise.

(7) The "enforcing authority", in relation to England and Wales, is the chief inspector or the local authority by whom, under section 4 below, the functions conferred or imposed by this Part otherwise than on the Secretary of State are for the time being exercisable in relation respectively to releases of substances into the environment or into the air; and "local enforcing authority" means any such local authority.

(8) The "enforcing authority", in relation to Scotland, is—

(a) in relation to releases of substances into the environment, the chief inspector or the river purification authority (which in this Part means a river purification authority within the meaning of the Rivers (Prevention of Pollution) (Scotland) Act 1951),

(b) in relation to releases of substances into the air, the local authority,

by whom, under section 4 below, the functions conferred or imposed by this Part otherwise than on the Secretary of State are for the time being exercisable; and "local enforcing authority" means any such local authority.

(9) "Authorisation" means an authorisation for a process (whether on premises or by means of mobile plant) granted under section 6 below; and a reference to the conditions of an authorisation is a reference to the conditions subject to which at any time the authorisation has effect.

(10) A substance is "released" into any environmental medium whenever it is released directly into that medium whether it is released into it within or outside Great Britain and "release" includes—

(a) in relation to air, any emission of the substance into the air;

(b) in relation to water, any entry (including any discharge) of the substance into water;

(c) in relation to land, any deposit, keeping or disposal of the substance in or on land;

and for this purpose "water" and "land" shall be construed in accordance with subsections (11) and (12) below.

(11) For the purpose of determining into what medium a substance is released—

(a) any release into—

(i) the sea or the surface of the seabed,

(ii) any river, watercourse, lake, loch or pond (whether natural or artificial or above or below ground) or reservoir or the surface of the riverbed or of other land supporting such waters, or

(iii) ground waters,

is a release into water;

(b) any release into—

(i) land covered by water falling outside paragraph (a) above or the water covering such land; or

(ii) the land beneath the surface of the seabed or of other land supporting waters falling within paragraph (a)(ii) above,

is a release into land; and

(c) any release into a sewer (within the meaning of the Public Health Act 1936 or, in relation to Scotland, of the Sewerage (Scotland) Act 1968) shall be treated as a release into water;

but a sewer and its contents shall be disregarded in determining whether there is pollution of the environment at any time.

(12) In subsection (11) above "ground waters" means any waters contained in underground strata, or in—

(a) a well, borehole or similar work sunk into underground strata, including any adit or passage constructed in connection with the well, borehole or work for facilitating the collection of water in the well, borehole or work; or

(b) any excavation into underground strata where the level of water in the excavation depends wholly or mainly on water entering it from the strata.

(13) "Substance" shall be treated as including electricity or heat and "prescribed substance" has the meaning given by section 2(7) below.

2 Prescribed processes and prescribed substances

(1) The Secretary of State may, by regulations, prescribe any description of process as a process for the carrying on of which after a prescribed date an authorisation is required under section 6 below.

(2) Regulations under subsection (1) above may frame the description of a process by reference to any characteristics of the process or the area or other circumstances in which the process is carried on or the description of person carrying it on.

(3) Regulations under subsection (1) above may prescribe or provide for the determination under the regulations of different dates for different descriptions of persons and may include such transitional provisions as the Secretary of State considers necessary or expedient as respects the making of applications for authorisations and suspending the application of section 6(1) below until the determination of applications made within the period allowed by the regulations.

(4) Regulations under subsection (1) above shall, as respects each description of process, designate it as one for central control or one for local control.

(5) The Secretary of State may, by regulations, prescribe any description of substance as a substance the release of which into the environment is subject to control under sections 6 and 7 below.

(6) Regulations under subsection (5) above may—

(a) prescribe separately, for each environmental medium, the substances the release of which into that medium is to be subject to control; and

(b) provide that a description of substance is only prescribed, for any environmental medium, so far as it is released into that medium in such amounts over such periods, in such concentrations or in such other circumstances as may be specified in the regulations;

and in relation to a substance of a description which is prescribed for releases into the air, the regulations may designate the substance as one for central control or one for local control.

(7) In this Part "prescribed substance" means any substance of a description prescribed in regulations under subsection (5) above or, in the case of a substance of a description prescribed only for releases in circumstances specified under subsection (6)(b) above, means any substance of that description which is released in those circumstances.

3 Emission etc. limits and quality objectives

(1) The Secretary of State may make regulations under subsection (2) or (4) below establishing standards, objectives or requirements in relation to particular prescribed processes or particular substances.

(2) Regulations under this subsection may—

(a) in relation to releases of any substance from prescribed processes into any environmental medium, prescribe standard limits for—
   (i) the concentration, the amount or the amount in any period of that substance which may be so released; and
   (ii) any other characteristic of that substance in any circumstances in which it may be so released;

(b) prescribe standard requirements for the measurement or analysis of, or of releases of, substances for which limits have been set under paragraph (a) above; and

(c) in relation to any prescribed process, prescribe standards or requirements as to any aspect of the process.

(3) Regulations under subsection (2) above may make different provision in relation to different cases, including different provision in relation to different processes, descriptions of person, localities or other circumstances.

(4) Regulations under this subsection may establish for any environmental medium (in all areas or in specified areas) quality objectives or quality standards in relation to any substances which may be released into that or any other medium from any process.

(5) The Secretary of State may make plans for—

(a) establishing limits for the total amount, or the total amount in any period, of any substance which may be released into the environment in, or in any area within, the United Kingdom;

(b) allocating quotas as respects the release of substances to persons carrying on processes in respect of which any such limit is established;

(c) establishing limits of the descriptions specified in subsection (2)(a) above so as progressively to reduce pollution of the environment;

(d) the progressive improvement in the quality objectives and quality standards established by regulations under subsection (4) above;

and the Secretary of State may, from time to time, revise any plan so made.

(6) Regulations or plans under this section may be made for any purposes of this Part or for other purposes.

(7) The Secretary of State shall give notice in the London, Edinburgh and Belfast Gazettes of the making and the revision of any plan under subsection (5) above and shall make the documents containing the plan, or the plan as so revised, available for inspection by members of the public at the places specified in the notice.

(8) Subject to any Order made after the passing of this Act by virtue of subsection (1)(a) of section 3 of the Northern Ireland Constitution Act 1973, the making and revision of plans under subsection (5) above shall not be a transferred matter for the purposes of that Act but shall for the purposes of subsection (2) of that section be treated as specified in Schedule 3 to that Act.

4 Discharge and scope of functions

(1) This section determines the authority by whom the functions conferred or imposed by this Part otherwise than on the Secretary of State are exercisable and the purposes for which they are exercisable.

(2) Those functions, in their application to prescribed processes designated for central control, shall be functions of the chief inspector appointed for England and Wales by the Secretary of State under section 16 below and, in relation to Scotland, of the chief inspector so appointed for Scotland or of the river purification authority, as determined under regulations made under section 5(1) below, and shall be exercisable for the purpose of preventing or minimising pollution of the environment due to the release of substances into any environmental medium.

(3) Subject to subsection (4) below, those functions, in their application to prescribed processes designated for local control, shall be functions of—

(a) in the case of a prescribed process carried on (or to be carried on) by means of mobile plant, the local authority in whose area the person carrying on the process has his principal place of business; and

(b) in any other cases, the local authority in whose area the prescribed processes are (or are to be) carried on;

and the functions applicable to such processes shall be exercisable for the purpose of preventing or minimising pollution of the environment due to the release of substances into the air (but not into any other environmental medium).

(4) The Secretary of State may, as respects the functions under this Part being exercised by a local authority specified in the direction, direct that those functions shall be exercised instead by the chief inspector while the direction remains in force or during a period specified in the direction.

(5) A transfer of functions under subsection (4) above to the chief inspector does not make them exercisable by him for the purpose of preventing or minimising pollution of the environment due to releases of substances into any other environmental medium than the air.

(6) A direction under subsection (4) above may transfer those functions as exercisable in relation to all or any description of prescribed processes carried on by all or any description of persons (a "general direction") or in relation to a prescribed process carried on by a specified person (a "specific direction").

(7) A direction under subsection (4) above may include such saving and transitional provisions as the Secretary of State considers necessary or expedient.

(8) The Secretary of State, on giving or withdrawing a direction under subsection (4) above, shall—

(a) in the case of a general direction—

(i) forthwith serve notice of it on the chief inspector and on the local enforcing authorities affected by the direction; and

(ii) cause notice of it to be published as soon as practicable in the London Gazette or, as the case may be, in the Edinburgh Gazette and in at least one newspaper circulating in the area of each authority affected by the direction;

(b) in the case of a specific direction—

(i) forthwith serve notice of it on the chief inspector, the local enforcing authority and the person carrying on or appearing to the Secretary of State to be carrying on the process affected, and

(ii) cause notice of it to be published as soon as practicable in the London Gazette or, as the case may be, in the Edinburgh Gazette and in at least one newspaper circulating in the authority's area;

and any such notice shall specify the date at which the direction is to take (or took) effect and (where appropriate) its duration.

(9) It shall be the duty of the chief inspector or, in Scotland, of the chief inspector and river purification authorities to follow developments in technology and techniques for preventing or reducing pollution of the environment due to releases of substances from prescribed processes; and the local enforcing authorities shall follow such of those developments as concern releases into the air of substances from prescribed processes designated for local control.

(10) It shall be the duty of the chief inspector, river purification authorities and the local enforcing authorities to give effect to any directions given to them under any provision of this Part.

(11) In this Part "local authority" means, subject to subsection (12) below—

(a) in Greater London, a London borough council, the Common Council of the City of London, the Sub-Treasurer of the Inner Temple and the Under Treasurer of the Middle Temple;

(b) outside Greater London, a district council and the Council of the Isles of Scilly; and

(c) in Scotland, an islands or district council.

(12) Where, by an order under section 2 of the Public Health (Control of Disease) Act 1984, a port health authority has been constituted for any port health district, the port health authority shall have by virtue of this subsection, as respects its district, the functions conferred or imposed by this Part and no such order shall be made assigning those functions; and "local authority" and "area" shall be construed accordingly.

5 Further provision as to discharge and scope of functions: Scotland

(1) For the purposes of section 4(2) above in its application to Scotland, the Secretary of State shall make regulations prescribing—

(a) the method and arrangements for determining whether the functions referred to in that subsection shall be functions of the chief inspector or of a river purification authority;

(b) if the functions are determined under paragraph (a) above to be functions of a river purification authority, the river purification authority by whom they are to be exercised.

(2) The Secretary of State may make regulations prescribing—

(a) the circumstances and manner in which consultation shall be carried out between—

(i) whichever of the chief inspector or river purification authority is determined under regulations made under subsection (1) above to be the enforcing authority, and

(ii) the other (the "consulted authority"),

before granting, varying, transferring or revoking an authorisation or serving an enforcement or prohibition notice;

(b) the circumstances in which the consulted authority may require the enforcing authority to include, in an authorisation, conditions which the consulted authority reasonably believe will achieve the objectives specified in section 7(2) below.

(3) Regulations under this section may contain such incidental, supplemental and consequential provision as the Secretary of State considers appropriate.

(4) This section applies to Scotland only.

Authorisations

6 Authorisations: general provisions

(1) No person shall carry on a prescribed process after the date prescribed or determined for that description of process by or under regulations under section 2(1) above (but subject to any transitional provision made by the regulations) except under an authorisation granted by the enforcing authority and in accordance with the conditions to which it is subject.

(2) An application for an authorisation shall be made to the enforcing authority in accordance with Part I of Schedule 1 to this Act and shall be accompanied by the fee prescribed under section 8(2)(a) below.

(3) Where an application is duly made to the enforcing authority, the authority shall either grant the authorisation subject to the conditions required or authorised to be imposed by section 7 below or refuse the application.

(4) An application shall not be granted unless the enforcing authority considers that the applicant will be able to carry on the process so as to comply with the conditions which would be included in the authorisation.

(5) The Secretary of State may, if he thinks fit in relation to any application for an authorisation, give to the enforcing authority directions as to whether or not the authority should grant the authorisation.

(6) The enforcing authority shall, as respects each authorisation in respect of which it has functions under this Part, from time to time but not less frequently than once in every period of four years, carry out a review of the conditions of the authorisation.

(7) The Secretary of State may, by regulations, substitute for the period for the time being specified in subsection (6) above such other period as he thinks fit.

(8) Schedule 1 to this Act (supplementary provisions) shall have effect in relation to authorisations.

7 Conditions of authorisations

(1) There shall be included in an authorisation—

(a) subject to paragraph (b) below, such specific conditions as the enforcing authority considers appropriate, when taken with the general condition implied by subsection (4) below, for achieving the objectives specified in subsection (2) below;

(b) such conditions as are specified in directions given by the Secretary of State under subsection (3) below; and

(c) such other conditions (if any) as appear to the enforcing authority to be appropriate;

but no conditions shall be imposed for the purpose only of securing the health of persons at work (within the meaning of Part I of the Health and Safety at Work etc. Act 1974).

(2) Those objectives are—

(a) ensuring that, in carrying on a prescribed process, the best available techniques not entailing excessive cost will be used—

(i) for preventing the release of substances prescribed for any environmental medium into that medium or, where that is not practicable by such means, for reducing the release of such substances to a minimum and for rendering harmless any such substances which are so released; and

(ii) for rendering harmless any other substances which might cause harm if released into any environmental medium;

(b) compliance with any directions by the Secretary of State given for the implementation of any obligations of the United Kingdom under the Community Treaties or international law relating to environmental protection;

(c) compliance with any limits or requirements and achievement of any quality standards or quality objectives prescribed by the Secretary of State under any of the relevant enactments;

(d) compliance with any requirements applicable to the grant of authorisations specified by or under a plan made by the Secretary of State under section 3(5) above.

(3) Except as respects the general condition implied by subsection (4) below, the Secretary of State may give directions to the enforcing authorities as to the conditions which are, or are not, to be included in all authorisations, in authorisations of any specified description or in any particular authorisation.

(4) Subject to subsections (5) and (6) below, there is implied in every authorisation a general condition that, in carrying on the process to which the authorisation applies, the person carrying it on must use the best available techniques not entailing excessive cost—

(a) for preventing the release of substances prescribed for any environmental medium into that medium or, where that is not practicable by such means, for reducing the release of such substances to a minimum and for rendering harmless any such substances which are so released; and

(b) for rendering harmless any other substances which might cause harm if released into any environmental medium.

(5) In the application of subsections (1) to (4) above to authorisations granted by a local enforcing authority references to the release of substances into any environmental medium are to be read as references to the release of substances into the air.

(6) The obligation implied by virtue of subsection (4) above shall not apply in relation to any aspect of the process in question which is regulated by a condition imposed under subsection (1) above.

(7) The objectives referred to in subsection (2) above shall, where the process—

(a) is one designated for central control; and

(b) is likely to involve the release of substances into more than one environmental medium;

include the objective of ensuring that the best available techniques not entailing excessive cost will be used for minimising the pollution which may be caused to the environment taken as a whole by the releases having regard to the best practicable environmental option available as respects the substances which may be released.

(8) An authorisation for carrying on a prescribed process may, without prejudice to the generality of subsection (1) above, include conditions—

(a) imposing limits on the amount or composition of any substance produced by or utilised in the process in any period; and

(b) requiring advance notification of any proposed change in the manner of carrying on the process.

(9) This section has effect subject to section 28 below and, in relation to Scotland, to any regulations made under section 5(2) above.

(10) References to the best available techniques not entailing excessive cost, in relation to a process, include (in addition to references to any technical means and technology) references to the number, qualifications, training and supervision of persons employed in the process and the design, construction, lay-out and maintenance of the buildings in which it is carried on.

(11) It shall be the duty of enforcing authorities to have regard to any guidance issued to them by the Secretary of State for the purposes of the application of subsections (2) and (7) above as to the techniques and environmental options that are appropriate for any description of prescribed process.

(12) In subsection (2) above "the relevant enactments" are any enactments or instruments contained in or made for the time being under—

(a) section 2 of the Clean Air Act 1968;

(b) section 2 of the European Communities Act 1972;

(c) Part I of the Health and Safety at Work etc. Act 1974;

(d) Parts II, III or IV of the Control of Pollution Act 1974;

(e) Part III of the Water Act 1989; and

(f) section 3 of this Act.

8 Fees and charges for authorisations

(1) There shall be charged by and paid to the enforcing authority such fees and charges as may be prescribed from time to time by a scheme under subsection (2) below (whether by being specified in or made calculable under the scheme).

(2) The Secretary of State may, with the approval of the Treasury, make, and from time to time revise, a scheme prescribing—

(a) fees payable in respect of applications for authorisations;

(b) fees payable by persons holding authorisations in respect of, or of applications for, the variation of authorisations; and

(c) charges payable by such persons in respect of the subsistence of their authorisations.

(3) The Secretary of State shall, on making or revising a scheme under subsection (2) above, lay a copy of the scheme or of the alterations made in the scheme or, if he considers it more appropriate, the scheme as revised, before each House of Parliament.

(4) The Secretary of State may make separate schemes for fees and charges payable to the chief inspector or, as the case may be, river purification authority and fees and charges payable to local enforcing authorities under this Part.

(5) A scheme under subsection (2) above may, in particular—

(a) make different provision for different cases, including different provision in relation to different persons, circumstances or localities;

(b) allow for reduced fees or charges to be payable in respect of authorisations for a number of prescribed processes carried on by the same person;

(c) provide for the times at which and the manner in which the payments required by the scheme are to be made; and

(d) make such incidental, supplementary and transitional provision as appears to the Secretary of State to be appropriate.

(6) The Secretary of State, in framing a scheme under subsection (2) above, shall, so far as practicable, secure that the fees and charges payable under the scheme are sufficient, taking one financial year with another, to cover the relevant expenditure attributable to authorisations.

(7) The "relevant expenditure attributable to authorisations" is the expenditure incurred by the enforcing authorities in exercising their functions under this Part in relation to authorisations together with the expenditure incurred by the National Rivers Authority in exercising the Authority's functions in relation to authorisations for processes which may involve the release of any substance into water.

(8) If it appears to the enforcing authority that the holder of an authorisation has failed to pay a charge due in consideration of the subsistence of the authorisation, it may, by notice in writing served on the holder, revoke the authorisation.

(9) The Secretary of State may make to the National Rivers Authority payments of such amounts as appear to him to be required to meet the estimated relevant expenditure of the Authority attributable to authorisations.

(10) Subsections (7) and (9) above shall not apply to Scotland, but in relation to Scotland the "relevant expenditure attributable to authorisations" is the expenditure incurred by the enforcing authorities in exercising their functions under this Part or in relation to consultation carried out under regulations made under section 5(2) above.

(11) In Scotland, the chief inspector may make to a river purification authority and a river purification authority may make to the chief inspector payments of such amounts as are appropriate to meet their estimated relevant expenditure attributable to authorisations, such amounts to be determined by the Secretary of State if the chief inspector and the authority fail to agree on an appropriate amount of payment.

9 Transfer of authorisations

(1) An authorisation for the carrying on of any prescribed process may be transferred by the holder to a person who proposes to carry on the process in the holder's place.

(2) Where an authorisation is transferred under this section, the person to whom it is transferred shall notify the enforcing authority in writing of that fact not later than the end of the period of twenty-one days beginning with the date of the transfer.

(3) An authorisation which is transferred under this section shall have effect on and after the date of the transfer as if it had been granted to that person under section 6 above, subject to the same conditions as were attached to it immediately before that date.

10 Variation of authorisations by enforcing authority

(1) The enforcing authority may at any time, subject to the requirements of section 7 above, and, in cases to which they apply, the requirements of Part II of Schedule 1 to this Act, vary an authorisation and shall do so if it appears to the authority at that time that that section requires conditions to be included which are different from the subsisting conditions.

(2) Where the enforcing authority has decided to vary an authorisation under subsection (1) above the authority shall notify the holder of the authorisation and serve a variation notice on him.

(3) In this Part a "variation notice" is a notice served by the enforcing authority on the holder of an authorisation—

(a) specifying variations of the authorisation which the enforcing authority has decided to make; and

(b) specifying the date or dates on which the variations are to take effect;

and, unless the notice is withdrawn, the variations specified in a variation notice shall take effect on the date or dates so specified.

(4) A variation notice served under subsection (2) above shall also—

(a) require the holder of the authorisation, within such period as may be specified in the notice, to notify the authority what action (if any) he proposes to take to ensure that the process is carried on in accordance with the authorisation as varied by the notice; and

(b) require the holder to pay the fee (if any) prescribed by a scheme under section 8 above within such period as may be specified in the notice.

(5) Where in the opinion of the enforcing authority any action to be taken by the holder of an authorisation in consequence of a variation notice served under subsection (2) above will involve a substantial change in the manner in which the process is being carried on, the enforcing authority shall notify the holder of its opinion.

(6) The Secretary of State may, if he thinks fit in relation to authorisations of any description or particular authorisations, direct the enforcing authorities—

(a) to exercise their powers under this section, or to do so in such circumstances as may be specified in the directions, in such manner as may be so specified; or

(b) not to exercise those powers, or not to do so in such circumstances or such manner as may be so specified;

and the Secretary of State shall have the corresponding power of direction in respect of the powers of the enforcing authorities to vary authorisations under section 11 below.

(7) In this section and section 11 below a "substantial change", in relation to a prescribed process being carried on under an authorisation, means a substantial change in the substances released from the process or in the amount or any other characteristic of any substance so released; and the Secretary of State may give directions to the enforcing authorities as to what does or does not constitute a substantial change in relation to processes generally, any description of process or any particular process.

(8) In this section and section 11 below—

"prescribed" means prescribed in regulations made by the Secretary of State;

"vary", in relation to the subsisting conditions or other provisions of an authorisation, means adding to them or varying or rescinding any of them;

and "variation" shall be construed accordingly.

11 Variation of conditions etc: applications by holders of authorisations

(1) A person carrying on a prescribed process under an authorisation who wishes to make a relevant change in the process may at any time—

(a) notify the enforcing authority in the prescribed form of that fact, and

(b) request the enforcing authority to make a determination, in relation to the proposed change, of the matters mentioned in subsection (2) below;

and a person making a request under paragraph (b) above shall furnish the enforcing authority with such information as may be prescribed or as the authority may by notice require.

(2) On receiving a request under subsection (1) above the enforcing authority shall determine—

(a) whether the proposed change would involve a breach of any condition of the authorisation;

(b) if it would not involve such a breach, whether the authority would be likely to vary the conditions of the authorisation as a result of the change;

(c) if it would involve such a breach, whether the authority would consider varying the conditions of the authorisation so that the change may be made; and

(d) whether the change would involve a substantial change in the manner in which the process is being carried on;

and the enforcing authority shall notify the holder of the authorisation of its determination of those matters.

(3) Where the enforcing authority has determined that the proposed change would not involve a substantial change, but has also determined under paragraph (b) or (c) of subsection (2) above that the change would lead to or require the variation of the conditions of the authorisation, then—

(a) the enforcing authority shall (either on notifying its determination under that subsection or on a subsequent occasion) notify the holder of the authorisation of the variations which the authority is likely to consider making; and

(b) the holder may apply in the prescribed form to the enforcing authority for the variation of the conditions of the authorisation so that he may make the proposed change.

(4) Where the enforcing authority has determined that a proposed change would involve a substantial change that would lead to or require the variation of the conditions of the authorisation, then—

(a) the authority shall (either on notifying its determination under subsection (2) above or on a subsequent occasion) notify the holder of the authorisation of the variations which the authority is likely to consider making; and

(b) the holder of the authorisation shall, if he wishes to proceed with the change, apply in the prescribed form to the enforcing authority for the variation of the conditions of the authorisation.

(5) The holder of an authorisation may at any time, unless he is carrying on a prescribed process under the authorisation and wishes to make a relevant change in the process, apply to the enforcing authority in the prescribed form for the variation of the conditions of the authorisation.

(6) A person carrying on a process under an authorisation who wishes to make a relevant change in the process may, where it appears to him that the change will require the variation of the conditions of the authorisation, apply to the enforcing authority in the prescribed form for the variation of the conditions of the authorisation specified in the application.

(7) A person who makes an application for the variation of the conditions of an authorisation shall furnish the authority with such information as may be prescribed or as the authority may by notice require.

(8) On an application for variation of the conditions of an authorisation under any provision of this section—

(a) the enforcing authority may, having fulfilled the requirements of Part II of Schedule 1 to this Act in cases to which they apply, as it thinks fit either refuse the application or, subject to the requirements of section 7 above, vary the conditions or, in the case of an application under subsection (6) above, treat the application as a request for a determination under subsection (2) above; and

(b) if the enforcing authority decides to vary the conditions, it shall serve a variation notice on the holder of the authorisation.

(9) Any application to the enforcing authority under this section shall be accompanied by the applicable fee (if any) prescribed by a scheme made under section 8 above.

(10) This section applies to any provision other than a condition which is contained in an authorisation as it applies to a condition with the modification that any reference to the breach of a condition shall be read as a reference to acting outside the scope of the authorisation.

(11) For the purposes of this section a relevant change in a prescribed process is a change in the manner of carrying on the process which is capable of altering the substances released from the process or of affecting the amount or any other characteristic of any substance so released.

12 Revocation of authorisation

(1) The enforcing authority may at any time revoke an authorisation by notice in writing to the person holding the authorisation.

(2) Without prejudice to the generality of subsection (1) above, the enforcing authority may revoke an authorisation where it has reason to believe that a prescribed process for which the authorisation is in force has not been carried on or not for a period of twelve months.

(3) The revocation of an authorisation under this section shall have effect from the date specified in the notice; and the period between the date on which the notice is served and the date so specified shall not be less than twenty-eight days.

(4) The enforcing authority may, before the date on which the revocation of an authorisation takes effect, withdraw the notice or vary the date specified in it.

(5) The Secretary of State may, if he thinks fit in relation to an authorisation, give to the enforcing authority directions as to whether the authority should revoke the authorisation under this section.

Enforcement

13 Enforcement notices

(1) If the enforcing authority is of the opinion that the person carrying on a prescribed process under an authorisation is contravening any condition of the authorisation, or is likely to contravene any such condition, the authority may serve on him a notice ("an enforcement notice").

(2) An enforcement notice shall—

(a) state that the authority is of the said opinion;

(b) specify the matters constituting the contravention or the matters making it likely that the contravention will arise, as the case may be;

(c) specify the steps that must be taken to remedy the contravention or to remedy the matters making it likely that the contravention will arise, as the case may be; and

(d) specify the period within which those steps must be taken.

(3) The Secretary of State may, if he thinks fit in relation to the carrying on by any person of a prescribed process, give to the enforcing authority directions as to whether the authority should exercise its powers under this section and as to the steps which are to be required to be taken under this section.

14 Prohibition notices

(1) If the enforcing authority is of the opinion, as respects the carrying on of a prescribed process under an authorisation, that the continuing to carry it on, or the continuing to carry it on in a particular manner, involves an imminent risk of serious pollution of the environment the authority shall serve a notice (a "prohibition notice") on the person carrying on the process.

(2) A prohibition notice may be served whether or not the manner of carrying on the process in question contravenes a condition of the authorisation and may relate to any aspects of the process, whether regulated by the conditions of the authorisation or not.

(3) A prohibition notice shall—

(a) state the authority's opinion;

(b) specify the risk involved in the process;

(c) specify the steps that must be taken to remove it and the period within which they must be taken; and

(d) direct that the authorisation shall, until the notice is withdrawn, wholly or to the extent specified in the notice cease to have effect to authorise the carrying on of the process;

and where the direction applies to part only of the process it may impose conditions to be observed in carrying on the part which is authorised to be carried on.

(4) The Secretary of State may, if he thinks fit in relation to the carrying on by any person of a prescribed process, give to the enforcing authority directions as to—

(a) whether the authority should perform its duties under this section; and

(b) the matters to be specified in any prohibition notice in pursuance of subsection (3) above which the authority is directed to issue.

(5) The enforcing authority shall, as respects any prohibition notice it has issued to any person, by notice in writing served on that person, withdraw the notice when it is satisfied that the steps required by the notice have been taken.

15 Appeals as respects authorisations and against variation, enforcement and prohibition notices

(1) The following persons, namely—

(a) a person who has been refused the grant of an authorisation under section 6 above;

(b) a person who is aggrieved by the conditions attached, under any provision of this Part, to his authorisation;

(c) a person who has been refused a variation of an authorisation on an application under section 11 above;

(d) a person whose authorisation has been revoked under section 12 above;

may appeal against the decision of the enforcing authority to the Secretary of State (except where the decision implements a direction of his).

(2) A person on whom a variation notice, an enforcement notice or a prohibition notice is served may appeal against the notice to the Secretary of State.

(3) Where an appeal under this section is made to the Secretary of State—

(a) the Secretary of State may refer any matter involved in the appeal to a person appointed by him for the purpose; or

(b) the Secretary of State may, instead of determining the appeal himself, direct that the appeal or any matter involved in it shall be determined by a person appointed by him for the purpose;

and a person appointed under paragraph (b) above for the purpose of an appeal shall have the same powers under subsection (5), (6) or (7) below as the Secretary of State.

(4) An appeal under this section shall, if and to the extent required by regulations under subsection (10) below, be advertised in such manner as may be prescribed by regulations under that subsection.

(5) If either party to the appeal so requests or the Secretary of State so decides, an appeal shall be or continue in the form of a hearing (which may, if the person hearing the appeal so decides, be held, or held to any extent, in private).

(6) On determining an appeal against a decision of an enforcing authority under subsection (1) above, the Secretary of State—

(a) may affirm the decision;

(b) where the decision was a refusal to grant an authorisation or a variation of an authorisation, may direct the enforcing authority to grant the authorisation or to vary the authorisation, as the case may be;

(c) where the decision was as to the conditions attached to an authorisation, may quash all or any of the conditions of the authorisation;

(d) where the decision was to revoke an authorisation, may quash the decision;

and where he exercises any of the powers in paragraphs (b), (c) or (d) above, he may give directions as to the conditions to be attached to the authorisation.

(7) On the determination of an appeal under subsection (2) above the Secretary of State may either quash or affirm the notice and, if he affirms it, may do so either in its original form or with such modifications as he may in the circumstances think fit.

(8) Where an appeal is brought under subsection (1) above against the revocation of an authorisation, the revocation shall not take effect pending the final determination or the withdrawal of the appeal.

(9) Where an appeal is brought under subsection (2) above against a notice, the bringing of the appeal shall not have the effect of suspending the operation of the notice.

(10) Provision may be made by the Secretary of State by regulations with respect to appeals under this section and in particular—

(a) as to the period within which and the manner in which appeals are to be brought; and

(b) as to the manner in which appeals are to be considered.

16 Appointment of chief inspector and other inspectors

(1) The Secretary of State may appoint as inspectors (under whatever title he may determine) such persons having suitable qualifications as he thinks necessary for carrying this Part into effect in relation to prescribed processes designated for central control or for the time being transferred under section 4(4) above to central control, and may terminate any appointment made under this subsection.

(2) The Secretary of State may make to or in respect of any person so appointed such payments by way of remuneration, allowances or otherwise as he may with the approval of the Treasury determine.

(3) In relation to England and Wales the Secretary of State shall constitute one of the inspectors appointed under subsection (1) above to be the chief inspector for England and Wales and in relation to Scotland the Secretary of State shall constitute one of the said inspectors to be the chief inspector for Scotland.

(4) The functions conferred or imposed by or under this Part on the chief inspector as the enforcing authority may, to any extent, be delegated by him to any other inspector appointed under subsection (1) above.

(5) A river purification authority may appoint as inspectors (under whatever title the authority may determine) such persons having suitable qualifications as the authority thinks necessary for carrying this Part into effect in relation to prescribed processes designated for central control and may terminate any appointment made under this subsection.

(6) Any local authority may appoint as inspectors (under whatever title the authority may determine) such persons having suitable qualifications as the authority think necessary for carrying this Part into effect in the authority's area in relation to prescribed processes designated for local control (and not so transferred), and may terminate any appointment made under this subsection.

(7) An inspector shall not be liable in any civil or criminal proceedings for anything done in the purported performance of his functions under section 17 or 18 below if the court is satisfied that the act was done in good faith and that there were reasonable grounds for doing it.

(8) In the following provisions of this Part "inspector" means a person appointed as an inspector under subsection (1), (5) or (6) above.

17 Powers of inspectors and others

(1) An inspector may, on production (if so required) of his authority, exercise any of the powers in subsection (3) below for the purposes of the discharge of the functions of the enforcing authority.

(2) Those powers, so far as exercisable in relation to premises, are exercisable in relation—

- (a) to premises on which a prescribed process is, or is believed (on reasonable grounds) to be, carried on; and
- (b) to premises on which a prescribed process has been carried on (whether or not the process was a prescribed process when it was carried on) the condition of which is believed (on reasonable grounds) to be such as to give rise to a risk of serious pollution of the environment.

(3) The powers of an inspector referred to above are—

- (a) at any reasonable time (or, in a situation in which in his opinion there is an immediate risk of serious pollution of the environment, at any time) to enter premises which he has reason to believe it is necessary for him to enter;
- (b) on entering any premises by virtue of paragraph (a) above to take with him—
  - (i) any person duly authorised by the chief inspector, the river purification authority or, as the case may be, the local enforcing authority and, if the inspector has reasonable cause to apprehend any serious obstruction in the execution of his duty, a constable; and
  - (ii) any equipment or materials required for any purpose for which the power of entry is being exercised;
- (c) to make such examination and investigation as may in any circumstances be necessary;
- (d) as regards any premises which he has power to enter, to direct that those premises or any part of them, or anything in them, shall be left undisturbed (whether generally or in particular respects) for so long as is reasonably necessary for the purpose of any examination or investigation under paragraph (c) above;
- (e) to take such measurements and photographs and make such recordings as he considers necessary for the purpose of any examination or investigation under paragraph (c) above;
- (f) to take samples of any articles or substances found in or on any premises which he has power to enter, and of the air, water or land in, on, or in the vicinity of, the premises;
- (g) in the case of any article or substance found in or on any premises which he has power to enter, being an article or substance which appears to him to have caused or to be likely to cause pollution of the environment, to cause it to

be dismantled or subjected to any process or test (but not so as to damage or destroy it unless this is necessary);

(h) in the case of any such article or substance as is mentioned in paragraph (g) above, to take possession of it and detain it for so long as is necessary for all or any of the following purposes, namely—

(i) to examine it and do to it anything which he has power to do under that paragraph;

(ii) to ensure that it is not tampered with before his examination of it is completed;

(iii) to ensure that it is available for use as evidence in any proceedings for an offence under section 23 below or any other proceedings relating to a variation notice, an enforcement notice or a prohibition notice;

(i) to require any person whom he has reasonable cause to believe to be able to give any information relevant to any examination or investigation under paragraph (c) above to answer (in the absence of persons other than a person nominated to be present and any persons whom the inspector may allow to be present) such questions as the inspector thinks fit to ask and to sign a declaration of the truth of his answers;

(j) to require the production of, or where the information is recorded in computerised form, the furnishing of extracts from, any records which are required to be kept under this Part or it is necessary for him to see for the purposes of an examination or investigation under paragraph (c) above and to inspect and take copies of, or of any entry in, the records;

(k) to require any person to afford him such facilities and assistance with respect to any matters or things within that person's control or in relation to which that person has responsibilities as are necessary to enable the inspector to exercise any of the powers conferred on him by this section;

(l) any other power for the purpose mentioned in subsection (1) above which is conferred by regulations made by the Secretary of State;

and in so far as any of the powers specified above are applicable in relation to mobile plant an inspector shall have, in circumstances corresponding to those specified in subsection (2) above, powers corresponding to those powers.

(4) The Secretary of State may by regulations make provision as to the procedure to be followed in connection with the taking of, and the dealing with, samples under subsection (3)(f) above.

(5) Where an inspector proposes to exercise the power conferred by subsection (3)(g) above in the case of an article or substance found on any premises, he shall, if so requested by a person who at the time is present on and has responsibilities in relation to those premises, cause anything which is to be done by virtue of that power to be done in the presence of that person.

(6) Before exercising the power conferred by subsection (3)(g) above in the case of any article or substance, an inspector shall consult such persons as appear to him appropriate for the purpose of ascertaining what dangers, if any, there may be in doing anything which he proposes to do under the power.

(7) Where under the power conferred by subsection (3)(h) above an inspector takes possession of any article or substance found on any premises, he shall leave there, either with a responsible person or, if that is impracticable, fixed in a conspicuous position, a notice giving particulars of that article or substance sufficient to identify it and stating that he has taken possession of it under that power; and before taking

possession of any such substance under that power an inspector shall, if it is practical for him to do so, take a sample of it and give to a responsible person at the premises a portion of the sample marked in a manner sufficient to identify it.

(8) No answer given by a person in pursuance of a requirement imposed under subsection (3)(i) above shall be admissible in evidence in England and Wales against that person in any proceedings, or in Scotland against that person in any criminal proceedings.

(9) The powers conferred by subsection (3)(a), (b)(ii), (c), (e) and (f) above shall also be exercisable (subject to subsection (4) above) by any person authorised for the purpose in writing by the Secretary of State.

(10) Nothing in this section shall be taken to compel the production by any person of a document of which he would on grounds of legal professional privilege be entitled to withhold production on an order for discovery in an action in the High Court or, in relation to Scotland, on an order for the production of documents in an action in the Court of Session.

18 Power to deal with cause of imminent danger of serious harm

(1) Where, in the case of any article or substance found by him on any premises which he has power to enter, an inspector has reasonable cause to believe that, in the circumstances in which he finds it, the article or substance is a cause of imminent danger of serious harm he may seize it and cause it to be rendered harmless (whether by destruction or otherwise).

(2) Before there is rendered harmless under this section—

- (a) any article that forms part of a batch of similar articles; or
- (b) any substance,

the inspector shall, if it is practicable for him to do so, take a sample of it and give to a responsible person at the premises where the article or substance was found by him a portion of the sample marked in a manner sufficient to identify it.

(3) As soon as may be after any article or substance has been seized and rendered harmless under this section, the inspector shall prepare and sign a written report giving particulars of the circumstances in which the article or substance was seized and so dealt with by him, and shall—

- (a) give a signed copy of the report to a responsible person at the premises where the article or substance was found by him; and
- (b) unless that person is the owner of the article or substance, also serve a signed copy of the report on the owner;

and if, where paragraph (b) above applies, the inspector cannot after reasonable inquiry ascertain the name or address of the owner, the copy may be served on him by giving it to the person to whom a copy was given under paragraph (a) above.

19 Obtaining of information from persons and authorities

(1) For the purposes of the discharge of his functions under this Part, the Secretary of State may, by notice in writing served on an enforcing authority, require the authority to furnish such information about the discharge of its functions as an enforcing authority under this Part as he may require.

(2) For the purposes of the discharge of their respective functions under this Part, the following authorities, that is to say—

(a) the Secretary of State,

(b) a local enforcing authority,

(c) the chief inspector, and

(d) in relation to Scotland, a river purification authority,

may, by notice in writing served on any person, require that person to furnish to the authority such information which the authority reasonably considers that it needs as is specified in the notice, in such form and within such period following service of the notice as is so specified.

(3) For the purposes of this section the discharge by the Secretary of State of an obligation of the United Kingdom under the Community Treaties or any international agreement relating to environmental protection shall be treated as a function of his under this Part.

Publicity

20 Public registers of information

(1) It shall be the duty of each enforcing authority, as respects prescribed processes for which it is the enforcing authority, to maintain, in accordance with regulations made by the Secretary of State, a register containing prescribed particulars of or relating to—

(a) applications for authorisations made to that authority;

(b) the authorisations which have been granted by that authority or in respect of which the authority has functions under this Part;

(c) variation notices, enforcement notices and prohibition notices issued by that authority;

(d) revocations of authorisations effected by that authority;

(e) appeals under section 15 above;

(f) convictions for such offences under section 23(1) below as may be prescribed;

(g) information obtained or furnished in pursuance of the conditions of authorisations or under any provision of this Part;

(h) directions given to the authority under any provision of this Part by the Secretary of State; and

(i) such other matters relating to the carrying on of prescribed processes or any pollution of the environment caused thereby as may be prescribed;

but that duty is subject to sections 21 and 22 below.

(2) Subject to subsection (4) below, the register maintained by a local enforcing authority shall also contain prescribed particulars of such information contained in any register maintained by the chief inspector or river purification authority as relates to the carrying on in the area of the authority of prescribed processes in relation to which the chief inspector or river purification authority has functions under this Part; and the chief inspector or river purification authority shall furnish each authority with the particulars which are necessary to enable it to discharge its duty under this subsection.

(3) In Scotland, the register maintained by—

(a) the chief inspector shall also contain prescribed particulars of such information contained in any register maintained by a river purification authority as relates to the carrying on in the area of the authority of prescribed processes in relation to which the authority has functions under this Part, and each authority shall furnish the chief inspector with the particulars which are necessary to enable him to discharge his duty under this section;

(b) each river purification authority shall also contain prescribed particulars of such information contained in any register maintained by the chief inspector as relates to the carrying on in the area of the authority of prescribed processes in relation to which the chief inspector has functions under this Part, and the chief inspector shall furnish each authority with the particulars which are necessary to enable them to discharge their duty under this section.

(4) Subsection (2) above does not apply to port health authorities but each local enforcing authority whose area adjoins that of a port health authority shall include corresponding information in the register maintained by it; and the chief inspector shall furnish each such local enforcing authority with the particulars which are necessary to enable it to discharge its duty under this subsection.

(5) Where information of any description is excluded from any register by virtue of section 22 below, a statement shall be entered in the register indicating the existence of information of that description.

(6) The Secretary of State may give to enforcing authorities directions requiring the removal from any register of theirs of any specified information not prescribed for inclusion under subsection (1) or (2) above or which, by virtue of section 21 or 22 below, ought to have been excluded from the register.

(7) It shall be the duty of each enforcing authority—

(a) to secure that the registers maintained by them under this section are available, at all reasonable times, for inspection by the public free of charge; and(b) to afford to members of the public facilities for obtaining copies of entries, on payment of reasonable charges.

(8) Registers under this section may be kept in any form.

(9) For the purpose of enabling the National Rivers Authority to discharge its duty under section 117(l)(f) of the Water Act 1989 to keep corresponding particulars in registers under that section, the chief inspector shall furnish the Authority with the particulars contained in any register maintained by him under this section.

(10) In this section "prescribed" means prescribed in regulations under this section.

21 Exclusion from registers of information affecting national security

(1) No information shall be included in a register maintained under section 20 above if and so long as, in the opinion of the Secretary of State, the inclusion in the register of that information, or information of that description, would be contrary to the interests of national security.

(2) The Secretary of State may, for the purpose of securing the exclusion from registers of information to which subsection (1) above applies, give to enforcing authorities directions—

(a) specifying information, or descriptions of information, to be excluded from their registers; or

(b) specifying descriptions of information to be referred to the Secretary of State for his determination;

and no information referred to the Secretary of State in pursuance of paragraph (b) above shall be included in any such register until the Secretary of State determines that it should be so included.

(3) The enforcing authority shall notify the Secretary of State of any information it excludes from the register in pursuance of directions under subsection (2) above.

(4) A person may, as respects any information which appears to him to be information to which subsection (1) above may apply, give a notice to the Secretary of State specifying the information and indicating its apparent nature; and, if he does so—

(a) he shall notify the enforcing authority that he has done so; and

(b) no information so notified to the Secretary of State shall be included in any such register until the Secretary of State has determined that it should be so included.

22 Exclusion from registers of certain confidential information

(1) No information relating to the affairs of any individual or business shall be included in a register maintained under section 20 above, without the consent of that individual or the person for the time being carrying on that business, if and so long as the information—

(a) is, in relation to him, commercially confidential; and

(b) is not required to be included in the register in pursuance of directions under subsection (7) below;

but information is not commercially confidential for the purposes of this section unless it is determined under this section to be so by the enforcing authority or, on appeal, by the Secretary of State.

(2) Where information is furnished to an enforcing authority for the purpose of—

(a) an application for an authorisation or for the variation of an authorisation;

(b) complying with any condition of an authorisation; or

(c) complying with a notice under section 19(2) above;

then, if the person furnishing it applies to the authority to have the information excluded from the register on the ground that it is commercially confidential (as regards himself or another person), the authority shall determine whether the information is or is not commercially confidential.

(3) A determination under subsection (2) above must be made within the period of fourteen days beginning with the date of the application and if the enforcing authority fails to make a determination within that period it shall be treated as having determined that the information is commercially confidential.

(4) Where it appears to an enforcing authority that any information (other than information furnished in circumstances within subsection (2) above) which has been obtained by the authority under or by virtue of any provision of this Part might be commercially confidential, the authority shall—

(a) give to the person to whom or whose business it relates notice that that information is required to be included in the register unless excluded under this section; and

(b) give him a reasonable opportunity—

(i) of objecting to the inclusion of the information on the ground that it is commercially confidential; and

(ii) of making representations to the authority for the purpose of justifying any such objection;

and, if any representations are made, the enforcing authority shall, having taken the representations into account, determine whether the information is or is not commercially confidential.

(5) Where, under subsection (2) or (4) above, an authority determines that information is not commercially confidential—

(a) the information shall not be entered on the register until the end of the period of twenty-one days beginning with the date on which the determination is notified to the person concerned;

(b) that person may appeal to the Secretary of State against the decision;

and, where an appeal is brought in respect of any information, the information shall not be entered on the register pending the final determination or withdrawal of the appeal.

(6) Subsections (3), (5) and (10) of section 15 above shall apply in relation to appeals under subsection (5) above.

(7) The Secretary of State may give to the enforcing authorities directions as to specified information, or descriptions of information, which the public interest requires to be included in registers maintained under section 20 above notwithstanding that the information may be commercially confidential.

(8) Information excluded from a register shall be treated as ceasing to be commercially confidential for the purposes of this section at the expiry of the period of four years beginning with the date of the determination by virtue of which it was excluded; but the person who furnished it may apply to the authority for the information to remain excluded from the register on the ground that it is still commercially confidential and the authority shall determine whether or not that is the case.

(9) Subsections (5) and (6) above shall apply in relation to a determination under subsection (8) above as they apply in relation to a determination under subsection (2) or (4) above.

(10) The Secretary of State may, by order, substitute for the period for the time being specified in subsection (3) above such other period as he considers appropriate.

(11) Information is, for the purposes of any determination under this section, commercially confidential, in relation to any individual or person, if its being contained in the register would prejudice to an unreasonable degree the commercial interests of that individual or person.

Provisions as to offences

23 Offences

(1) It is an offence for a person—

(a) to contravene section 6(1) above;

(b) to fail to give the notice required by section 9(2) above;

(c) to fail to comply with or contravene any requirement or prohibition imposed by an enforcement notice or a prohibition notice;

(d) without reasonable excuse, to fail to comply with any requirement imposed under section 17 above;

(e) to prevent any other person from appearing before or from answering any question to which an inspector may by virtue of section 17(3) require an answer;

(f) intentionally to obstruct an inspector in the exercise or performance of his powers or duties;

(g) to fail, without reasonable excuse, to comply with any requirement imposed by a notice under section 19(2) above;

(h) to make a statement which he knows to be false or misleading in a material particular, or recklessly to make a statement which is false or misleading in a material particular, where the statement is made—

(i) in purported compliance with a requirement to furnish any information imposed by or under any provision of this Part; or

(ii) for the purpose of obtaining the grant of an authorisation to himself or any other person or the variation of an authorisation;

(i) intentionally to make a false entry in any record required to be kept under section 7 above;

(j) with intent to deceive, to forge or use a document issued or authorised to be issued under section 7 above or required for any purpose thereunder or to make or have in his possession a document so closely resembling any such document as to be likely to deceive;

(k) falsely to pretend to be an inspector;

(l) to fail to comply with an order made by a court under section 26 below.

(2) A person guilty of an offence under paragraph (a), (c) or (l) of subsection (1) above shall be liable:

(a) on summary conviction, to a fine not exceeding £20,000;

(b) on conviction on indictment, to a fine or to imprisonment for a term not exceeding two years, or to both.

(3) A person guilty of an offence under paragraph (b), (g), (h), (i) or (j) of subsection (1) above shall be liable—

(a) on summary conviction, to a fine not exceeding the statutory maximum;

(b) on conviction on indictment, to a fine or to imprisonment for a term not exceeding two years, or to both.

(4) A person guilty of an offence under paragraph (d), (e), (f) or (k) of subsection (1) above shall be liable, on summary conviction, to a fine not exceeding the statutory maximum.

(5) In England and Wales an inspector, if authorised to do so by the Secretary of State, may, although not of counsel or a solicitor, prosecute before a magistrates' court proceedings for an offence under subsection (1) above.

24 Enforcement by High Court

If the enforcing authority is of the opinion that proceedings for an offence under section 23(1)(c) above would afford an ineffectual remedy against a person who has failed to comply with the requirements of an enforcement notice or a prohibition notice, the authority may take proceedings in the High Court or, in Scotland, in any court of competent jurisdiction for the purpose of securing compliance with the notice.

25 Onus of proof as regards techniques and evidence

(1) In any proceedings for an offence under section 23(1)(a) above consisting in a failure to comply with the general condition implied in every authorisation by section 7(4) above, it shall be for the accused to prove that there was no better available technique not entailing excessive cost than was in fact used to satisfy the condition.

(2) Where—

(a) an entry is required under section 7 above to be made in any record as to the observance of any condition of an authorisation; and

(b) the entry has not been made;

that fact shall be admissible as evidence that that condition has not been observed.

26 Power of court to order cause of offence to be remedied

(1) Where a person is convicted of an offence under section 23(1)(a) or (c) above in respect of any matters which appear to the court to be matters which it is in his power to remedy, the court may, in addition to or instead of imposing any punishment, order him, within such time as may be fixed by the order, to take such steps as may be specified in the order for remedying those matters.

(2) The time fixed by an order under subsection (1) above may be extended or further extended by order of the court on an application made before the end of the time as originally fixed or as extended under this subsection, as the case may be.

(3) Where a person is ordered under subsection (1) above to remedy any matters, that person shall not be liable under section 23 above in respect of those matters in so far as they continue during the time fixed by the order or any further time allowed under subsection (2) above.

27 Power of chief inspector to remedy harm

(1) Where the commission of an offence under section 23(1)(a) or (c) above causes any harm which it is possible to remedy, the chief inspector or, in Scotland, a river purification authority may, subject to subsection (2) below—

(a) arrange for any reasonable steps to be taken towards remedying the harm; and

(b) recover the cost of taking those steps from any person convicted of that offence.

(2) The chief inspector or, as the case may be, the river purification authority shall not exercise their powers under this section except with the approval in writing of the Secretary of State and, where any of the steps are to be taken on or will affect land in the occupation of any person other than the person on whose land the prescribed process is being carried on, with the permission of that person.

Authorisations and other statutory controls

28 Authorisations and other statutory controls

(1) No condition shall at any time be attached to an authorisation so as to regulate the final disposal by deposit in or on land of controlled waste (within the meaning of Part II), nor shall any condition apply to such a disposal; but the enforcing authority shall notify the authority which is the waste regulation authority under that Part for the area

in which the process is to be carried on of the fact that the process involves the final disposal of controlled waste by deposit in or on land.

(2) Where any of the activities comprising a prescribed process are regulated both by an authorisation granted by the enforcing authority under this Part and by a registration or authorisation under the Radioactive Substances Act 1960, then, if different obligations are imposed as respects the same matter by a condition attached to the authorisation under this Part and a condition attached to the registration or authorisation under that Act, the condition imposed by the authorisation under this Part shall be treated as not binding the person carrying on the process.

(3) Where the activities comprising a prescribed process designated for central control include the release of any substances into water included in waters which are controlled waters for the purposes of Chapter I of Part III of the Water Act 1989, then—

(a) the enforcing authority shall not grant an authorisation under this Part if the National Rivers Authority certifies to the enforcing authority its opinion that the release will result in or contribute to a failure to achieve any water quality objective in force under Part III of that Act; and

(b) any authorisation that is granted shall, as respects such releases, include (with or without others appearing to the enforcing authority to be appropriate) such conditions as appear to the National Rivers Authority to be appropriate for the purposes of this Part as that Authority requires by notice in writing given to the enforcing authority;

but the enforcing authority may, if it appears to be appropriate to do so, make the authorisation subject to conditions more onerous than those (if any) notified to it under paragraph (b) above.

(4) Where the activities comprising a prescribed process carried on under an authorisation include the release of any substances into water as mentioned in subsection (3) above then, if at any time it appears to the National Rivers Authority appropriate for the purposes of this Part that the conditions of the authorisation should be varied, the enforcing authority shall exercise its powers under section 10 above so as to vary the conditions of the authorisation as required by the National Rivers Authority by notice in writing given to the enforcing authority.

PART II

WASTE ON LAND

Preliminary

29 Preliminary

(1) The following provisions have effect for the interpretation of this Part.

(2) The "environment" consists of all, or any, of the following media, namely land, water and the air.

(3) "Pollution of the environment" means pollution of the environment due to the release or escape (into any environmental medium) from—

(a) the land on which controlled waste is treated,

(b) the land on which controlled waste is kept,

(c) the land in or on which controlled waste is deposited,

(d) fixed plant by means of which controlled waste is treated, kept or disposed of,

of substances or articles constituting or resulting from the waste and capable (by reason of the quantity or concentrations involved) of causing harm to man or any other living organisms supported by the environment.

(4) Subsection (3) above applies in relation to mobile plant by means of which controlled waste is treated or disposed of as it applies to plant on land by means of which controlled waste is treated or disposed of.

(5) For the purposes of subsections (3) and (4) above "harm" means harm to the health of living organisms or other interference with the ecological systems of which they form part and in the case of man includes offence to any of his senses or harm to his property; and "harmless" has a corresponding meaning.

(6) The "disposal" of waste includes its disposal by way of deposit in or on land and, subject to subsection (7) below, waste is "treated" when it is subjected to any process, including making it re-usable or reclaiming substances from it and "recycle" (and cognate expressions) shall be construed accordingly.

(7) Regulations made by the Secretary of State may prescribe activities as activities which constitute the treatment of waste for the purposes of this Part or any provision of this Part prescribed in the regulations.

(8) "Land" includes land covered by waters where the land is above the low water mark of ordinary spring tides and references to land on which controlled waste is treated, kept or deposited are references to the surface of the land (including any structure set into the surface).

(9) "Mobile plant" means, subject to subsection (10) below, plant which is designed to move or be moved whether on roads or other land.

(10) Regulations made by the Secretary of State may prescribe descriptions of plant which are to be treated as being, or as not being, mobile plant for the purposes of this Part.

(11) "Substance" means any natural or artificial substance, whether in solid or liquid form or in the form of a gas or vapour.

30 Authorities for purposes of this Part

(1) For the purposes of this Part the following authorities are, subject to section 31 below, waste regulation authorities, namely—

(a) for any non-metropolitan county in England, the county council;

(b) for Greater London, the authority constituted as the London Waste Regulation Authority;

(c) for the metropolitan county of Greater Manchester, the authority constituted as the Greater Manchester Waste Disposal Authority;

(d) for the metropolitan county of Merseyside, the authority constituted as the Merseyside Waste Disposal Authority;

(e) for any district in any other metropolitan county in England, the council of the district;

(f) for any district in Wales, the council of the district;

(g) in Scotland, an islands or district council;

and the authorities mentioned in paragraph (c) and (d) above shall for the purposes of their functions as waste regulation authorities be known as the Greater Manchester Waste Regulation Authority and the Merseyside Waste Regulation Authority respectively.

(2) For the purposes of this Part the following authorities are waste disposal authorities, namely—

(a) for any non-metropolitan county in England, the county council;

(b) in Greater London, the following—

(i) for the area of a London waste disposal authority, the authority constituted as the waste disposal authority for that area;

(ii) for the City of London, the Common Council;

(iii) for any other London borough, the council of the borough;

(c) in the metropolitan county of Greater Manchester, the following—

(i) for the metropolitan district of Wigan, the district council;

(ii) for all other areas in the county, the authority constituted as the Greater Manchester Waste Disposal Authority;

(d) for the metropolitan county of Merseyside, the authority constituted as the Merseyside Waste Disposal Authority;

(e) for any district in any other metropolitan county in England, the council of the district;

(f) for any district in Wales, the council of the district;

(g) in Scotland, an islands or district council.

(3) For the purposes of this Part the following authorities are waste collection authorities—

(a) for any district in England and Wales not within Greater London, the council of the district;

(b) in Greater London, the following—

(i) for any London borough, the council of the borough;

(ii) for the City of London, the Common Council;

(iii) for the Temples, the Sub-Treasurer of the Inner Temple and the Under Treasurer of the Middle Temple respectively;

(c) in Scotland, an islands or district council.

(4) In this section references to particular authorities having been constituted as waste disposal or regulation authorities are references to their having been so constituted by the Waste Regulation and Disposal (Authorities) Order 1985 made by the Secretary of State under section 10 of the Local Government Act 1985 and the reference to London waste disposal authorities is a reference to the authorities named in Parts I, II, III, IV and V of Schedule 1 to that Order and this section has effect subject to any order made under the said section 10 establishing authorities to discharge any functions to which that section applies.

(5) In this Part "waste disposal contractor" means a person who in the course of a business collects, keeps, treats or disposes of waste, being either—

(a) a company formed for all or any of those purposes by a waste disposal authority whether in pursuance of section 32 below or otherwise; or

(b) either a company formed for all or any of those purposes by other persons or a partnership or an individual;

and "company" has the same meaning as in the Companies Act 1985 and "formed", in relation to a company formed by other persons, includes the alteration of the objects of the company.

(6) In this Part, in its application to Scotland, "river purification authority" means a river purification authority within the meaning of the Rivers (Prevention of Pollution) (Scotland) Act 1951.

(7) It shall be the duty of each authority which is both a waste regulation authority and a waste disposal authority—

(a) to make administrative arrangements for keeping its functions as a waste regulation authority separate from its functions as a waste disposal authority; and

(b) to submit details of the arrangements which it has made to the Secretary of State.

(8) The Secretary of State may give to an authority to which subsection (7) above applies directions as to the arrangements which it is to make for the purpose of keeping its functions as a waste regulation authority separate from its functions as a waste disposal authority; and it shall be the duty of the authority to give effect to the directions.

31 Power to create regional authorities for purposes of waste regulation

(1) If it appears to the Secretary of State in the case of any two or more of the authorities mentioned in section 30(1) above that those authorities (in this section referred to as "relevant authorities") could with advantage make joint arrangements for the discharge of all or any of their functions as waste regulation authorities, he may by order establish a single authority (a "regional authority") to discharge such of those functions as may be specified in the order for the area comprising the areas of those authorities.

(2) A regional authority shall exercise the functions specified in the order establishing it on and after a day specified in the order and, so far as the exercise of those functions (if not withdrawn) and any subsequently-conferred functions is concerned, shall (in place of the relevant authorities) be the waste regulation authority for the purposes of this Part.

(3) The members of a regional authority shall be appointed by the relevant authorities in accordance with the order establishing it and no person shall be such a member unless he is a member of one of the relevant authorities.

(4) The Secretary of State may by order made with respect to any regional authority—

(a) confer or impose on it further functions;

(b) withdraw from it any functions previously conferred or imposed; or

(c) dissolve it;

and functions may be so conferred or imposed or withdrawn as respects the whole or any part of the authority's area.

(5) An order under this section may contain such supplementary and transitional provisions as the Secretary of State thinks necessary or expedient, including provision for the transfer of property, staff, rights and liabilities.

32 Transition to waste disposal companies etc

(1) In this section "existing disposal authority" means any authority (including any joint authority) constituted as a waste disposal authority for any area before the day appointed for this section to come into force.

(2) The Secretary of State shall, subject to subsection (3) below, give directions to existing disposal authorities or, in the case of joint authorities, to the constituent authorities requiring them, before specified dates, to—

(a) form or participate in forming waste disposal companies; and

(b) transfer to the companies so formed, by and in accordance with a scheme made in accordance with Schedule 2 to this Act, the relevant part of their undertakings;

and a waste disposal authority shall accordingly have power to form, and hold securities in, any company so established.

(3) Subject to subsection (4) below, the Secretary of State shall not give any direction under subsection (2) above to an existing disposal authority, or to the constituent authorities of an existing disposal authority, as respects which or each of which he is satisfied that the authority—

(a) has formed or participated in forming a waste disposal company and transferred to it the relevant part of its undertaking;

(b) has, in pursuance of arrangements made with other persons, ceased to carry on itself the relevant part of its undertaking;

(c) has made arrangements with other persons to cease to carry on itself the relevant part of its undertaking; or

(d) has, in pursuance of arrangements made with other persons, ceased to provide places at which and plant and equipment by means of which controlled waste can be disposed of or deposited for the purposes of disposal.

(4) Subsection (3) above does not apply in a case falling within paragraph (a) unless it appears to the Secretary of State that—

(a) the form of the company and the undertaking transferred are satisfactory; and

(b) the requirements of subsections (8) and (9) below are fulfilled;

and "satisfactory" means satisfactory by reference to the corresponding arrangements to which he would give his approval for the purposes of a transfer scheme under Schedule 2 to this Act.

(5) Where the Secretary of State is precluded from giving a direction under subsection (2) above to any authority by reason of his being satisfied as to the arrangements mentioned in subsection (3)(c) above, then, if those arrangements are not implemented within what appears to him to be a reasonable time, he may exercise his power to give directions under subsection (2) above as respects that authority.

(6) Part I of Schedule 2 to this Act has effect for the purposes of this section and Part II for regulating the functions of waste disposal authorities and the activities of waste disposal contractors.

(7) Subject to subsection (8) below, the activities of a company which a waste disposal authority has formed or participated in forming (whether in pursuance of subsection (2)(a) above or otherwise) may include activities which are beyond the powers of the authority to carry on itself, but, in the case of a company formed otherwise than in pursuance of subsection (2)(a) above, only if the Secretary of State

has determined under subsection (4)(a) above that the form of the company and the undertaking transferred to it are satisfactory.

(8) A waste disposal authority shall, for so long as it controls a company which it has formed or participated in forming (whether in pursuance of subsection (2)(a) above or otherwise), so exercise its control as to secure that the company does not engage in activities other than the following activities or any activities incidental or conducive to, or calculated to facilitate, them, that is to say, the disposal, keeping or treatment of waste and the collection of waste.

(9) Subject to subsection (10) below, a waste disposal authority shall, for so long as it controls a company which it has formed or participated in forming (whether in pursuance of subsection (2)(a) above or otherwise), so exercise its control as to secure that, for the purposes of Part V of the Local Government and Housing Act 1989, the company is an arm's length company.

(10) Subsection (9) above shall not apply in the case of a company which a waste disposal authority has formed or participated in forming in pursuance of subsection (2)(a) above until after the vesting date for that company.

(11) In this section and Schedule 2 to this Act—

"control" (and cognate expressions) is to be construed in accordance with section 68 or, as the case requires, section 73 of the Local Government and Housing Act 1989;

"the relevant part" of the undertaking of an existing disposal authority is that part which relates to the disposal, keeping or treatment or the collection of waste;

and in this section "securities" and "vesting date" have the same meaning as in Schedule 2.

(12) This section shall not apply to Scotland.

Prohibition on unauthorised or harmful depositing, treatment or disposal of waste

33 Prohibition on unauthorised or harmful deposit, treatment or disposal etc. of waste

(1) Subject to subsection (2) and (3) below and, in relation to Scotland, to section 54 below, a person shall not—

(a) deposit controlled waste, or knowingly cause or knowingly permit controlled waste to be deposited in or on any land unless a waste management licence authorising the deposit is in force and the deposit is in accordance with the licence;

(b) treat, keep or dispose of controlled waste, or knowingly cause or knowingly permit controlled waste to be treated, kept or disposed of—

(i) in or on any land, or

(ii) by means of any mobile plant,

except under and in accordance with a waste management licence;

(c) treat, keep or dispose of controlled waste in a manner likely to cause pollution of the environment or harm to human health.

(2) Subsection (1) above does not apply in relation to household waste from a domestic property which is treated, kept or disposed of within the curtilage of the dwelling by or with the permission of the occupier of the dwelling.

(3) Subsection (1)(a), (b) or (c) above do not apply in cases prescribed in regulations made by the Secretary of State and the regulations may make different exceptions for different areas.

(4) The Secretary of State, in exercising his power under subsection (3) above, shall have regard in particular to the expediency of excluding from the controls imposed by waste management licences—

- (a) any deposits which are small enough or of such a temporary nature that they may be so excluded;
- (b) any means of treatment or disposal which are innocuous enough to be so excluded;
- (c) cases for which adequate controls are provided by another enactment than this section.

(5) Where controlled waste is carried in and deposited from a motor vehicle, the person who controls or is in a position to control the use of the vehicle shall, for the purposes of subsection (1)(a) above, be treated as knowingly causing the waste to be deposited whether or not he gave any instructions for this to be done.

(6) A person who contravenes subsection (1) above or any condition of a waste management licence commits an offence.

(7) It shall be a defence for a person charged with an offence under this section to prove—

- (a) that he took all reasonable precautions and exercised all due diligence to avoid the commission of the offence; or
- (b) that he acted under instructions from his employer and neither knew nor had reason to suppose that the acts done by him constituted a contravention of subsection (1) above; or
- (c) that the acts alleged to constitute the contravention were done in an emergency in order to avoid danger to the public and that, as soon as reasonably practicable after they were done, particulars of them were furnished to the waste regulation authority in whose area the treatment or disposal of the waste took place.

(8) Except in a case falling within subsection (9) below, a person who commits an offence under this section shall be liable—

- (a) on summary conviction, to imprisonment for a term not exceeding six months or a fine not exceeding £20,000 or both; and
- (b) on conviction on indictment, to imprisonment for a term not exceeding two years or a fine or both.

(9) A person who commits an offence under this section in relation to special waste shall be liable—

- (a) on summary conviction, to imprisonment for a term not exceeding six months or a fine not exceeding £20,000 or both;
- (b) on conviction on indictment, to imprisonment for a term not exceeding five years or a fine or both.

Duty of care etc. as respects waste

34 Duty of care etc. as respects waste

(1) Subject to subsection (2) below, it shall be the duty of any person who imports, produces, carries, keeps, treats or disposes of controlled waste or, as a broker, has control of such waste, to take all such measures applicable to him in that capacity as are reasonable in the circumstances—

(a) to prevent any contravention by any other person of section 33 above;

(b) to prevent the escape of the waste from his control or that of any other person; and

(c) on the transfer of the waste, to secure—

(i) that the transfer is only to an authorised person or to a person for authorised transport purposes; and

(ii) that there is transferred such a written description of the waste as will enable other persons to avoid a contravention of that section and to comply with the duty under this subsection as respects the escape of waste.

(2) The duty imposed by subsection (1) above does not apply to an occupier of domestic property as respects the household waste produced on the property.

(3) The following are authorised persons for the purpose of subsection (1)(c) above—

(a) any authority which is a waste collection authority for the purposes of this Part;

(b) any person who is the holder of a waste management licence under section 35 below or of a disposal licence under section 5 of the Control of Pollution Act 1974;

(c) any person to whom section 33(1) above does not apply by virtue of regulations under subsection (3) of that section;

(d) any person registered as a carrier of controlled waste under section 2 of the Control of Pollution (Amendment) Act 1989;

(e) any person who is not required to be so registered by virtue of regulations under section 1(3) of that Act; and

(f) a waste disposal authority in Scotland.

(4) The following are authorised transport purposes for the purposes of subsection (1)(c) above—

(a) the transport of controlled waste within the same premises between different places in those premises;

(b) the transport to a place in Great Britain of controlled waste which has been brought from a country or territory outside Great Britain not having been landed in Great Britain until it arrives at that place; and

(c) the transport by air or sea of controlled waste from a place in Great Britain to a place outside Great Britain;

and "transport" has the same meaning in this subsection as in the Control of Pollution (Amendment) Act 1989.

(5) The Secretary of State may, by regulations, make provision imposing requirements on any person who is subject to the duty imposed by subsection (1) above as respects

the making and retention of documents and the furnishing of documents or copies of documents.

(6) Any person who fails to comply with the duty imposed by subsection (1) above or with any requirement imposed under subsection (5) above shall be liable—

(a) on summary conviction, to a fine not exceeding the statutory maximum; and

(b) on conviction on indictment, to a fine.

(7) The Secretary of State shall, after consultation with such persons or bodies as appear to him representative of the interests concerned, prepare and issue a code of practice for the purpose of providing to persons practical guidance on how to discharge the duty imposed on them by subsection (1) above.

(8) The Secretary of State may from time to time revise a code of practice issued under subsection (7) above by revoking, amending or adding to the provisions of the code.

(9) The code of practice prepared in pursuance of subsection (7) above shall be laid before both Houses of Parliament.

(10) A code of practice issued under subsection (7) above shall be admissible in evidence and if any provision of such a code appears to the court to be relevant to any question arising in the proceedings it shall be taken into account in determining that question.

(11) Different codes of practice may be prepared and issued under subsection (7) above for different areas.

Waste Management Licences

35 Waste management licences: general

(1) A waste management licence is a licence granted by a waste regulation authority authorising the treatment, keeping or disposal of any specified description of controlled waste in or on specified land or the treatment or disposal of any specified description of controlled waste by means of specified mobile plant.

(2) A licence shall be granted to the following person, that is to say—

(a) in the case of a licence relating to the treatment, keeping or disposal of waste in or on land, to the person who is in occupation of the land; and

(b) in the case of a licence relating to the treatment or disposal of waste by means of mobile plant, to the person who operates the plant.

(3) A licence shall be granted on such terms and subject to such conditions as appear to the waste regulation authority to be appropriate and the conditions may relate—

(a) to the activities which the licence authorises, and

(b) to the precautions to be taken and works to be carried out in connection with or in consequence of those activities;

and accordingly requirements may be imposed in the licence which are to be complied with before the activities which the licence authorises have begun or after the activities which the licence authorises have ceased.

(4) Conditions may require the holder of a licence to carry out works or do other things notwithstanding that he is not entitled to carry out the works or do the thing and any person whose consent would be required shall grant, or join in granting, the holder of

the licence such rights in relation to the land as will enable the holder of the licence to comply with any requirements imposed on him by the licence.

(5) Conditions may relate, where waste other than controlled waste is to be treated, kept or disposed of, to the treatment, keeping or disposal of that other waste.

(6) The Secretary of State may, by regulations, make provision as to the conditions which are, or are not, to be included in a licence; and regulations under this subsection may make different provision for different circumstances.

(7) The Secretary of State may, as respects any licence for which an application is made to a waste regulation authority, give to the authority directions as to the terms and conditions which are, or are not, to be included in the licence; and it shall be the duty of the authority to give effect to the directions.

(8) It shall be the duty of waste regulation authorities to have regard to any guidance issued to them by the Secretary of State with respect to the discharge of their functions in relation to licences.

(9) A licence may not be surrendered by the holder except in accordance with section 39 below.

(10) A licence is not transferable by the holder but the waste regulation authority may transfer it to another person under section 40 below.

(11) A licence shall continue in force until it is revoked entirely by the waste regulation authority under section 38 below or it is surrendered or its surrender is accepted under section 39 below.

(12) In this Part "licence" means a waste management licence and "site licence" and "mobile plant licence" mean, respectively, a licence authorising the treatment, keeping or disposal of waste in or on land and a licence authorising the treatment or disposal of waste by means of mobile plant.

36 Grant of licences

(1) An application for a licence shall be made—

(a) in the case of an application for a site licence, to the waste regulation authority in whose area the land is situated; and

(b) in the case of an application for a mobile plant licence, to the waste regulation authority in whose area the operator of the plant has his principal place of business;

and shall be made in the form prescribed by the Secretary of State in regulations and accompanied by the prescribed fee payable under section 41 below.

(2) A licence shall not be issued for a use of land for which planning permission is required in pursuance of the Town and Country Planning Act 1990 or the Town and Country Planning (Scotland) Act 1972 unless—

(a) such planning permission is in force in relation to that use of the land, or

(b) an established use certificate is in force under section 192 of the said Act of 1990 or section 90 of the said Act of 1972 in relation to that use of the land.

(3) Subject to subsection (2) above and subsection (4) below, a waste regulation authority to which an application for a licence has been duly made shall not reject the application

if it is satisfied that the applicant is a fit and proper person unless it is satisfied that its rejection is necessary for the purpose of preventing—

(a) pollution of the environment;

(b) harm to human health; or

(c) serious detriment to the amenities of the locality;

but paragraph (c) above is inapplicable where planning permission is in force in relation to the use to which the land will be put under the licence.

(4) Where the waste regulation authority proposes to issue a licence, the authority must, before it does so,—

(a) refer the proposal to the National Rivers Authority and the Health and Safety Executive; and

(b) consider any representations about the proposal which the Authority or the Executive makes to it during the allowed period.

(5) If, following the referral of a proposal to the National Rivers Authority under subsection (4)(a) above, the Authority requests that the licence be not issued or disagrees about the conditions of the proposed licence either of them may refer the matter to the Secretary of State and the licence shall not be issued except in accordance with his decision.

(6) Subsection (4) above shall not apply to Scotland, but in Scotland where a waste regulation authority (other than an islands council) proposes to issue a licence, the authority must, before it does so,—

(a) refer the proposal to—

(i) the river purification authority whose area includes any of the relevant land;

(ii) the Health and Safety Executive;

(iii) where the waste regulation authority is not also a district planning authority within the meaning of section 172 of the Local Government (Scotland) Act 1973, the general planning authority within the meaning of that section whose area includes any of the relevant land; and

(b) consider any representations about the proposal which the river purification authority, the Executive or the general planning authority makes to it during the allowed period,

and if the river purification authority requests that the licence be not issued or disagrees with the waste regulation authority about the conditions of the proposed licence either of them may refer the matter to the Secretary of State and the licence shall not be issued except in accordance with his decision.

(7) Where any part of the land to be used is land which has been notified under section 28(1) of the Wildlife and Countryside Act 1981 (protection for certain areas) and the waste regulation authority proposes to issue a licence, the authority must, before it does so—

(a) refer the proposal to the appropriate nature conservation body; and

(b) consider any representations about the proposal which the body makes to it during the allowed period;

and in this section any reference to the appropriate nature conservation body is a reference to the Nature Conservancy Council for England, the Nature Conservancy

Council for Scotland or the Countryside Council for Wales, according as the land is situated in England, Scotland or Wales.

(8) Until the date appointed under section 131(3) below any reference in subsection (7) above to the appropriate nature conservation body is a reference to the Nature Conservancy Council.

(9) If within the period of four months beginning with the date on which a waste regulation authority received an application for the grant of a licence, or within such longer period as the authority and the applicant may at any time agree in writing, the authority has neither granted the licence in consequence of the application nor given notice to the applicant that the authority has rejected the application, the authority shall be deemed to have rejected the application.

(10) The period allowed to the National Rivers Authority, the Health and Safety Executive, the appropriate nature conservancy body, a river purification authority or general planning authority for the making of representations under subsection (4), (6) or (7) above about a proposal is the period of twenty-one days beginning with that on which the proposal is received by the authority or such longer period as the waste regulation authority and the Authority, the Executive, the body, the river purification authority or the general planning authority, as the case may be, agree in writing.

37 Variation of licences

(1) While a licence issued by a waste regulation authority is in force, the authority may, subject to regulations under section 35(6) above and to subsection (3) below,—

- (a) on its own initiative, modify the conditions of the licence to any extent which, in the opinion of the authority, is desirable and is unlikely to require unreasonable expense on the part of the holder; and
- (b) on the application of the licence holder accompanied by the prescribed fee payable under section 41 below, modify the conditions of his licence to the extent requested in the application.

(2) While a licence issued by a waste regulation authority is in force, the authority shall, except where it revokes the licence entirely under section 38 below, modify the conditions of the licence—

- (a) to the extent which in the opinion of the authority is required for the purpose of ensuring that the activities authorised by the licence do not cause pollution of the environment or harm to human health or become seriously detrimental to the amenities of the locality affected by the activities; and
- (b) to the extent required by any regulations in force under section 35(6) above.

(3) The Secretary of State may, as respects any licence issued by a waste regulation authority, give to the authority directions as to the modifications which are to be made in the conditions of the licence under subsection (1)(a) or (2)(a) above; and it shall be the duty of the authority to give effect to the directions.

(4) Any modification of a licence under this section shall be effected by notice served on the holder of the licence and the notice shall state the time at which the modification is to take effect.

(5) Section 36(4), (5), (6), (7), (8) and (10) above shall with the necessary modifications apply to a proposal by a waste regulation authority to modify a licence under

subsection (1) or (2)(a) above as they apply to a proposal to issue a licence, except that—

(a) the authority may postpone the reference so far as the authority considers that by reason of an emergency it is appropriate to do so; and

(b) the authority need not consider any representations as respects a modification which, in the opinion of the waste regulation authority, will not affect any authority mentioned in the subsections so applied.

(6) If within the period of two months beginning with the date on which a waste regulation authority received an application by the holder of a licence for a modification of it, or within such longer period as the authority and the applicant may at any time agree in writing, the authority has neither granted a modification of the licence in consequence of the application nor given notice to the applicant that the authority has rejected the application, the authority shall be deemed to have rejected the application.

38 Revocation and suspension of licences

(1) Where a licence granted by a waste regulation authority is in force and it appears to the authority—

(a) that the holder of the licence has ceased to be a fit and proper person by reason of his having been convicted of a relevant offence; or

(b) that the continuation of the activities authorised by the licence would cause pollution of the environment or harm to human health or would be seriously detrimental to the amenities of the locality affected; and

(c) that the pollution, harm or detriment cannot be avoided by modifying the conditions of the licence;

the authority may exercise, as it thinks fit, either of the powers conferred by subsections (3) and (4) below.

(2) Where a licence granted by a waste regulation authority is in force and it appears to the authority that the holder of the licence has ceased to be a fit and proper person by reason of the management of the activities authorised by the licence having ceased to be in the hands of a technically competent person, the authority may exercise the power conferred by subsection (3) below.

(3) The authority may, under this subsection, revoke the licence so far as it authorises the carrying on of the activities specified in the licence or such of them as the authority specifies in revoking the licence.

(4) The authority may, under this subsection, revoke the licence entirely.

(5) A licence revoked under subsection (3) above shall cease to have effect to authorise the carrying on of the activities specified in the licence or, as the case may be, the activities specified by the authority in revoking the licence but shall not affect the requirements imposed by the licence which the authority, in revoking the licence, specify as requirements which are to continue to bind the licence holder.

(6) Where a licence granted by a waste regulation authority is in force and it appears to the authority—

(a) that the holder of the licence has ceased to be a fit and proper person by reason of the management of the activities authorised by the licence having ceased to be in the hands of a technically competent person; or

(b) that serious pollution of the environment or serious harm to human health has resulted from, or is about to be caused by, the activities to which the licence relates or the happening or threatened happening of an event affecting those activities; and

(c) that the continuing to carry on those activities, or any of those activities, in the circumstances will continue or, as the case may be, cause serious pollution of the environment or serious harm to human health;

the authority may suspend the licence so far as it authorises the carrying on of the activities specified in the licence or such of them as the authority specifies in suspending the licence.

(7) The Secretary of State may, if he thinks fit in relation to a licence granted by a waste regulation authority, give to the authority directions as to whether and in what manner the authority should exercise its powers under this section; and it shall be the duty of the authority to give effect to the directions.

(8) A licence suspended under subsection (6) above shall, while the suspension has effect, be of no effect to authorise the carrying on of the activities specified in the licence or, as the case may be, the activities specified by the authority in suspending the licence.

(9) Where a licence is suspended under subsection (6) above, the authority, in suspending it or at any time while it is suspended, may require the holder of the licence to take such measures to deal with or avert the pollution or harm as the authority considers necessary.

(10) A person who, without reasonable excuse, fails to comply with any requirement imposed under subsection (9) above otherwise than in relation to special waste shall be liable—

(a) on summary conviction, to a fine of an amount not exceeding the statutory maximum; and

(b) on conviction on indictment, to imprisonment for a term not exceeding two years or a fine or both.

(11) A person who, without reasonable excuse, fails to comply with any requirement imposed under subsection (9) above in relation to special waste shall be liable—

(a) on summary conviction, to imprisonment for a term not exceeding six months or a fine not exceeding the statutory maximum or both; and

(b) on conviction on indictment, to imprisonment for a term not exceeding five years or a fine or both.

(12) Any revocation or suspension of a licence or requirement imposed during the suspension of a licence under this section shall be effected by notice served on the holder of the licence and the notice shall state the time at which the revocation or suspension or the requirement is to take effect and, in the case of suspension, the period at the end of which, or the event on the occurrence of which, the suspension is to cease.

39 Surrender of licences

(1) A licence may be surrendered by its holder to the authority which granted it but, in the case of a site licence, only if the authority accepts the surrender.

(2) The following provisions apply to the surrender and acceptance of the surrender of a site licence.

(3) The holder of a site licence who desires to surrender it shall make an application for that purpose to the authority in such form, giving such information and accompanied by such evidence as the Secretary of State prescribes by regulations and accompanied by the prescribed fee payable under section 41 below.

(4) An authority which receives an application for the surrender of a site licence—

(a) shall inspect the land to which the licence relates, and

(b) may require the holder of the licence to furnish to it further information or further evidence.

(5) The authority shall determine whether it is likely or unlikely that the condition of the land, so far as that condition is the result of the use of the land for the treatment, keeping or disposal of waste (whether or not in pursuance of the licence), will cause pollution of the environment or harm to human health.

(6) If the authority is satisfied that the condition of the land is unlikely to cause the pollution or harm mentioned in subsection (5) above, the authority shall, subject to subsection (7) below, accept the surrender of the licence; but otherwise the authority shall refuse to accept it.

(7) Where the authority proposes to accept the surrender of a site licence, the authority must, before it does so,—

(a) refer the proposal to the National Rivers Authority; and

(b) consider any representations about the proposal which the Authority makes to it during the allowed period;

and if the Authority requests that the surrender of the licence be not accepted either of them may refer the matter to the Secretary of State and the surrender shall not be accepted except in accordance with his decision.

(8) Subsection (7) above shall not apply to Scotland, but in Scotland where the authority (not being an islands council) proposes to accept the surrender of a licence, the authority must, before it does so,—

(a) refer the proposal to—

(i) the river purification authority whose area includes any of the relevant land;

(ii) where the waste regulation authority is not also a district planning authority within the meaning of section 172 of the Local Government (Scotland) Act 1973, the general planning authority within the meaning of that section whose area includes any of the relevant land; and

(b) consider any representations about the proposal which the river purification authority or the general planning authority makes to it during the allowed period,

and if the river purification authority requests that the surrender of the licence be not accepted by the waste regulation authority either of them may refer the matter to the Secretary of State and the surrender shall not be accepted except in accordance with his decision.

(9) Where the surrender of a licence is accepted under this section the authority shall issue to the applicant, with the notice of its determination, a certificate (a "certificate of completion") stating that it is satisfied as mentioned in subsection (6) above and, on the issue of that certificate, the licence shall cease to have effect.

(10) If within the period of three months beginning with the date on which an authority receives an application to surrender a licence, or within such longer period as the authority and the applicant may at any time agree in writing, the authority has neither issued a certificate of completion nor given notice to the applicant that the authority has rejected the application, the authority shall be deemed to have rejected the application.

(11) Section 36(10) above applies for the interpretation of the "allowed period" in subsections (7) and (8) above.

40 Transfer of licences

(1) A licence may be transferred to another person in accordance with subsections (2) to (6) below and may be so transferred whether or not the licence is partly revoked or suspended under any provision of this Part.

(2) Where the holder of a licence desires that the licence be transferred to another person ("the proposed transferee") the licence holder and the proposed transferee shall jointly make an application to the waste regulation authority which granted the licence for a transfer of it.

(3) An application under subsection (2) above for the transfer of a licence shall be made in such form and shall include such information as the Secretary of State prescribes by regulations and shall be accompanied by the prescribed fee payable under section 41 below and the licence.

(4) If, on such an application, the authority is satisfied that the proposed transferee is a fit and proper person the authority shall effect a transfer of the licence to the proposed transferee.

(5) The authority shall effect a transfer of a licence under the foregoing provisions of this section by causing the licence to be endorsed with the name and other particulars of the proposed transferee as the holder of the licence from such date specified in the endorsement as may be agreed with the applicants.

(6) If within the period of two months beginning with the date on which the authority receives an application for the transfer of a licence, or within such longer period as the authority and the applicants may at any time agree in writing, the authority has neither effected a transfer of the licence nor given notice to the applicants that the authority has rejected the application, the authority shall be deemed to have rejected the application.

41 Fees and charges for licences

(1) There shall be charged by and paid to waste regulation authorities, in respect of applications for licences or relevant applications in respect of licences, and in respect of the holding of licences, such fees and charges as may be provided for from time to time by a scheme under subsection (2) below.

(2) The Secretary of State may, with the approval of the Treasury, make, and from time to time revise, a scheme prescribing—

(a) fees payable in respect of applications for licences or relevant applications in respect of licences, and

(b) charges payable in respect of the subsistence of licences,

to waste regulation authorities by persons making applications for or in respect of licences, or holding licences, as the case may be.

(3) The applications in respect of licences which are relevant for the purposes of this section are—

(a) applications for a modification of the conditions of a licence;

(b) applications to surrender a licence; and

(c) applications for the transfer of a licence.

(4) The Secretary of State shall, on making or revising a scheme under subsection (2) above, lay a copy of the scheme or of the modifications made in the scheme before each House of Parliament.

(5) A waste regulation authority in England and Wales shall pay to the National Rivers Authority, and a waste regulation authority in Scotland shall pay to any river purification authority which it consults in relation to a licence, out of any fee or charge which—

(a) is payable to the authority under a scheme under subsection (2) above; and

(b) is of a description prescribed in such a scheme for the purposes of this subsection,

such amount as may be prescribed in the scheme in relation to fees or charges of that description.

(6) A scheme under subsection (2) above may in particular—

(a) provide for different fees or charges to be payable according to the description of activities authorised by licences and the descriptions and amounts of controlled waste to which those activities relate;

(b) provide for the times at which and manner in which payments of fees or charges are to be made; and

(c) make such incidental, supplementary and transitional provision as appears to the Secretary of State to be appropriate;

and different schemes may be made and revised for different areas.

(7) If it appears to the waste regulation authority that the holder of a licence has failed to pay a charge due in consideration of the subsistence of the licence, the authority may, by notice in writing served on the holder, revoke the licence so far as it authorises the carrying on of the activities specified in the licence.

(8) Section 38(5) above applies for the purposes of subsection (7) above as it applies for the purposes of subsection (3) of that section.

42 Supervision of licensed activities

(1) While a licence is in force it shall be the duty of the waste regulation authority which granted the licence to take the steps needed—

(a) for the purpose of ensuring that the activities authorised by the licence do not cause pollution of the environment or harm to human health or become seriously detrimental to the amenities of the locality affected by the activities; and

(b) for the purpose of ensuring that the conditions of the licence are complied with.

(2) Where, at any time during the subsistence of a licence, it appears to the waste regulation authority that pollution of water is likely to be caused by the activities to which the licence relates, it shall be the duty of the authority to consult the National

Rivers Authority or, in Scotland, the river purification authority whose area includes any of the relevant land as to the discharge by the authority of the duty imposed on it by subsection (1) above.

(3) For the purpose of performing the duty imposed on it by subsection (1) above, any officer of the authority authorised in writing for the purpose by the authority may, if it appears to him that by reason of an emergency it is necessary to do so, carry out work on the land or in relation to plant or equipment on the land to which the licence relates or, as the case may be, in relation to the mobile plant to which the licence relates.

(4) Where a waste regulation authority incurs any expenditure by virtue of subsection (3) above, the authority may recover the amount of the expenditure from the holder of the licence or, if the licence has been surrendered, from the former holder of it, except where the holder or former holder of the licence shows that there was no emergency requiring any work or except such of the expenditure as he shows was unnecessary.

(5) Where it appears to a waste regulation authority that a condition of a licence granted by it is not being complied with, then, without prejudice to any proceedings under section 33(6) above, the authority may—

(a) require the licence holder to comply with the condition within a specified time; and

(b) if in the opinion of the authority the licence holder has not complied with the condition within that time, exercise any of the powers specified in subsection (6) below.

(6) The powers which become exercisable in the event mentioned in subsection (5)(b) above are the following—

(a) to revoke the licence so far as it authorises the carrying on of the activities specified in the licence or such of them as the authority specifies in revoking the licence;

(b) to revoke the licence entirely; and

(c) to suspend the licence so far as it authorises the carrying on of the activities specified in the licence or, as the case may be, the activities specified by the authority in suspending the licence.

(7) Where a licence is revoked or suspended under subsection (6) above, subsections (5) or (8) and (9), (10) and (12) of section 38 above shall apply with the necessary modifications as they respectively apply to revocations or suspensions of licences under that section; and the power to make a requirement under subsection (5)(a) above shall be exercisable by notice served on the holder of the licence (and "specified" shall be construed accordingly).

(8) The Secretary of State may, if he thinks fit in relation to a licence granted by a waste regulation authority, give to the authority directions as to whether and in what manner the authority should exercise its powers under this section; and it shall be the duty of the authority to give effect to the directions.

43 Appeals to Secretary of State from decisions with respect to licences

(1) Where, except in pursuance of a direction given by the Secretary of State,—

(a) an application for a licence or a modification of the conditions of a licence is rejected;

(b) a licence is granted subject to conditions;

(c) the conditions of a licence are modified;
(d) a licence is suspended;
(e) a licence is revoked under section 38 or 42 above;
(f) an application to surrender a licence is rejected; or
(g) an application for the transfer of a licence is rejected;

then, except in the case of an application for a transfer, the applicant for the licence or, as the case may be, the holder or former holder of it may appeal from the decision to the Secretary of State and, in the case of an application for a transfer, the proposed transferee may do so.

(2) Where an appeal is made to the Secretary of State—
(a) the Secretary of State may refer any matter involved in the appeal to a person appointed by him for the purpose;
(b) the Secretary of State may, instead of determining the appeal himself, direct that the appeal or any matter involved in it shall be determined by a person appointed by him for the purpose (who shall have the same powers as the Secretary of State);
(c) if a party to the appeal so requests, or the Secretary of State so decides, the appeal shall be or continue in the form of a hearing (which may, if the person hearing the appeal so decides, be held or held to any extent in private).

(3) Where, on such an appeal, the Secretary of State or other person determining the appeal determines that the decision of the authority shall be altered it shall be the duty of the authority to give effect to the determination.

(4) While an appeal is pending in a case falling within subsection (1)(c) or (e) above, the decision in question shall, subject to subsection (6) below, be ineffective; and if the appeal is dismissed or withdrawn the decision shall become effective from the end of the day on which the appeal is dismissed or withdrawn.

(5) Where an appeal is made in a case falling within subsection (1)(d) above, the bringing of the appeal shall have no effect on the decision in question.

(6) Subsection (4) above shall not apply to a decision modifying the conditions of a licence under section 37 above or revoking a licence under section 38 or 42 above in the case of which the notice effecting the modification or revocation includes a statement that in the opinion of the authority it is necessary for the purpose of preventing or, where that is not practicable, minimising pollution of the environment or harm to human health that that subsection should not apply.

(7) Where the decision under appeal is one falling within subsection (6) above or is a decision to suspend a licence, if, on the application of the holder or former holder of the licence, the Secretary of State or other person determining the appeal determines that the authority acted unreasonably in excluding the application of subsection (4) above or, as the case may be, in suspending the licence, then—
(a) if the appeal is still pending at the end of the day on which the determination is made, subsection (4) above shall apply to the decision from the end of that day; and
(b) the holder or former holder of the licence shall be entitled to recover compensation from the authority in respect of any loss suffered by him in consequence of the exclusion of the application of that subsection or the suspension of the licence;

and any dispute as to a person's entitlement to such compensation or as to the amount of it shall be determined by arbitration or in Scotland by a single arbiter appointed, in default of agreement between the parties concerned, by the Secretary of State on the application of any of the parties.

(8) Provision may be made by the Secretary of State by regulations with respect to appeals under this section and in particular—

(a) as to the period within which and the manner in which appeals are to be brought; and

(b) as to the manner in which appeals are to be considered.

44 Offences of making false statements

A person who, in an application for a licence, for a modification of the conditions of a licence or for the surrender or transfer of a licence, makes any statement which he knows to be false in a material particular or recklessly makes any statement which is false in a material particular shall be liable—

(a) on summary conviction, to a fine not exceeding the statutory maximum; and

(b) on conviction on indictment, to imprisonment for a term not exceeding two years or to a fine or both.

Collection, disposal or treatment of controlled waste

45 Collection of controlled waste

(1) It shall be the duty of each waste collection authority—

(a) to arrange for the collection of household waste in its area except waste—

(i) which is situated at a place which in the opinion of the authority is so isolated or inaccessible that the cost of collecting it would be unreasonably high, and

(ii) as to which the authority is satisfied that adequate arrangements for its disposal have been or can reasonably be expected to be made by a person who controls the waste; and

(b) if requested by the occupier of premises in its area to collect any commercial waste from the premises, to arrange for the collection of the waste.

(2) Each waste collection authority may, if requested by the occupier of premises in its area to collect any industrial waste from the premises, arrange for the collection of the waste; but a collection authority in England and Wales shall not exercise the power except with the consent of the waste disposal authority whose area includes the area of the waste collection authority.

(3) No charge shall be made for the collection of household waste except in cases prescribed in regulations made by the Secretary of State; and in any of those cases—

(a) the duty to arrange for the collection of the waste shall not arise until a person who controls the waste requests the authority to collect it; and

(b) the authority may recover a reasonable charge for the collection of the waste from the person who made the request.

(4) A person at whose request waste other than household waste is collected under this section shall be liable to pay a reasonable charge for the collection and disposal of the

waste to the authority which arranged for its collection; and it shall be the duty of that authority to recover the charge unless in the case of a charge in respect of commercial waste the authority considers it inappropriate to do so.

(5) It shall be the duty of each waste collection authority—

(a) to make such arrangements for the emptying, without charge, of privies serving one or more private dwellings in its area as the authority considers appropriate;

(b) if requested by the person who controls a cesspool serving only one or more private dwellings in its area to empty the cesspool, to remove such of the contents of the cesspool as the authority considers appropriate on payment, if the authority so requires, of a reasonable charge.

(6) A waste collection authority may, if requested by the person who controls any other privy or cesspool in its area to empty the privy or cesspool, empty the privy or, as the case may be, remove from the cesspool such of its contents as the authority consider appropriate on payment, if the authority so requires, of a reasonable charge.

(7) A waste collection authority may—

(a) construct, lay and maintain, within or outside its area, pipes and associated works for the purpose of collecting waste;

(b) contribute towards the cost incurred by another person in providing or maintaining pipes or associated works connecting with pipes provided by the authority under paragraph (a) above.

(8) A waste collection authority may contribute towards the cost incurred by another person in providing or maintaining plant or equipment intended to deal with commercial or industrial waste before it is collected under arrangements made by the authority under subsection (1)(b) or (2) above.

(9) Subject to section 48(1) below, anything collected under arrangements made by a waste collection authority under this section shall belong to the authority and may be dealt with accordingly.

(10) In relation to Scotland, sections 2, 3, 4 and 41 of the Sewerage (Scotland) Act 1968 (maintenance of public sewers etc.) shall apply in relation to pipes and associated works provided or to be provided under subsection (7)(a) above as those sections apply in relation to public sewers but as if—

(a) the said section 2 conferred a power and did not impose a duty on a local authority to do the things mentioned in that section;

(b) in the said section 4, the words from "but before any person" to the end were omitted,

and the Pipe-lines Act 1962 shall not apply to pipes and associated works provided or to be provided under the said subsection (7)(a).

(11) In the application of this section to Scotland, subsection (5)(b) and the references to a cesspool occurring in subsection (6) shall be omitted.

(12) In this section "privy" means a latrine which has a moveable receptacle and "cesspool" includes a settlement tank or other tank for the reception or disposal of foul matter from buildings.

46 Receptacles for household waste

(1) Where a waste collection authority has a duty by virtue of section 45(1)(a) above to arrange for the collection of household waste from any premises, the authority may, by notice served on him, require the occupier to place the waste for collection in receptacles of a kind and number specified.

(2) The kind and number of the receptacles required under subsection (1) above to be used shall be such only as are reasonable but, subject to that, separate receptacles or compartments of receptacles may be required to be used for waste which is to be recycled and waste which is not.

(3) In making requirements under subsection (1) above the authority may, as respects the provision of the receptacles—

- (a) determine that they be provided by the authority free of charge;
- (b) propose that they be provided, if the occupier agrees, by the authority on payment by him of such a single payment or such periodical payments as he agrees with the authority;
- (c) require the occupier to provide them if he does not enter into an agreement under paragraph (b) above within a specified period; or
- (d) require the occupier to provide them.

(4) In making requirements as respects receptacles under subsection (1) above, the authority may, by the notice under that subsection, make provision with respect to—

- (a) the size, construction and maintenance of the receptacles;
- (b) the placing of the receptacles for the purpose of facilitating the emptying of them, and access to the receptacles for that purpose;
- (c) the placing of the receptacles for that purpose on highways or, in Scotland, roads;
- (d) the substances or articles which may or may not be put into the receptacles or compartments of receptacles of any description and the precautions to be taken where particular substances or articles are put into them; and
- (e) the steps to be taken by occupiers of premises to facilitate the collection of waste from the receptacles.

(5) No requirement shall be made under subsection (1) above for receptacles to be placed on a highway or, as the case may be, road, unless—

- (a) the relevant highway authority or roads authority have given their consent to their being so placed; and
- (b) arrangements have been made as to the liability for any damage arising out of their being so placed.

(6) A person who fails, without reasonable excuse, to comply with any requirements imposed under subsection (1), (3)(c) or (d) or (4) above shall be liable on summary conviction to a fine not exceeding level 3 on the standard scale.

(7) Where an occupier is required under subsection (1) above to provide any receptacles he may, within the period allowed by subsection (8) below, appeal to a magistrates' court or, in Scotland, to the sheriff by way of summary application against any requirement imposed under subsection (1), subsection (3)(c) or (d) or (4) above on the ground that—

- (a) the requirement is unreasonable; or

(b) the receptacles in which household waste is placed for collection from the premises are adequate.

(8) The period allowed to the occupier of premises for appealing against such a requirement is the period of twenty-one days beginning—

(a) in a case where a period was specified under subsection (3)(c) above, with the end of that period; and

(b) where no period was specified, with the day on which the notice making the requirement was served on him.

(9) Where an appeal against a requirement is brought under subsection (7) above—

(a) the requirement shall be of no effect pending the determination of the appeal;

(b) the court shall either quash or modify the requirement or dismiss the appeal; and

(c) no question as to whether the requirement is, in any respect, unreasonable shall be entertained in any proceedings for an offence under subsection (6) above.

(10) In this section—

"receptacle" includes a holder for receptacles; and

"specified" means specified in a notice under subsection (1) above.

47 Receptacles for commercial or industrial waste

(1) A waste collection authority may, at the request of any person, supply him with receptacles for commercial or industrial waste which he has requested the authority to arrange to collect and shall make a reasonable charge for any receptacle supplied unless in the case of a receptacle for commercial waste the authority considers it appropriate not to make a charge.

(2) If it appears to a waste collection authority that there is likely to be situated, on any premises in its area, commercial waste or industrial waste of a kind which, if the waste is not stored in receptacles of a particular kind, is likely to cause a nuisance or to be detrimental to the amenities of the locality, the authority may, by notice served on him, require the occupier of the premises to provide at the premises receptacles for the storage of such waste of a kind and number specified.

(3) The kind and number of the receptacles required under subsection (2) above to be used shall be such only as are reasonable.

(4) In making requirements as respects receptacles under subsection (2) above, the authority may, by the notice under that subsection, make provision with respect to—

(a) the size, construction and maintenance of the receptacles;

(b) the placing of the receptacles for the purpose of facilitating the emptying of them, and access to the receptacles for that purpose;

(c) the placing of the receptacles for that purpose on highways or, in Scotland, roads;

(d) the substances or articles which may or may not be put into the receptacles and the precautions to be taken where particular substances or articles are put into them; and

(e) the steps to be taken by occupiers of premises to facilitate the collection of waste from the receptacles.

(5) No requirement shall be made under subsection (2) above for receptacles to be placed on a highway or, as the case may be, road unless—

(a) the relevant highway authority or roads authority have given their consent to their being so placed; and

(b) arrangements have been made as to the liability for any damage arising out of their being so placed.

(6) A person who fails, without reasonable excuse, to comply with any requirements imposed under subsection (2) or (4) above shall be liable on summary conviction to a fine not exceeding level 3 on the standard scale.

(7) Where an occupier is required under subsection (2) above to provide any receptacles he may, within the period allowed by subsection (8) below, appeal to a magistrates' court or, in Scotland, to the sheriff by way of summary application against any requirement imposed under subsection (2) or (4) above on the ground that—

(a) the requirement is unreasonable; or

(b) the waste is not likely to cause a nuisance or be detrimental to the amenities of the locality.

(8) The period allowed to the occupier of premises for appealing against such a requirement is the period of twenty-one days beginning with the day on which the notice making the requirement was served on him.

(9) Where an appeal against a requirement is brought under subsection (7) above—

(a) the requirement shall be of no effect pending the determination of the appeal;

(b) the court shall either quash or modify the requirement or dismiss the appeal; and

(c) no question as to whether the requirement is, in any respect, unreasonable shall be entertained in any proceedings for an offence under subsection (6) above.

(10) In this section—

"receptacle" includes a holder for receptacles; and

"specified" means specified in a notice under subsection (2) above.

48 Duties of waste collection authorities as respects disposal of waste collected

(1) Subject to subsections (2) and (6) below, it shall be the duty of each waste collection authority to deliver for disposal all waste which is collected by the authority under section 45 above to such places as the waste disposal authority for its area directs.

(2) The duty imposed on a waste collection authority by subsection (1) above does not, except in cases falling within subsection (4) below, apply as respects household waste or commercial waste for which the authority decides to make arrangements for recycling the waste; and the authority shall have regard, in deciding what recycling arrangements to make, to its waste recycling plan under section 49 below.

(3) A waste collection authority which decides to make arrangements under subsection (2) above for recycling waste collected by it shall, as soon as reasonably practicable, by notice in writing, inform the waste disposal authority for the area which includes its area of the arrangements which it proposes to make.

(4) Where a waste disposal authority has made with a waste disposal contractor arrangements, as respects household waste or commercial waste in its area or any part

of its area, for the contractor to recycle the waste, or any of it, the waste disposal authority may, by notice served on the waste collection authority, object to the waste collection authority having the waste recycled; and the objection may be made as respects all the waste, part only of the waste or specified descriptions of the waste.

(5) Where an objection is made under subsection (4) above, subsection (2) above shall not be available to the waste collection authority to the extent objected to.

(6) A waste collection authority may, subject to subsection (7) below, provide plant and equipment for the sorting and baling of waste retained by the authority under subsection (2) above.

(7) Subsection (6) above does not apply to an authority which is also a waste disposal authority; but, in such a case, the authority may make arrangements with a waste disposal contractor for the contractor to deal with the waste as mentioned in that subsection.

(8) A waste collection authority may permit another person to use facilities provided by the authority under subsection (6) above and may provide for the use of another person any such facilities as the authority has power to provide under that subsection; and—

- (a) subject to paragraph (b) below, it shall be the duty of the authority to make a reasonable charge in respect of the use by another person of the facilities, unless the authority considers it appropriate not to make a charge;
- (b) no charge shall be made under this subsection in respect of household waste; and
- (c) anything delivered to the authority by another person in the course of using the facilities shall belong to the authority and may be dealt with accordingly.

(9) This section shall not apply to Scotland.

49 Waste recycling plans by collection authorities

(1) It shall be the duty of each waste collection authority, as respects household and commercial waste arising in its area—

- (a) to carry out an investigation with a view to deciding what arrangements are appropriate for dealing with the waste by separating, baling or otherwise packaging it for the purpose of recycling it;
- (b) to decide what arrangements are in the opinion of the authority needed for that purpose;
- (c) to prepare a statement ("the plan") of the arrangements made and proposed to be made by the authority and other persons for dealing with waste in those ways;
- (d) to carry out from time to time further investigations with a view to deciding what changes in the plan are needed; and
- (e) to make any modification of the plan which the authority thinks appropriate in consequence of any such further investigation.

(2) In considering any arrangements or modification for the purposes of subsection (1) (c) or (e) above it shall be the duty of the authority to have regard to the effect which the arrangements or modification would be likely to have on the amenities of any locality and the likely cost or saving to the authority attributable to the arrangements or modification.

(3) It shall be the duty of a waste collection authority to include in the plan information as to—

(a) the kinds and quantities of controlled waste which the authority expects to collect during the period specified in the plan;

(b) the kinds and quantities of controlled waste which the authority expects to purchase during that period;

(c) the kinds and quantities of controlled waste which the authority expects to deal with in the ways specified in subsection (1)(a) above during that period;

(d) the arrangements which the authority expects to make during that period with waste disposal contractors or, in Scotland, waste disposal authorities and waste disposal contractors for them to deal with waste in those ways;

(e) the plant and equipment which the authority expects to provide under section 48(6) above or 53 below; and

(f) the estimated costs or savings attributable to the methods of dealing with the waste in the ways provided for in the plan.

(4) It shall be the duty of a waste collection authority, before finally determining the content of the plan or a modification, to send a copy of it in draft to the Secretary of State for the purpose of enabling him to determine whether subsection (3) above has been complied with; and, if the Secretary of State gives any directions to the authority for securing compliance with that subsection, it shall be the duty of the authority to comply with the direction.

(5) When a waste collection authority has determined the content of the plan or a modification it shall be the duty of the authority—

(a) to take such steps as in the opinion of the authority will give adequate publicity in its area to the plan or modification; and

(b) to send to the waste disposal authority and waste regulation authority for the area which includes its area a copy of the plan or, as the case may be, particulars of the modification.

(6) It shall be the duty of each waste collection authority to keep a copy of the plan and particulars of any modifications to it available at all reasonable times at its principal offices for inspection by members of the public free of charge and to supply a copy of the plan and of the particulars of any modifications to it to any person who requests one, on payment by that person of such reasonable charge as the authority requires.

(7) The Secretary of State may give to any waste collection authority directions as to the time by which the authority is to perform any duty imposed by this section specified in the direction; and it shall be the duty of the authority to comply with the direction.

50 Waste disposal plans of waste regulation authorities

(1) It shall be the duty of each waste regulation authority—

(a) to carry out an investigation with a view to deciding what arrangements are needed for the purpose of treating or disposing of controlled waste which is situated in its area and controlled waste which is likely to be so situated so as to prevent or minimise pollution of the environment or harm to human health;

(b) to decide what arrangements are in the opinion of the authority needed for that purpose and how it should discharge its functions in relation to licences;

(c) to prepare a statement ("the plan") of the arrangements made and proposed to be made by waste disposal contractors, or, in Scotland, waste disposal authorities and waste disposal contractors, for the treatment or disposal of such waste;

(d) to carry out from time to time further investigations with a view to deciding what changes in the plan are needed; and

(e) to make any modification of the plan which the authority thinks appropriate in consequence of any such further investigation.

(2) In considering any arrangements or modification for the purposes of subsection (1)(c) or (e) above it shall be the duty of the authority to have regard both to the likely cost of the arrangements or modification and to their likely beneficial effects on the environment.

(3) It shall be the duty of the authority to include in the plan information as to—

(a) the kinds and quantities of controlled waste which the authority expects to be situated in its area during the period specified in the plan;

(b) the kinds and quantities of controlled waste which the authority expects to be brought into or taken for disposal out of its area during that period;

(c) the kinds and quantities of controlled waste which the authority expects to be disposed of within its area during that period;

(d) the methods and the respective priorities for the methods by which in the opinion of the authority controlled waste in its area should be disposed of or treated during that period;

(e) the policy of the authority as respects the discharge of its functions in relation to licences and any relevant guidance issued by the Secretary of State;

(f) the sites and equipment which persons are providing and which during that period are expected to provide for disposing of controlled waste; and

(g) the estimated costs of the methods of disposal or treatment provided for in the plan;

but provision may be made by the Secretary of State by regulations for modifying the foregoing paragraphs and for requiring waste regulation authorities to take into account in preparing plans and any modifications of plans under this section such factors as may be prescribed in the regulations.

(4) In considering what information to include in the plan under subsection (3)(d) above, it shall be the duty of the authority to have regard to the desirability, where reasonably practicable, of giving priority to recycling waste.

(5) It shall be the duty of the authority—

(a) in preparing the plan and any modification of it, to consult—

(i) the National Rivers Authority or, in Scotland, any river purification authority any part of whose area is included in the area of the waste regulation authority;

(ii) the waste collection authorities whose areas are included in the area of the authority;

(iii) in a case where the plan or modification is prepared by a waste regulation authority in Wales, the county council whose area includes that of the authority;

(iv) in a case where the plan or modification is prepared by a Scottish waste regulation authority other than an islands council, the council of the region in which the area of the authority is included;

(v) in a case where provisions of the plan or modification relate to the taking of waste for disposal or treatment into the area of another waste regulation authority, that other authority; and

(vi) in any case, such persons as the authority considers it appropriate to consult from among persons who in the opinion of the authority are or are likely to be, or are representative of persons who are or are likely to be, engaged by way of trade or business in the disposal or treatment of controlled waste situated in the area of the authority; and

(b) before finally determining the content of the plan or modification, to take, subject to subsection (6) below, such steps as in the opinion of the authority will—

(i) give adequate publicity in its area to the plan or modification; and

(ii) provide members of the public with opportunities of making representations to the authority about it;

and to consider any representations made by the public and make any change in the plan or modification which the authority considers appropriate.

(6) No steps need be taken under subsection (5)(b) above in respect of a modification which in the opinion of the waste regulation authority is such that no person will be prejudiced if those steps are not taken.

(7) Without prejudice to the duty of authorities under subsection (5) above, it shall be the duty of the authority, in preparing the plan and any modification of it, to consider, in consultation with the waste collection authorities in its area and any other persons,—

(a) what arrangements can reasonably be expected to be made for recycling waste; and

(b) what provisions should be included in the plan for that purpose.

(8) An authority shall not finally determine the content of the plan or modification in a case falling within subsection (5)(a)(v) above except with the consent of the other waste regulation authority or, if the other authority withholds its consent, with the consent of the Secretary of State.

(9) It shall be the duty of the authority, before finally determining the content of the plan or modification, to send a copy of it in draft to the Secretary of State for the purpose of enabling him to determine whether subsection (3) above has been complied with; and, if the Secretary of State gives any directions to the authority for securing compliance with that subsection, it shall be the duty of the authority to comply with the direction.

(10) When an authority has finally determined the content of the plan or a modification it shall be the duty of the authority—

(a) to take such steps as in the opinion of the authority will give adequate publicity in its area to the plan or modification; and

(b) to send to the Secretary of State a copy of the plan or, as the case may be, particulars of the modification.

(11) The Secretary of State may give to any waste regulation authority directions as to the time by which the authority is to perform any duty imposed by this section specified in the direction; and it shall be the duty of the authority to comply with the direction.

51 Functions of waste disposal authorities

(1) It shall be the duty of each waste disposal authority to arrange—

(a) for the disposal of the controlled waste collected in its area by the waste collection authorities; and

(b) for places to be provided at which persons resident in its area may deposit their household waste and for the disposal of waste so deposited;

in either case by means of arrangements made (in accordance with Part II of Schedule 2 to this Act) with waste disposal contractors, but by no other means.

(2) The arrangements made by a waste disposal authority under subsection (1)(b) above shall be such as to secure that—

(a) each place is situated either within the area of the authority or so as to be reasonably accessible to persons resident in its area;

(b) each place is available for the deposit of waste at all reasonable times (including at least one period on the Saturday or following day of each week except a week in which the Saturday is 25th December or 1st January);

(c) each place is available for the deposit of waste free of charge by persons resident in the area;

but the arrangements may restrict the availability of specified places to specified descriptions of waste.

(3) A waste disposal authority may include in arrangements made under subsection (1)(b) above arrangements for the places provided for its area for the deposit of household waste free of charge by residents in its area to be available for the deposit of household or other controlled waste by other persons on such terms as to payment (if any) as the authority determines.

(4) For the purpose of discharging its duty under subsection (1)(a) above as respects controlled waste collected as mentioned in that paragraph a waste disposal authority—

(a) shall give directions to the waste collection authorities within its area as to the persons to whom and places at which such waste is to be delivered;

(b) may arrange for the provision, within or outside its area, by waste disposal contractors of places at which such waste may be treated or kept prior to its removal for treatment or disposal;

(c) may make available to waste disposal contractors (and accordingly own) plant and equipment for the purpose of enabling them to keep such waste prior to its removal for disposal or to treat such waste in connection with so keeping it or for the purpose of facilitating its transportation;

(d) may make available to waste disposal contractors (and accordingly hold) land for the purpose of enabling them to treat, keep or dispose of such waste in or on the land;

(e) may contribute towards the cost incurred by persons who produce commercial or industrial waste in providing and maintaining plant or equipment intended to deal with such waste before it is collected; and

(f) may contribute towards the cost incurred by persons who produce commercial or industrial waste in providing or maintaining pipes or associated works connecting with pipes provided by a waste collection authority within the area of the waste disposal authority.

(5) For the purpose of discharging its duties under subsection (1)(b) above as respects household waste deposited as mentioned in that paragraph a waste disposal authority—

(a) may arrange for the provision, within or outside its area, by waste disposal contractors of places at which such waste may be treated or kept prior to its removal for treatment or disposal;

(b) may make available to waste disposal contractors (and accordingly own) plant and equipment for the purpose of enabling them to keep such waste prior to its removal for disposal or to treat such waste in connection with so keeping it or for the purpose of facilitating its transportation; and

(c) may make available to waste disposal contractors (and accordingly hold) land for the purpose of enabling them to treat, keep or dispose of such waste in or on the land.

(6) Where the arrangements made under subsection (1)(b) include such arrangements as are authorised by subsection (3) above, subsection (5) above applies as respects household or other controlled waste as it applies as respects household waste.

(7) Subsection (1) above is subject to section 77.

(8) This section shall not apply to Scotland.

52 Payments for recycling and disposal etc. of waste

(1) Where, under section 48(2) above, a waste collection authority retains for recycling waste collected by it under section 45 above, the waste disposal authority for the area which includes the area of the waste collection authority shall make to that authority payments, in respect of the waste so retained, of such amounts representing its net saving of expenditure on the disposal of the waste as the authority determines.

(2) Where, by reason of the discharge by a waste disposal authority of its functions, waste arising in its area does not fall to be collected by a waste collection authority under section 45 above, the waste collection authority shall make to the waste disposal authority payments, in respect of the waste not falling to be so collected, of such amounts representing its net saving of expenditure on the collection of the waste as the authority determines.

(3) Where a person other than a waste collection authority, for the purpose of recycling it, collects waste arising in the area of a waste disposal authority which would fall to be collected under section 45 above, the waste disposal authority may make to that person payments, in respect of the waste so collected, of such amounts representing its net saving of expenditure on the disposal of the waste as the authority determines.

(4) Where a person other than a waste collection authority, for the purpose of recycling it, collects waste which would fall to be collected under section 45 above, the waste collection authority may make to that person payments, in respect of the waste so collected, of such amounts representing its net saving of expenditure on the collection of the waste as the authority determines.

(5) The Secretary of State may, by regulations, impose on waste disposal authorities a duty to make payments corresponding to the payments which are authorised by subsection (3) above to such persons in such circumstances and in respect of such descriptions or quantities of waste as are specified in the regulations.

(6) For the purposes of subsections (1), (3) and (5) above the net saving of expenditure of a waste disposal authority on the disposal of any waste retained or collected for recycling is the amount of the expenditure which the authority would, but for the retention or collection, have incurred in having it disposed of less any amount payable by the authority to any person in consequence of the retention or collection for recycling (instead of the disposal) of the waste.

(7) For the purposes of subsections (2) and (4) above the net saving of expenditure of a waste collection authority on the collection of any waste not falling to be collected by it is the amount of the expenditure which the authority would, if it had had to collect the waste, have incurred in collecting it .

(8) The Secretary of State shall, by regulations, make provision for the determination of the net saving of expenditure for the purposes of subsections (1), (2), (3), (4) and (5) above.

(9) A waste disposal authority shall be entitled to receive from a waste collection authority such sums as are needed to reimburse the waste disposal authority the reasonable cost of making arrangements under section 51(1) above for the disposal of commercial and industrial waste collected in the area of the waste disposal authority.

(10) A waste disposal authority shall pay to a waste collection authority a reasonable contribution towards expenditure reasonably incurred by the waste collection authority in delivering waste, in pursuance of a direction under section 51(4)(a) above, to a place which is unreasonably far from the waste collection authority's area.

(11) Any question arising under subsection (9) or (10) above shall, in default of agreement between the two authorities in question, be determined by arbitration.

53 Duties of authorities as respects disposal of waste collected: Scotland

(1) It shall be the duty of each waste disposal authority to arrange for the disposal of any waste collected by it, in its capacity as a waste collection authority, under section 45 above; and without prejudice to the authority's powers apart from the following provisions of this subsection, the powers exercisable by the authority for the purpose of performing that duty shall include power—

- (a) to provide, within or outside its area, places at which to deposit waste before the authority transfers it to a place or plant or equipment provided under the following paragraph; and
- (b) to provide, within or outside its area, places at which to dispose of or recycle the waste and plant or equipment for processing, recycling or otherwise disposing of it.

(2) Subsections (7) and (10) of section 45 above shall have effect in relation to a waste disposal authority as if the reference in paragraph (a) of the said subsection (7) to the collection of waste included the disposal of waste under this section and the disposal of anything produced from waste belonging to the authority.

(3) A waste disposal authority may permit another person to use facilities provided by the authority under the preceding provisions of this section and may provide for the use of another person any such facilities as the authority has power to provide under those provisions, and—

(a) subject to the following paragraph, it shall be the duty of the authority to make a reasonable charge in respect of the use by another person of the facilities unless the authority considers it appropriate not to make a charge;
(b) no charge shall be made under this section in respect of household waste; and
(c) anything delivered to the authority by another person in the course of using the facilities shall belong to the authority and may be dealt with accordingly.

(4) References to waste in subsection (1) above do not include matter removed from privies under section 45(5)(a) or (6) above, and it shall be the duty of a waste collection authority (other than an islands council) by which matter is so removed—
(a) to deliver the matter, in accordance with any directions of the regional council, at a place specified in the directions (which must be in or within a reasonable distance from the waste collection authority's area), to the regional council or another person so specified;
(b) to give to the regional council from time to time a notice stating the quantity of the matter which the waste collection authority expects to deliver to or as directed by the regional council under the preceding paragraph during a period specified in the notice.

(5) Any question arising under paragraph (a) of the preceding subsection as to whether a place is within a reasonable distance from a waste collection authority's area shall, in default of agreement between the waste collection authority and the regional council in question, be determined by a single arbiter appointed, in default of agreement between the parties concerned, by the Secretary of State on the application of any of the parties; and anything delivered to a regional council under that subsection shall belong to the council and may be dealt with accordingly.

(6) This section applies to Scotland only.

54 Special provisions for land occupied by disposal authorities: Scotland

(1) Nothing in subsection (1)(a) and (b) of section 33 above shall apply to—
(a) the deposit of controlled waste in or on land in the area of a waste disposal authority which is occupied by the authority; or
(b) the treating, keeping or disposing of controlled waste—
(i) in or on land so occupied;
(ii) by means of any mobile plant operated by the waste disposal authority,

if the requirements of subsection (3) below are satisfied.

(2) If any land occupied by a waste disposal authority is used by the authority as a site in or on which to deposit, treat, keep or dispose of or permit other persons to deposit, treat, keep or dispose of controlled waste or if the authority operates their mobile plant for the purpose aforesaid, it shall be the duty of the waste regulation authority to ensure that the land is used and the mobile plant operated in accordance with conditions which are—
(a) calculated to prevent the use from causing pollution of the environment or harm to human health or serious detriment to the amenities of the locality in which the land is situated or the mobile plant may be operated; and
(b) specified in a resolution passed by the waste regulation authority in accordance with the following provisions of this section.

(3) The requirements mentioned in subsection (1) above are, where the deposit is made, or the treating, keeping or disposing is carried out—

(a) by the waste disposal authority that, as respects the land or as the case may be the mobile plant, conditions have been specified by the waste regulation authority by virtue of subsection (2)(b) above and (in so far as current) are complied with;

(b) by another person, that it is with the consent of the waste disposal authority and in accordance with any conditions to which the consent is subject.

(4) Where a waste disposal authority proposes that any land which the waste disposal authority occupies or intends to occupy should be used by that authority or that any mobile plant should be operated by the authority as mentioned in the preceding subsection, it shall be the duty of the waste regulation authority before it gives effect to the proposal—

(a) to prepare a statement of the conditions which the waste regulation authority intends to specify in a resolution to be passed by that authority under paragraph (d) below;

(b) to refer the proposal and the statement—

(i) to the river purification authority whose area includes any of the land in question;

(ii) to the Health and Safety Executive;

(iii) where the waste regulation authority is not also a district planning authority (within the meaning of section 172 of the Local Government (Scotland) Act 1973), to the general planning authority (within the meaning of that section) whose area includes any of the land; and

(iv) in the case of a proposal to operate mobile plant, to the river purification authority whose area includes the area of the waste disposal authority;

(c) to consider any representations about the proposal and statement which the river purification authority, the Health and Safety Executive or the general planning authority makes to it during the allowed period;

(d) subject to subsection (7) of this section, to pass a resolution—

(i) authorising the deposit, keeping, treatment or disposal of any specified description of controlled waste in or on specified land occupied or to be occupied by the waste disposal authority or the treatment or disposal of any specified description of controlled waste by means of specified mobile plant;

(ii) specifying the conditions in accordance with which the land in question or the mobile plant is to be used by the waste disposal authority as mentioned in the preceding subsection;

(e) where any part of the land to be used is land which has been notified under section 28(1) of the Wildlife and Countryside Act 1981, to—

(i) refer the proposal and the statement to the appropriate nature conservation body, and

(ii) consider any representations about the proposal and the statement which that body makes to it during the allowed period,

and in this subsection and subsection (13) of this section any reference to the appropriate nature conservation body is a reference, until the date appointed under section 131(3) below, to the Nature Conservancy Council or, after that date, to the Nature Conservancy Council for Scotland.

(5) In subsection (4) above, paragraphs (a) to (c), and in paragraph (d) the words "subject to subsection (7) of this section", shall have effect only in a case where the proposal is made by a waste disposal authority other than an islands council.

(6) A separate resolution under subsection (4)(d) above shall be passed by the authority—

(a) in respect of each item of mobile plant; and

(b) in relation to each site.

(7) If a river purification authority to which a proposal is referred by a waste regulation authority under paragraph (b) of subsection (4) of this section requests the authority not to proceed with the resolution or disagrees with the authority as to the conditions to be specified in the resolution under paragraph (d) of that subsection, either of them may refer the matter to the Secretary of State and it shall be the duty of the authority not to pass a resolution under that paragraph except in accordance with his decision.

(8) A waste regulation authority by which a resolution has been passed under paragraph (d) of subsection (4) of this section or this subsection may vary or rescind the resolution by a subsequent resolution of the authority.

(9) Paragraphs (a) to (c) of subsection (4) and subsection (7) of this section shall with the necessary modifications apply to a proposal to pass a resolution under subsection (8) above and to such a resolution as they apply to such a proposal as is mentioned in those provisions and to a resolution under the said paragraph (d), except that—

(a) those provisions shall not apply to a resolution, or to a proposal to pass a resolution, which only rescinds a previous resolution; and

(b) the waste regulation authority may postpone the reference under the said subsection (4) so far as the authority considers that by reason of an emergency it is appropriate to do so; and

(c) the waste regulation authority may disregard any other authority or the Health and Safety Executive for the purposes of the preceding provisions of this subsection in relation to a resolution which, in the opinion of the waste regulation authority, will not affect the other authority.

(10) If while a resolution is in force under the preceding provisions of this section it appears to the authority which passed the resolution—

(a) that the continuation of activities to which the resolution relates would cause pollution of the environment or harm to human health or would be seriously detrimental to the amenities of the locality affected; and

(b) that the pollution, harm or detriment cannot be avoided by modifying the conditions relating to the carrying on of the activities,

it shall be the duty of the waste disposal authority to discontinue the activities and of the waste regulation authority to rescind the resolution.

(11) If it appears to a river purification authority that activities to which a resolution under this section relates are causing or likely to cause pollution to controlled waters (within the meaning of Part II of the Control of Pollution Act 1974) in the area of the authority, the authority may, without prejudice to the provisions of the preceding subsection or the said Part II, request the Secretary of State to direct the waste regulation authority which passed the resolution to rescind it and the waste disposal authority to discontinue the activities; and it shall be the duty of a waste disposal authority and a waste regulation authority to comply with a direction given to it under this subsection.

(12) It shall be the duty of waste regulation authorities to have regard to any guidance issued to them by the Secretary of State with regard to the discharge of their functions under this section.

(13) The period allowed to the river purification authority, the Health and Safety Executive and the general planning authority for the making of representations under subsection (4)(c) above or to the appropriate nature conservation body for the making of representations under subsection (4)(e) above about a proposal is the period of twenty-one days beginning with that on which the proposal is received by that body or such longer period as the waste regulation authority and that body agree in writing.

(14) The Secretary of State may, by regulations, make provision as to conditions which are, or are not, to be included in a resolution; and regulations under this subsection may make different provision for different circumstances.

(15) The Secretary of State may as respects any resolution made or to be made by the authority give to the authority directions—

- (a) as to the conditions which are or are not to be included in the resolution;
- (b) as to the modifications which it would be appropriate to make in the conditions included in a resolution by virtue of subsection (7) above;
- (c) as to the rescinding of the resolution;

and it shall be the duty of the authority to give effect to the directions.

(16) Any resolution of a waste disposal authority under Part I of the Control of Pollution Act 1974 effective immediately before the commencement of this section shall have effect as if it were a resolution of a waste regulation authority under this section.

(17) This section applies to Scotland only.

55 Powers for recycling waste

(1) This section has effect for conferring on waste disposal authorities and waste collection authorities powers for the purposes of recycling waste.

(2) A waste disposal authority may—

- (a) make arrangements with waste disposal contractors for them to recycle waste as respects which the authority has duties under section 51(1) above or agrees with another person for its disposal or treatment;
- (b) make arrangements with waste disposal contractors for them to use waste for the purpose of producing from it heat or electricity or both;
- (c) buy or otherwise acquire waste with a view to its being recycled;
- (d) use, sell or otherwise dispose of waste as respects which the authority has duties under section 51(1) above or anything produced from such waste.

(3) A waste collection authority may—

- (a) buy or otherwise acquire waste with a view to recycling it;
- (b) use, or dispose of by way of sale or otherwise to another person, waste belonging to the authority or anything produced from such waste.

(4) This section shall not apply to Scotland.

56 Powers for recycling waste: Scotland

(1) Without prejudice to the powers of waste disposal authorities apart from this section, a waste disposal authority may—

(a) do such things as the authority considers appropriate for the purpose of—

(i) enabling waste belonging to the authority, or belonging to another person who requests the authority to deal with it under this section, to be recycled; or

(ii) enabling waste to be used for the purpose of producing from it heat or electricity or both;

(b) buy or otherwise acquire waste with a view to its being recycled;

(c) use, sell or otherwise dispose of waste belonging to the authority or anything produced from such waste.

(2) This section applies to Scotland only.

57 Power of Secretary of State to require waste to be accepted, treated, disposed of or delivered

(1) The Secretary of State may, by notice in writing, direct the holder of any waste management licence to accept and keep, or accept and treat or dispose of, controlled waste at specified places on specified terms.

(2) The Secretary of State may, by notice in writing, direct any person who is keeping controlled waste on any land to deliver the waste to a specified person on specified terms with a view to its being treated or disposed of by that other person.

(3) A direction under this section may impose a requirement as respects waste of any specified kind or as respects any specified consignment of waste.

(4) A direction under subsection (2) above may require the person who is directed to deliver the waste to pay to the specified person his reasonable costs of treating or disposing of the waste.

(5) A person who fails, without reasonable excuse, to comply with a direction under this section shall be liable on summary conviction to a fine not exceeding level 5 on the standard scale.

(6) A person shall not be guilty of an offence under any other enactment prescribed by the Secretary of State by regulations made for the purposes of this subsection by reason only of anything necessarily done or omitted in order to comply with a direction under this section.

(7) The Secretary of State may, where the costs of the treatment or disposal of waste are not paid or not fully paid in pursuance of subsection (4) above to the person treating or disposing of the waste, pay the costs or the unpaid costs, as the case may be, to that person.

(8) In this section “specified” means specified in a direction under this section.

58 Power of Secretary of State to require waste to be accepted, treated, disposed of or delivered: Scotland

In relation to Scotland, the Secretary of State may give directions to a waste disposal authority to accept and keep, or accept and treat or dispose of, controlled waste at specified places on specified terms; and it shall be the duty of the authority to give effect to the directions.

59 Powers to require removal of waste unlawfully deposited

(1) If any controlled waste is deposited in or on any land in the area of a waste regulation authority or waste collection authority in contravention of section 33(1) above, the authority may, by notice served on him, require the occupier to do either or both of the following, that is—

(a) to remove the waste from the land within a specified period not less than a period of twenty-one days beginning with the service of the notice;

(b) to take within such a period specified steps with a view to eliminating or reducing the consequences of the deposit of the waste.

(2) A person on whom any requirements are imposed under subsection (1) above may, within the period of twenty-one days mentioned in that subsection, appeal against the requirement to a magistrates' court or, in Scotland, to the sheriff by way of summary application.

(3) On any appeal under subsection (2) above the court shall quash the requirement if it is satisfied that—

(a) the appellant neither deposited nor knowingly caused nor knowingly permitted the deposit of the waste; or

(b) there is a material defect in the notice;

and in any other case shall either modify the requirement or dismiss the appeal.

(4) Where a person appeals against any requirement imposed under subsection (1) above, the requirement shall be of no effect pending the determination of the appeal; and where the court modifies the requirement or dismisses the appeal it may extend the period specified in the notice.

(5) If a person on whom a requirement imposed under subsection (1) above fails, without reasonable excuse, to comply with the requirement he shall be liable, on summary conviction, to a fine not exceeding level 5 on the standard scale and to a further fine of an amount equal to one-tenth of level 5 on the standard scale for each day on which the failure continues after conviction of the offence and before the authority has begun to exercise its powers under subsection (6) below.

(6) Where a person on whom a requirement has been imposed under subsection (1) above by an authority fails to comply with the requirement the authority may do what that person was required to do and may recover from him any expenses reasonably incurred by the authority in doing it.

(7) If it appears to a waste regulation authority or waste collection authority that waste has been deposited in or on any land in contravention of section 33(1) above and that—

(a) in order to remove or prevent pollution of land, water or air or harm to human health it is necessary that the waste be forthwith removed or other steps taken to eliminate or reduce the consequences of the deposit or both; or

(b) there is no occupier of the land; or

(c) the occupier neither made nor knowingly permitted the deposit of the waste;

the authority may remove the waste from the land or take other steps to eliminate or reduce the consequences of the deposit or, as the case may require, to remove the waste and take those steps.

(8) Where an authority exercises any of the powers conferred on it by subsection (7) above it shall be entitled to recover the cost incurred by it in removing the waste or taking the steps or both and in disposing of the waste—

(a) in a case falling within subsection (7)(a) above, from the occupier of the land unless he proves that he neither made nor knowingly caused nor knowingly permitted the deposit of the waste;

(b) in any case, from any person who deposited or knowingly caused or knowingly permitted the deposit of any of the waste;

except such of the cost as the occupier or that person shows was incurred unnecessarily.

(9) Any waste removed by an authority under subsection (7) above shall belong to that authority and may be dealt with accordingly.

60 Interference with waste sites and receptacles for waste

(1) No person shall sort over or disturb—

(a) anything deposited at a place for the deposit of waste provided by a waste collection authority, by a waste disposal contractor under arrangements made with a waste disposal authority or by any other local authority or person or, in Scotland, by a waste disposal authority;

(b) anything deposited in a receptacle for waste, whether for public or private use, provided by a waste collection authority, by a waste disposal contractor under arrangements made with a waste disposal authority, by a parish or community council or by a holder of a waste management licence or, in Scotland, by a waste disposal authority or a roads authority; or

(c) the contents of any receptacle for waste which, in accordance with a requirement under section 46 or 47 above, is placed on any highway or, in Scotland, road or in any other place with a view to its being emptied;

unless he has the relevant consent or right to do so specified in subsection (2) below.

(2) The consent or right that is relevant for the purposes of subsection (1)(a), (b) or (c) above is—

(a) in the case of paragraph (a), the consent of the authority, contractor or other person who provides the place for the deposit of the waste;

(b) in the case of paragraph (b), the consent of the authority, contractor or other person who provides the receptacle for the deposit of the waste;

(c) in the case of paragraph (c), the right to the custody of the receptacle, the consent of the person having the right to the custody of the receptacle or the right conferred by the function by or under this Part of emptying such receptacles.

(3) A person who contravenes subsection (1) above shall be liable on summary conviction to a fine of an amount not exceeding level 3 on the standard scale.

61 Duty of waste regulation authorities as respects closed landfills

(1) Except as respects land in relation to which a site licence is in force, it shall be the duty of every waste regulation authority to cause its area to be inspected from time to time to detect whether any land is in such a condition, by reason of the relevant matters affecting the land, that it may cause pollution of the environment or harm to human health.

(2) The matters affecting land relevant for the purposes of this section are the concentration or accumulation in, and emission or discharge from, the land of noxious gases or noxious liquids caused by deposits of controlled waste in the land.

(3) For the purpose of discharging the duty imposed by subsection (1) above on a waste regulation authority, the authority may enter and inspect any land—

(a) in or on which controlled waste has been deposited at any time under the authority of a waste management licence or a disposal licence under section 5 of the Control of Pollution Act 1974; or

(b) as respects which the authority has reason to believe that controlled waste has been deposited in the land at any time (whether before or after 1st January 1976); or

(c) in which there are, or the authority has reason to believe there may be, concentrations or accumulations of noxious gases or noxious liquids.

In this subsection "controlled waste" means household, industrial or commercial waste as defined in section 75(5), (6) and (7) below (subject, if the regulations so provide, to regulations under section 63(1) or 75(8) below).

(4) Where it appears to a waste regulation authority that the condition of any land in its area is such as is specified in subsection (1) above it shall be the duty of the authority, from time to time during the period of its responsibility for the land, to enter and inspect the land for the purpose of keeping its condition under review.

(5) Where, at any time during the period of its responsibility for any land, it appears to a waste regulation authority that the condition of the land is, by reason of the relevant matters affecting the land, such that pollution of water is likely to be caused, it shall be the duty of the authority to consult the National Rivers Authority or, in Scotland, the river purification authority whose area includes the land in question as to the discharge by the authority of the duty imposed on it in relation to the land by subsection (7) below.

(6) The "period of responsibility" for any land for the purposes of subsections (4) and (5) above extends from the time at which the condition of the land first appears to the authority to be such as is referred to in that subsection until the authority is satisfied that no pollution of the environment or harm to human health will be caused by reason of the relevant matters affecting the land.

(7) Where, on an inspection by a waste regulation authority of any land under this section, it appears to the authority that the condition of the land is, by reason of the relevant matters affecting the land, such that pollution of the environment or harm to human health is likely to be caused it shall be the duty of the authority to do such works and take such other steps (whether on the land affected or on adjacent land) as appear to the authority to be reasonable to avoid such pollution or harm.

(8) Where an authority exercises in relation to waste on any land the duty imposed by subsection (7) above, the authority shall, except in a case falling within subsection (9) below, be entitled to recover the cost or part of the cost incurred in doing so from the person who is for the time being the owner of the land, except such of the cost as that person shows was incurred unreasonably.

(9) Subsection (8) above does not apply in a case where the authority accepted the surrender under section 39 above of the waste management licence which authorised the activities in the course of which the waste was deposited.

(10) In deciding whether to recover the cost and, if so, how much to recover of the cost which it is entitled to recover under subsection (8) above, the authority shall have regard to any hardship which the recovery may cause to the owner of the land.

(11) It shall be the duty of waste regulation authorities to have regard to any guidance issued to them by the Secretary of State as respects the discharge of their functions under this section.

Special waste and non-controlled waste

62 Special provision with respect to certain dangerous or intractable waste

(1) If the Secretary of State considers that controlled waste of any kind is or may be so dangerous or difficult to treat, keep or dispose of that special provision is required for dealing with it he shall make provision by regulations for the treatment, keeping or disposal of waste of that kind ("special waste").

(2) Without prejudice to the generality of subsection (1) above, the regulations may include provision—

(a) for the giving of directions by waste regulation authorities with respect to matters connected with the treatment, keeping or disposal of special waste;

(b) for securing that special waste is not, while awaiting treatment or disposal in pursuance of the regulations, kept at any one place in quantities greater than those which are prescribed and in circumstances which differ from those which are prescribed;

(c) in connection with requirements imposed on consignors or consignees of special waste, imposing, in the event of non-compliance, requirements on any person carrying the consignment to re-deliver it as directed;

(d) for requiring the occupier of premises on which special waste is situated to give notice of that fact and other prescribed information to a prescribed authority;

(e) for the keeping of records by waste regulation authorities and by persons who import, export, produce, keep, treat or dispose of special waste or deliver it to another person for treatment or disposal, for the inspection of the records and for the furnishing by such persons to waste regulation authorities of copies of or information derived from the records;

(f) for the keeping in the register under section 64(1) below of copies of such of those records, or such information derived from those records, as may be prescribed;

(g) providing that a contravention of the regulations shall be an offence and prescribing the maximum penalty for the offence, which shall not exceed, on summary conviction, a fine at level 5 on the standard scale and, on conviction on indictment, imprisonment for a term of two years or a fine or both.

(3) Without prejudice to the generality of subsection (1) above, the regulations may include provision—

(a) for the supervision by waste regulation authorities of activities authorised by virtue of the regulations and for the recovery of the costs incurred by them from the persons carrying on the activities;

(b) as to the recovery of expenses or other charges for the treatment, keeping or disposal or the re-delivery of special waste in pursuance of the regulations;

(c) as to appeals to the Secretary of State from decisions of waste regulation authorities under the regulations.

(4) In the application of this section to Northern Ireland "waste regulation authority" means a district council established under the Local Government Act (Northern Ireland) 1972.

63 Waste other than controlled waste

(1) The Secretary of State may, after consultation with such bodies as he considers appropriate, make regulations providing that prescribed provisions of this Part shall have effect in a prescribed area—

(a) as if references in those provisions to controlled waste or controlled waste of a kind specified in the regulations included references to such waste as is mentioned in section 75(7)(c) below which is of a kind so specified; and

(b) with such modifications as may be prescribed;

and the regulations may make such modifications of other enactments as the Secretary of State considers appropriate.

(2) A person who—

(a) deposits any waste other than controlled waste, or

(b) knowingly causes or knowingly permits the deposit of any waste other than controlled waste,

in a case where, if the waste were special waste and any waste management licence were not in force, he would be guilty of an offence under section 33 above shall, subject to subsection (3) below, be guilty of that offence and punishable accordingly.

(3) No offence is committed by virtue of subsection (2) above if the act charged was done under and in accordance with any consent, licence, approval or authority granted under any enactment (excluding any planning permission under the enactments relating to town and country planning).

(4) Section 45(2) and section 47(1) above shall apply to waste other than controlled waste as they apply to controlled waste.

Publicity

64 Public registers

(1) Subject to sections 65 and 66 below, it shall be the duty of each waste regulation authority to maintain a register containing prescribed particulars of or relating to—

(a) current or recently current licences ("licences") granted by the authority;

(b) current or recently current applications to the authority for licences;

(c) applications made to the authority under section 37 above for the modification of licences;

(d) notices issued by the authority under section 37 above effecting the modification of licences;

(e) notices issued by the authority under section 38 above effecting the revocation or suspension of licences or imposing requirements on the holders of licences;

(f) appeals under section 43 above relating to decisions of the authority;

(g) certificates of completion issued by the authority under section 39(9) above;

(h) notices issued by the authority imposing requirements on the holders of licences under section 42(5) above;

(i) convictions of the holders of licences granted by the authority for any offence under this Part (whether in relation to a licence so granted or not);

(j) the occasions on which the authority has discharged any function under section 42 or 61 above;

(k) directions given to the authority under any provision of this Part by the Secretary of State;

(l) in Scotland, resolutions made by the authority under section 54 above;

(m) such matters relating to the treatment, keeping or disposal of waste in the area of the authority or any pollution of the environment caused thereby as may be prescribed;

and any other document or information required to be kept in the register under any provision of this Act.

(2) Where information of any description is excluded from any register by virtue of section 66 below, a statement shall be entered in the register indicating the existence of information of that description.

(3) For the purposes of subsection (1) above licences are "recently" current for the period of twelve months after they cease to be in force and applications for licences are "recently" current if they relate to a licence which is current or recently current or, in the case of an application which is rejected, for the period of twelve months beginning with the date on which the waste regulation authority gives notice of rejection or, as the case may be, on which the application is deemed by section 36(9) above to have been rejected.

(4) It shall be the duty of each waste collection authority in England which is not a waste regulation authority to maintain a register containing prescribed particulars of such information contained in any register maintained under subsection (1) above as relates to the treatment, keeping or disposal of controlled waste in the area of the authority.

(5) Waste regulation authorities in England which are not waste collection authorities shall furnish any waste collection authorities in their areas with the particulars necessary to enable them to discharge their duty under subsection (4) above.

(6) Each waste regulation authority and waste collection authority shall secure that any register maintained under this section is open to inspection at its principal office by members of the public free of charge at all reasonable hours and shall afford to members of the public reasonable facilities for obtaining, on payment of reasonable charges, copies of entries in the register.

(7) Registers under this section may be kept in any form.

(8) In this section "prescribed" means prescribed in regulations by the Secretary of State.

65 Exclusion from registers of information affecting national security

(1) No information shall be included in a register maintained under section 64 above (a "register") if and so long as, in the opinion of the Secretary of State, the inclusion in the register of that information, or information of that description, would be contrary to the interests of national security.

(2) The Secretary of State may, for the purpose of securing the exclusion from registers of information to which subsection (1) above applies, give to the authorities maintaining registers directions—

(a) specifying information, or descriptions of information, to be excluded from their registers; or

(b) specifying descriptions of information to be referred to the Secretary of State for his determination;

and no information referred to the Secretary of State in pursuance of paragraph (b) above shall be included in any such register until the Secretary of State determines that it should be so included.

(3) An authority maintaining a register shall notify the Secretary of State of any information it excludes from the register in pursuance of directions under subsection (2) above.

(4) A person may, as respects any information which appears to him to be information to which subsection (1) above may apply, give a notice to the Secretary of State specifying the information and indicating its apparent nature; and, if he does so—

(a) he shall notify the authority concerned that he has done so; and

(b) no information so notified to the Secretary of State shall be included in the register kept by that authority until the Secretary of State has determined that it should be so included.

66 Exclusion from registers of certain confidential information

(1) No information relating to the affairs of any individual or business shall be included in a register maintained under section 64 above (a "register"), without the consent of that individual or the person for the time being carrying on that business, if and so long as the information—

(a) is, in relation to him, commercially confidential; and

(b) is not required to be included in the register in pursuance of directions under subsection (7) below;

but information is not commercially confidential for the purposes of this section unless it is determined under this section to be so by the authority maintaining the register or, on appeal, by the Secretary of State.

(2) Where information is furnished to an authority maintaining a register for the purpose of—

(a) an application for, or for the modification of, a licence;

(b) complying with any condition of a licence; or

(c) complying with a notice under section 71(2) below;

then, if the person furnishing it applies to the authority to have the information excluded from the register on the ground that it is commercially confidential (as regards himself or another person), the authority shall determine whether the information is or is not commercially confidential.

(3) A determination under subsection (2) above must be made within the period of fourteen days beginning with the date of the application and if the authority fails to make a determination within that period it shall be treated as having determined that the information is commercially confidential.

(4) Where it appears to an authority maintaining a register that any information (other than information furnished in circumstances within subsection (2) above) which has been obtained by the authority under or by virtue of any provision of this Part might be commercially confidential, the authority shall—

(a) give to the person to whom or whose business it relates notice that that information is required to be included in the register unless excluded under this section; and

(b) give him a reasonable opportunity—

(i) of objecting to the inclusion of the information on the grounds that it is commercially confidential; and

(ii) of making representations to the authority for the purpose of justifying any such objection;

and, if any representations are made, the authority shall, having taken the representations into account, determine whether the information is or is not commercially confidential.

(5) Where, under subsection (2) or (4) above, an authority determines that information is not commercially confidential—

(a) the information shall not be entered in the register until the end of the period of twenty-one days beginning with the date on which the determination is notified to the person concerned;

(b) that person may appeal to the Secretary of State against the decision;

and, where an appeal is brought in respect of any information, the information shall not be entered in the register pending the final determination or withdrawal of the appeal.

(6) Subsections (2) and (8) of section 43 above shall apply in relation to appeals under subsection (5) above.

(7) The Secretary of State may give to the authorities maintaining registers directions as to specified information, or descriptions of information, which the public interest requires to be included in the registers notwithstanding that the information may be commercially confidential.

(8) Information excluded from a register shall be treated as ceasing to be commercially confidential for the purposes of this section at the expiry of the period of four years beginning with the date of the determination by virtue of which it was excluded; but the person who furnished it may apply to the authority for the information to remain excluded from the register on the ground that it is still commercially confidential and the authority shall determine whether or not that is the case.

(9) Subsections (5) and (6) above shall apply in relation to a determination under subsection (8) above as they apply in relation to a determination under subsection (2) or (4) above.

(10) The Secretary of State may, by order, substitute for the period for the time being specified in subsection (3) above such other period as he considers appropriate.

(11) Information is, for the purposes of any determination under this section, commercially confidential, in relation to any individual or person, if its being contained in the register would prejudice to an unreasonable degree the commercial interests of that individual or person.

67 Annual reports

(1) Each waste regulation authority shall, for each financial year of the authority, prepare and publish a report on the discharge by the authority of its functions under this Part or under any relevant instrument.

(2) A report under subsection (1) above shall include information as respects—

(a) the licences respectively applied for, granted, in force, modified, revoked, suspended, surrendered or transferred during the year and the appeals made against decisions taken in respect of them;

(b) the exercise by the authority of its powers under sections 42, 54, 61 or 62 of this Act or any relevant instrument;

(c) the implementation of the authority's plan under section 50 above, with particular reference to recycling waste;

(d) the number and description of prosecutions brought under this Part; and

(e) the cost incurred, and the sums received, by the authority in discharging its functions under this Part.

(3) Each waste regulation authority shall—

(a) arrange for the report for any year under subsection (1) above to be published not later than the end of the period of six months following the end of the year to which the report relates; and

(b) when it publishes it, send a copy of the report to the Secretary of State.

(4) In subsections (1) and (2) above "relevant instrument" means any instrument under section 2(2) of the European Communities Act 1972 under which waste regulation authorities have functions.

Supervision and enforcement

68 Functions of Secretary of State and appointment etc. of inspectors

(1) The Secretary of State shall have the function of keeping under review the discharge by waste regulation authorities of their functions under this Part.

(2) The Secretary of State may appoint as inspectors (under whatever title he may determine) such persons having suitable qualifications as he thinks necessary for assisting him in discharging his functions under this Part, and may terminate any appointment made under this subsection.

(3) Any waste regulation authority having functions under this Part may appoint as inspectors (under whatever title the authority may determine) such persons having suitable qualifications as the authority thinks necessary for carrying this Part into effect in the authority's area, and may terminate any appointment made under this subsection.

(4) An inspector shall not be liable in any civil or criminal proceedings for anything done in the purported performance of his functions under section 69 or 70 below if the court is satisfied that the act was done in good faith and that there were reasonable grounds for doing it.

(5) In the following provisions of this Part "inspector" means a person appointed as an inspector under subsection (2) or (3) above.

69 Powers of entry etc. of inspectors

(1) An inspector may, on production (if so required) of his authority, exercise any of the powers specified in subsection (3) below for the purpose of—

- (a) discharging any functions conferred or imposed by or under this Part on the Secretary of State or, as the case may be, a waste regulation authority or on the inspector;
- (b) determining whether, and if so in what manner, such a function should be discharged; or
- (c) determining whether any provision of this Part or of an instrument under it is being complied with.

(2) Those powers are exercisable in relation to—

- (a) land in or on which, or vessels in or by means of which, controlled waste is being or has been deposited, treated, kept or disposed of;
- (b) land in or on which, or vessels in or by means of which, controlled waste is (on reasonable grounds) believed to be being, or to have been, deposited, treated, kept or disposed of;
- (c) land which is or is (on reasonable grounds) believed to be affected by the deposit, treatment, keeping or disposal of controlled waste on other land;

and in this section "premises" means any such land or any such vessel.

(3) The powers of an inspector referred to above are—

- (a) at any reasonable time (or, in a situation in which in his opinion there is an immediate risk of serious pollution of the environment or serious harm to human health, at any time) to enter premises which he has reason to believe it is necessary for him to enter;
- (b) on entering any premises by virtue of paragraph (a) above to take with him—
  - (i) any person duly authorised by the Secretary of State or, as the case may be, the waste regulation authority and, if the inspector has reasonable cause to apprehend any serious obstruction in the execution of his duty, a constable; and
  - (ii) any equipment or materials required for any purpose for which the power of entry is being exercised;
- (c) to make such examination and investigation as may in any circumstances be necessary;
- (d) as regards any premises which he has power to enter, to direct that those premises or any part of them, or anything in them, shall be left undisturbed (whether generally or in particular respects) for so long as is reasonably necessary for the purpose of any examination or investigation under paragraph (c) above;
- (e) to take such measurements and photographs and make such recordings as he considers necessary for the purpose of any examination or investigation under paragraph (c) above;
- (f) to take samples of any articles or substances found on any premises which he has power to enter, and of the air, water or land in, on, or in the vicinity of, the premises;
- (g) in the case of any article or substance found in any premises which he has power to enter, being an article or substance which appears to him to have caused or to be likely to cause pollution of the environment or harm to human

health, to cause it to be dismantled or subjected to any process or test (but not so as to damage or destroy it unless this is necessary);

(h) in the case of any such article or substance as is mentioned in paragraph (g) above, to take possession of it and detain it for so long as is necessary for all or any of the following purposes, namely—

(i) to examine it and do to it anything which he has power to do under that paragraph;

(ii) to ensure that it is not tampered with before his examination of it is completed;

(iii) to ensure that it is available for use as evidence in any proceedings under this Part;

(i) to require any person whom he has reasonable cause to believe to be able to give any information relevant to any examination or investigation under paragraph (c) above to answer (in the absence of persons other than a person nominated to be present and any persons whom the inspector may allow to be present) such questions as the inspector thinks fit to ask and to sign a declaration of the truth of his answers;

(j) to require the production of, or where the information is recorded in computerised form, the furnishing of extracts from, any records which are required to be kept under this Part or it is necessary for him to see for the purposes of an examination or investigation under paragraph (c) above and to inspect, and takes copies of, or of any entry in, the records;

(k) to require any person to afford him such facilities and assistance with respect to any matters or things within that person's control or in relation to which that person has responsibilities as are necessary to enable the inspector to exercise any of the powers conferred on him by this section.

(4) The Secretary of State may by regulations make provision as to the procedure to be followed in connection with the taking of, and the dealing with, samples under subsection (3)(f) above.

(5) Where an inspector proposes to exercise the power conferred by subsection (3)(g) above in the case of an article or substance found on any premises, he shall, if so requested by a person who at the time is present on and has responsibilities in relation to those premises, cause anything which is to be done by virtue of that power to be done in the presence of that person.

(6) Before exercising the power conferred by subsection (3)(g) above in the case of any article or substance, an inspector shall consult such persons as appear to him appropriate for the purpose of ascertaining what dangers, if any, there may be in doing anything which he proposes to do under the power.

(7) Where under the power conferred by subsection (3)(h) above an inspector takes possession of any article or substance found on any premises, he shall leave there, either with a responsible person or, if that is impracticable, fixed in a conspicuous position, a notice giving particulars of that article or substance sufficient to identify it and stating that he has taken possession of it under that power; and before taking possession of any such substance under that power an inspector shall, if it is practical for him to do so, take a sample of it and give to a responsible person at the premises a portion of the sample marked in a manner sufficient to identify it.

(8) No answer given by a person in pursuance of a requirement imposed under subsection (3)(i) above shall be admissible in evidence in England and Wales against

that person in any proceedings or in Scotland against that person in any criminal proceedings.

(9) Any person who—

(a) fails, without reasonable excuse, to comply with any requirement imposed under this section;

(b) prevents any other person from appearing before or from answering any question to which an inspector may by virtue of subsection (3) above require an answer; or

(c) intentionally obstructs an inspector in the exercise or performance of his powers or duties;

shall be liable, on summary conviction, to a fine not exceeding level 5 on the standard scale.

(10) The powers conferred by subsection (3)(a), (c), (e) and (f) above shall also be exercisable by any person authorised for the purpose in writing by the Secretary of State.

(11) Nothing in this section shall be taken to compel the production by any person of a document of which he would on grounds of legal professional privilege be entitled to withhold production on an order for discovery in an action in the High Court or, in relation to Scotland, on an order for the production of documents in an action in the Court of Session.

70 Power to deal with cause of imminent danger of serious pollution etc

(1) Where, in the case of any article or substance found by him on any premises which he has power to enter, an inspector has reasonable cause to believe that, in the circumstances in which he finds it, the article or substance is a cause of imminent danger of serious pollution of the environment or serious harm to human health, he may seize it and cause it to be rendered harmless (whether by destruction or otherwise).

(2) Before there is rendered harmless under this section—

(a) any article that forms part of a batch of similar articles; or

(b) any substance,

the inspector shall, if it is practicable for him to do so, take a sample of it and give to a responsible person at the premises where the article or substance was found by him a portion of the sample marked in a manner sufficient to identify it.

(3) As soon as may be after any article or substance has been seized and rendered harmless under this section, the inspector shall prepare and sign a written report giving particulars of the circumstances in which the article or substance was seized and so dealt with by him, and shall—

(a) give a signed copy of the report to a responsible person at the premises where the article or substance was found by him; and

(b) unless that person is the owner of the article or substance, also serve a signed copy of the report on the owner;

and if, where paragraph (b) above applies, the inspector cannot after reasonable inquiry ascertain the name or address of the owner, the copy may be served on him by giving it to the person to whom a copy was given under paragraph (a) above.

(4) Any person who intentionally obstructs an inspector in the exercise of his powers under this section shall be liable—

(a) on summary conviction, to a fine not exceeding the statutory maximum;
(b) on conviction on indictment, to a fine or to imprisonment for a term not exceeding two years, or to both.

71 Obtaining of information from persons and authorities

(1) For the purpose of the discharge of his functions under this Part, the Secretary of State may, by notice in writing served on a waste regulation authority, require the authority to furnish such information about the discharge of its functions under this Part as he may require.

(2) For the purpose of the discharge of their respective functions under this Part—

(a) the Secretary of State, and
(b) a waste regulation authority,

may, by notice in writing served on him, require any person to furnish such information specified in the notice as the Secretary of State or the authority, as the case may be, reasonably considers he or it needs, in such form and within such period following service of the notice as is so specified.

(3) A person who—

(a) fails, without reasonable excuse, to comply with a requirement imposed under subsection (2) above; or
(b) in furnishing any information in compliance with such a requirement, makes any statement which he knows to be false or misleading in a material particular, or recklessly makes a statement which is false or misleading in a material particular;

shall be liable—

(i) on summary conviction, to a fine not exceeding the statutory maximum;
(ii) on conviction on indictment, to a fine or to imprisonment for a term not exceeding two years, or to both.

72 Default powers of Secretary of State

(1) If the Secretary of State is satisfied that a waste regulation authority has failed, in any respect, to discharge any function under this Part which it ought to have discharged, he may make an order declaring the authority to be in default.

(2) The failure to discharge any such function may be a failure in a class of case to which the function relates or a failure in a particular case.

(3) An order made under subsection (1) above which declares an authority to be in default may, for the purpose of remedying the default, direct the authority ("the defaulting authority") to perform any function specified in the order (whether in relation to a class of case or a particular case) and may specify the manner in which and the time or times within which the function is to be performed by the authority.

(4) If the defaulting authority fails to comply with any direction contained in such an order the Secretary of State may, instead of enforcing the order by mandamus, make an order transferring to himself any function of the authority specified in the order, whether in relation to all the classes of case to which the function relates or to such of those classes or, as the case may be, such particular case as is specified in the order.

(5) Where any function of a defaulting authority is transferred under subsection (4) above, the amount of any expenses which the Secretary of State certifies were incurred by him in performing the function shall on demand be paid to him by the defaulting authority.

(6) Any expenses required to be paid by a defaulting authority under subsection (5) above shall be defrayed by the authority in like manner, and shall be debited to the like account, as if the functions had not been transferred and the expenses had been incurred by the authority in performing them.

(7) The Secretary of State may by order vary or revoke any order previously made by him under this section.

(8) An order transferring any functions of a defaulting authority may provide for the transfer to the Secretary of State of such of the property, rights, liabilities and obligations of the authority as he considers appropriate; and where such an order is revoked the Secretary of State may, by the revoking order or a subsequent order, make such provision as he considers appropriate with respect to the property, rights, liabilities and obligations held by him for the purposes of the transferred function.

(9) Any order under this section may include such incidental, supplemental and transitional provisions as the Secretary of State considers appropriate.

(10) This section shall not apply to Scotland.

Supplemental

73 Appeals and other provisions relating to legal proceedings and civil liability

(1) An appeal against any decision of a magistrates' court under this Part (other than a decision made in criminal proceedings) shall lie to the Crown Court at the instance of any party to the proceedings in which the decision was given if such an appeal does not lie to the Crown Court by virtue of any other enactment.

(2) In Scotland an appeal against any decision of the sheriff under this Part (other than a decision made in criminal proceedings) shall lie to the Court of Session at the instance of any party to the proceedings in which the decision was given if such an appeal does not lie to the Court of Session by virtue of any other enactment.

(3) Where a person appeals to the Crown Court or the Court of Session against a decision of a magistrates' court or the sheriff dismissing an appeal against any requirement imposed under this Part which was suspended pending determination of that appeal, the requirement shall again be suspended pending the determination of the appeal to the Crown Court or Court of Session.

(4) Where an appeal against a decision of any authority lies to a magistrates' court or to the sheriff by virtue of any provision of this Part, it shall be the duty of the authority to include in any document by which it notifies the decision to the person concerned a statement indicating that such an appeal lies and specifying the time within which it must be brought.

(5) Where on an appeal to any court against or arising out of a decision of any authority under this Part the court varies or reverses the decision it shall be the duty of the authority to act in accordance with the court's decision.

(6) Where any damage is caused by waste which has been deposited in or on land, any person who deposited it, or knowingly caused or knowingly permitted it to be deposited, in either case so as to commit an offence under section 33(1) or 63(2) above, is liable for the damage except where the damage—

(a) was due wholly to the fault of the person who suffered it; or

(b) was suffered by a person who voluntarily accepted the risk of the damage being caused;

but without prejudice to any liability arising otherwise than under this subsection.

(7) The matters which may be proved by way of defence under section 33(7) above may be proved also by way of defence to an action brought under subsection (6) above.

(8) In subsection (6) above—

"damage" includes the death of, or injury to, any person (including any disease and any impairment of physical or mental condition); and

"fault" has the same meaning as in the Law Reform (Contributory Negligence) Act 1945.

(9) For the purposes of the following enactments—

(a) the Fatal Accidents Act 1976;

(b) the Law Reform (Contributory Negligence) Act 1945; and

(c) the Limitation Act 1980;

and for the purposes of any action of damages in Scotland arising out of the death of, or personal injury to, any person, any damage for which a person is liable under subsection (6) above shall be treated as due to his fault.

74 Meaning of "fit and proper person"

(1) The following provisions apply for the purposes of the discharge by a waste regulation authority of any function under this Part which requires the authority to determine whether a person is or is not a fit and proper person to hold a waste management licence.

(2) Whether a person is or is not a fit and proper person to hold a licence is to be determined by reference to the carrying on by him of the activities which are or are to be authorised by the licence and the fulfilment of the requirements of the licence.

(3) Subject to subsection (4) below, a person shall be treated as not being a fit and proper person if it appears to the authority—

(a) that he or another relevant person has been convicted of a relevant offence;

(b) that the management of the activities which are or are to be authorised by the licence are not or will not be in the hands of a technically competent person; or

(c) that the person who holds or is to hold the licence has not made and either has no intention of making or is in no position to make financial provision adequate to discharge the obligations arising from the licence.

(4) The authority may, if it considers it proper to do so in any particular case, treat a person as a fit and proper person notwithstanding that subsection (3)(a) above applies in his case.

(5) It shall be the duty of waste regulation authorities to have regard to any guidance issued to them by the Secretary of State with respect to the discharge of their functions of making the determinations to which this section applies.

(6) The Secretary of State may, by regulations, prescribe the offences that are relevant for the purposes of subsection (3)(a) above and the qualifications and experience required of a person for the purposes of subsection (3)(b) above.

(7) For the purposes of subsection (3)(a) above, another relevant person shall be treated, in relation to the licence holder or proposed licence holder, as the case may be, as having been convicted of a relevant offence if—

- (a) any person has been convicted of a relevant offence committed by him in the course of his employment by the holder or, as the case may be, the proposed holder of the licence or in the course of the carrying on of any business by a partnership one of the members of which was the holder or, as the case may be, the proposed holder of the licence;
- (b) a body corporate has been convicted of a relevant offence committed when the holder or, as the case may be, the proposed holder of the licence was a director, manager, secretary or other similar officer of that body corporate; or
- (c) where the holder or, as the case may be, the proposed holder of the licence is a body corporate, a person who is a director, manager, secretary or other similar officer of that body corporate—
  - (i) has been convicted of a relevant offence; or
  - (ii) was a director, manager, secretary or other similar officer of another body corporate at a time when a relevant offence for which that other body corporate has been convicted was committed.

75 Meaning of "waste" and household, commercial and industrial waste and special waste

(1) The following provisions apply for the interpretation of this Part.

(2) "Waste" includes—

- (a) any substance which constitutes a scrap material or an effluent or other unwanted surplus substance arising from the application of any process; and
- (b) any substance or article which requires to be disposed of as being broken, worn out, contaminated or otherwise spoiled;

but does not include a substance which is an explosive within the meaning of the Explosives Act 1875.

(3) Any thing which is discarded or otherwise dealt with as if it were waste shall be presumed to be waste unless the contrary is proved.

(4) "Controlled waste" means household, industrial and commercial waste or any such waste.

(5) Subject to subsection (8) below, "household waste" means waste from—

- (a) domestic property, that is to say, a building or self-contained part of a building which is used wholly for the purposes of living accommodation;
- (b) a caravan (as defined in section 29(1) of the Caravan Sites and Control of Development Act 1960) which usually and for the time being is situated on a caravan site (within the meaning of that Act);

(c) a residential home;

(d) premises forming part of a university or school or other educational establishment;

(e) premises forming part of a hospital or nursing home.

(6) Subject to subsection (8) below, "industrial waste" means waste from any of the following premises—

(a) any factory (within the meaning of the Factories Act 1961);

(b) any premises used for the purposes of, or in connection with, the provision to the public of transport services by land, water or air;

(c) any premises used for the purposes of, or in connection with, the supply to the public of gas, water or electricity or the provision of sewerage services; or

(d) any premises used for the purposes of, or in connection with, the provision to the public of postal or telecommunications services.

(7) Subject to subsection (8) below, "commercial waste" means waste from premises used wholly or mainly for the purposes of a trade or business or the purposes of sport, recreation or entertainment excluding—

(a) household waste;

(b) industrial waste;

(c) waste from any mine or quarry and waste from premises used for agriculture within the meaning of the Agriculture Act 1947 or, in Scotland, the Agriculture (Scotland) Act 1948; and

(d) waste of any other description prescribed by regulations made by the Secretary of State for the purposes of this paragraph.

(8) Regulations made by the Secretary of State may provide that waste of a description prescribed in the regulations shall be treated for the purposes of provisions of this Part prescribed in the regulations as being or not being household waste or industrial waste or commercial waste; but no regulations shall be made in respect of such waste as is mentioned in subsection (7)(c) above and references to waste in subsection (7) above and this subsection do not include sewage (including matter in or from a privy) except so far as the regulations provide otherwise.

(9) "Special waste" means controlled waste as respects which regulations are in force under section 62 above.

76 Application of this Part to Isles of Scilly

This Part shall have effect in its application to the Isles of Scilly with such modifications as the Secretary of State may by order specify.

77 Transition from Control of Pollution Act 1974 to this Part

(1) This section has effect for the purposes of the transition from the provisions of Part I of the Control of Pollution Act 1974 ("the 1974 Act") to the corresponding provisions of this Part of this Act and in this section—

"existing disposal authority" has the same meaning as in section 32 above;

"existing disposal licence" means a disposal licence under section 5 of the 1974 Act subsisting on the day appointed under section 164(3) below for the repeal of sections 3 to 10 of the 1974 Act and "relevant appointed day for licences" shall be construed accordingly;

"existing disposal plan" means a plan under section 2 of the 1974 Act subsisting on the day appointed under section 164(3) below for the repeal of that section and "relevant appointed day for plans" shall be construed accordingly;

"relevant part of its undertaking", in relation to an existing disposal authority, has the same meaning as in section 32 above; and

"the vesting date", in relation to an existing disposal authority and its waste disposal contractors, means the vesting date under Schedule 2 to this Act.

(2) An existing disposal licence shall, on and after the relevant appointed day for licences, be treated as a site licence until it expires or otherwise ceases to have effect; and accordingly it shall be variable and subject to revocation or suspension under this Part of this Act and may not be surrendered or transferred except under this Part of this Act.

(3) The restriction imposed by section 33(1) above shall not apply in relation to land occupied by an existing disposal authority for which a resolution of the authority subsists under section 11 of the 1974 Act on the relevant appointed day for licences until the following date, that is to say—

(a) in the case of an authority which transfers the relevant part of its undertaking in accordance with a scheme under Schedule 2 to this Act, the date which is the vesting date for that authority; and

(b) in any other case, the date on which the authority transfers, or ceases itself to carry on, the relevant part of its undertaking or ceases to provide places at which and plant and equipment by means of which controlled waste can be disposed of or deposited for the purposes of disposal.

(4) Any existing disposal plan of an existing disposal authority shall, on and after the relevant appointed day for plans, be treated as the plan of that authority under section 50 above and that section shall accordingly have effect as if references in it to "the plan" included the existing disposal plan of that authority.

(5) Subsection (4) above applies to Scotland and, for the purposes of that application, "existing disposal authority" means any authority constituted as a disposal authority for any area before the day appointed for this section to come into force and "that authority" means the waste disposal authority for that area under section 30(2) above.

(6) Subject to subsection (7) below, as respects any existing disposal authority—

(a) the restriction imposed by section 51(1) of this Act on the means whereby the authority arranges for the disposal of controlled waste shall not apply to the authority—

(i) in the case of an authority which transfers the relevant part of its undertaking in accordance with a scheme under Schedule 2 to this Act, until the date which is the vesting date for that authority; and

(ii) in any other case, until the date on which the authority transfers, or ceases itself to carry on, the relevant part of its undertaking or ceases to provide places at which and plant and equipment by means of which controlled waste can be disposed of or deposited for the purposes of disposal; and

(b) on and after that date, section 14(4) of the 1974 Act shall not authorise the authority to arrange for the disposal of controlled waste except by means of arrangements made (in accordance with Part II of Schedule 2 to this Act) with waste disposal contractors.

(7) The Secretary of State may, as respects any existing disposal authority, direct that the restriction imposed by section 51(1) above shall not apply in the case of that authority until such date as he specifies in the direction and where he does so paragraph (a) of subsection (6) above shall not apply and paragraph (b) shall be read as referring to the date so specified.

(8) In section 14(4) of the 1974 Act, after the words "this subsection", there shall be inserted the words "but subject to subsection (6) of section 77 of the Environmental Protection Act 1990 as respects any time after the date applicable to the authority under paragraph (a) or (b) of that subsection".

(9) As respects any existing disposal authority, until the date which is, under subsection (6)(a) above, the date until which the restriction imposed by section 51(1) of this Act is disapplied,—

- (a) the powers conferred on a waste disposal authority by section 55(2)(a) and (b) of this Act as respects the recycling of waste and the use of waste to produce heat or electricity shall be treated as powers which the authority may exercise itself; and
- (b) the power conferred on a waste disposal authority by section 48(4) of this Act to object to a waste collection authority having waste recycled where the disposal authority has made arrangements with a waste disposal contractor for the contractor to recycle the waste shall be available to the waste disposal authority where it itself has the waste recycled.

78 This Part and radioactive substances

Except as provided by regulations made by the Secretary of State under this section, nothing in this Part applies to radioactive waste within the meaning of the Radioactive Substances Act 1960; but regulations may—

- (a) provide for prescribed provisions of this Part to have effect with such modifications as the Secretary of State considers appropriate for the purposes of dealing with such radioactive waste;
- (b) make such modifications of the Radioactive Substances Act 1960 and any other Act as the Secretary of State considers appropriate.

PART III

STATUTORY NUISANCES AND CLEAN AIR

Statutory nuisances: England and Wales

79 Statutory nuisances and inspections therefor

(1) Subject to subsections (2) to (6) below, the following matters constitute "statutory nuisances" for the purposes of this Part, that is to say—

- (a) any premises in such a state as to be prejudicial to health or a nuisance;
- (b) smoke emitted from premises so as to be prejudicial to health or a nuisance;
- (c) fumes or gases emitted from premises so as to be prejudicial to health or a nuisance;

(d) any dust, steam, smell or other effluvia arising on industrial, trade or business premises and being prejudicial to health or a nuisance;

(e) any accumulation or deposit which is prejudicial to health or a nuisance;

(f) any animal kept in such a place or manner as to be prejudicial to health or a nuisance;

(g) noise emitted from premises so as to be prejudicial to health or a nuisance;

(h) any other matter declared by any enactment to be a statutory nuisance;

and it shall be the duty of every local authority to cause its area to be inspected from time to time to detect any statutory nuisances which ought to be dealt with under section 80 below and, where a complaint of a statutory nuisance is made to it by a person living within its area, to take such steps as are reasonably practicable to investigate the complaint.

(2) Subsection (1)(b) and (g) above do not apply in relation to premises—

(a) occupied on behalf of the Crown for naval, military or air force purposes or for the purposes of the department of the Secretary of State having responsibility for defence, or

(b) occupied by or for the purposes of a visiting force;

and "visiting force" means any such body, contingent or detachment of the forces of any country as is a visiting force for the purposes of any of the provisions of the Visiting Forces Act 1952.

(3) Subsection (1)(b) above does not apply to—

(i) smoke emitted from a chimney of a private dwelling within a smoke control area,

(ii) dark smoke emitted from a chimney of a building or a chimney serving the furnace of a boiler or industrial plant attached to a building or for the time being fixed to or installed on any land,

(iii) smoke emitted from a railway locomotive steam engine, or

(iv) dark smoke emitted otherwise than as mentioned above from industrial or trade premises.

(4) Subsection (1)(c) above does not apply in relation to premises other than private dwellings.

(5) Subsection (1)(d) above does not apply to steam emitted from a railway locomotive engine.

(6) Subsection (1)(g) above does not apply to noise caused by aircraft other than model aircraft.

(7) In this Part—

"chimney" includes structures and openings of any kind from or through which smoke may be emitted;

"dust" does not include dust emitted from a chimney as an ingredient of smoke;

"fumes" means any airborne solid matter smaller than dust;

"gas" includes vapour and moisture precipitated from vapour;

"industrial, trade or business premises" means premises used for any industrial, trade or business purposes or premises not so used on which matter is burnt in connection with any industrial, trade or business process, and premises are used for industrial purposes where they are used for the purposes of any treatment or process as well as where they are used for the purposes of manufacturing;

"local authority" means, subject to subsection (8) below,—

(a) in Greater London, a London borough council, the Common Council of the City of London and, as respects the Temples, the Sub-Treasurer of the Inner Temple and the Under-Treasurer of the Middle Temple respectively;

(b) outside Greater London, a district council; and

(c) the Council of the Isles of Scilly;

"noise" includes vibration;

"person responsible", in relation to a statutory nuisance, means the person to whose act, default or sufferance the nuisance is attributable;

"prejudicial to health" means injurious, or likely to cause injury, to health;

"premises" includes land and, subject to subsection (12) below, any vessel;

"private dwelling" means any building, or part of a building, used or intended to be used, as a dwelling;

"smoke" includes soot, ash, grit and gritty particles emitted in smoke;

and any expressions used in this section and in the Clean Air Act 1956 or the Clean Air Act 1968 have the same meaning in this section as in that Act and section 34(2) of the Clean Air Act 1956 shall apply for the interpretation of the expression "dark smoke" and the operation of this Part in relation to it.

(8) Where, by an order under section 2 of the Public Health (Control of Disease) Act 1984, a port health authority has been constituted for any port health district, the port health authority shall have by virtue of this subsection, as respects its district, the functions conferred or imposed by this Part in relation to statutory nuisances other than a nuisance falling within paragraph (g) of subsection (1) above and no such order shall be made assigning those functions; and "local authority" and "area" shall be construed accordingly.

(9) In this Part "best practicable means" is to be interpreted by reference to the following provisions—

(a) "practicable" means reasonably practicable having regard among other things to local conditions and circumstances, to the current state of technical knowledge and to the financial implications;

(b) the means to be employed include the design, installation, maintenance and manner and periods of operation of plant and machinery, and the design, construction and maintenance of buildings and structures;

(c) the test is to apply only so far as compatible with any duty imposed by law;

(d) the test is to apply only so far as compatible with safety and safe working conditions, and with the exigencies of any emergency or unforeseeable circumstances;

and, in circumstances where a code of practice under section 71 of the Control of Pollution Act 1974 (noise minimisation) is applicable, regard shall also be had to guidance given in it.

(10) A local authority shall not without the consent of the Secretary of State institute summary proceedings under this Part in respect of a nuisance falling within paragraph (b), (d) or (e) of subsection (1) above if proceedings in respect thereof might be instituted under Part I or the Alkali &c. Works Regulation Act 1906 or section 5 of the Health and Safety at Work etc. Act 1974.

(11) The area of a local authority which includes part of the seashore shall also include for the purposes of this Part the territorial sea lying seawards from that part of the shore; and subject to subsection (12) below, this Part shall have effect, in relation to any area included in the area of a local authority by virtue of this subsection—

(a) as if references to premises and the occupier of premises included respectively a vessel and the master of a vessel; and

(b) with such other modifications, if any, as are prescribed in regulations made by the Secretary of State.

(12) A vessel powered by steam reciprocating machinery is not a vessel to which this Part of this Act applies.

80 Summary proceedings for statutory nuisances

(1) Where a local authority is satisfied that a statutory nuisance exists, or is likely to occur or recur, in the area of the authority, the local authority shall serve a notice ("an abatement notice") imposing all or any of the following requirements—

(a) requiring the abatement of the nuisance or prohibiting or restricting its occurrence or recurrence;

(b) requiring the execution of such works, and the taking of such other steps, as may be necessary for any of those purposes,

and the notice shall specify the time or times within which the requirements of the notice are to be complied with.

(2) The abatement notice shall be served—

(a) except in a case falling within paragraph (b) or (c) below, on the person responsible for the nuisance;

(b) where the nuisance arises from any defect of a structural character, on the owner of the premises;

(c) where the person responsible for the nuisance cannot be found or the nuisance has not yet occurred, on the owner or occupier of the premises.

(3) The person served with the notice may appeal against the notice to a magistrates' court within the period of twenty-one days beginning with the date on which he was served with the notice.

(4) If a person on whom an abatement notice is served, without reasonable excuse, contravenes or fails to comply with any requirement or prohibition imposed by the notice, he shall be guilty of an offence.

(5) Except in a case falling within subsection (6) below, a person who commits an offence under subsection (4) above shall be liable on summary conviction to a fine not exceeding level 5 on the standard scale together with a further fine of an amount equal to one-tenth of that level for each day on which the offence continues after the conviction.

(6) A person who commits an offence under subsection (4) above on industrial, trade or business premises shall be liable on summary conviction to a fine not exceeding £20,000.

(7) Subject to subsection (8) below, in any proceedings for an offence under subsection (4) above in respect of a statutory nuisance it shall be a defence to prove that the best practicable means were used to prevent, or to counteract the effects of, the nuisance.

(8) The defence under subsection (7) above is not available—

(a) in the case of a nuisance falling within paragraph (a), (d), (e), (f) or (g) of section 79(1) above except where the nuisance arises on industrial, trade or business premises;

(b) in the case of a nuisance falling within paragraph (b) of section 79(1) above except where the smoke is emitted from a chimney; and

(c) in the case of a nuisance falling within paragraph (c) or (h) of section 79(1) above.

(9) In proceedings for an offence under subsection (4) above in respect of a statutory nuisance falling within paragraph (g) of section 79(1) above where the offence consists in contravening requirements imposed by virtue of subsection (1)(a) above it shall be a defence to prove—

(a) that the alleged offence was covered by a notice served under section 60 or a consent given under section 61 or 65 of the Control of Pollution Act 1974 (construction sites, etc); or

(b) where the alleged offence was committed at a time when the premises were subject to a notice under section 66 of that Act (noise reduction notice), that the level of noise emitted from the premises at that time was not such as to a constitute a contravention of the notice under that section; or

(c) where the alleged offence was committed at a time when the premises were not subject to a notice under section 66 of that Act, and when a level fixed under section 67 of that Act (new buildings liable to abatement order) applied to the premises, that the level of noise emitted from the premises at that time did not exceed that level.

(10) Paragraphs (b) and (c) of subsection (9) above apply whether or not the relevant notice was subject to appeal at the time when the offence was alleged to have been committed.

81 Supplementary provisions

(1) Where more than one person is responsible for a statutory nuisance section 80 above shall apply to each of those persons whether or not what any one of them is responsible for would by itself amount to a nuisance.

(2) Where a statutory nuisance which exists or has occurred within the area of a local authority, or which has affected any part of that area, appears to the local authority to be wholly or partly caused by some act or default committed or taking place outside the area, the local authority may act under section 80 above as if the act or default were wholly within that area, except that any appeal shall be heard by a magistrates' court having jurisdiction where the act or default is alleged to have taken place.

(3) Where an abatement notice has not been complied with the local authority may, whether or not they take proceedings for an offence under section 80(4) above, abate the nuisance and do whatever may be necessary in execution of the notice.

(4) Any expenses reasonably incurred by a local authority in abating, or preventing the recurrence of, a statutory nuisance under subsection (3) above may be recovered by them from the person by whose act or default the nuisance was caused and, if that person is the owner of the premises, from any person who is for the time being the owner thereof; and the court may apportion the expenses between persons by whose acts or defaults the nuisance is caused in such manner as the court consider fair and reasonable.

(5) If a local authority is of opinion that proceedings for an offence under section 80(4) above would afford an inadequate remedy in the case of any statutory nuisance , they may, subject to subsection (6) below, take proceedings in the High Court for the purpose of securing the abatement, prohibition or restriction of the nuisance, and the proceedings shall be maintainable notwithstanding the local authority have suffered no damage from the nuisance.

(6) In any proceedings under subsection (5) above in respect of a nuisance falling within paragraph (g) of section 79(1) above, it shall be a defence to prove that the noise was authorised by a notice under section 60 or a consent under section 61 (construction sites) of the Control of Pollution Act 1974.

(7) The further supplementary provisions in Schedule 3 to this Act shall have effect.

82 Summary proceedings by persons aggrieved by statutory nuisances

(1) A magistrates' court may act under this section on a complaint made by any person on the ground that he is aggrieved by the existence of a statutory nuisance.

(2) If the magistrates' court is satisfied that the alleged nuisance exists, or that although abated it is likely to recur on the same premises, the court shall make an order for either or both of the following purposes—

- (a) requiring the defendant to abate the nuisance, within a time specified in the order, and to execute any works necessary for that purpose;
- (b) prohibiting a recurrence of the nuisance, and requiring the defendant, within a time specified in the order, to execute any works necessary to prevent the recurrence;

and may also impose on the defendant a fine not exceeding level 5 on the standard scale.

(3) If the magistrates' court is satisfied that the alleged nuisance exists and is such as, in the opinion of the court, to render premises unfit for human habitation, an order under subsection (2) above may prohibit the use of the premises for human habitation until the premises are, to the satisfaction of the court, rendered fit for that purpose.

(4) Proceedings for an order under subsection (2) above shall be brought—

- (a) except in a case falling within paragraph (b) or (c) below, against the person responsible for the nuisance;
- (b) where the nuisance arises from any defect of a structural character, against the owner of the premises;
- (c) where the person responsible for the nuisance cannot be found, against the owner or occupier of the premises.

(5) Where more than one person is responsible for a statutory nuisance, subsections (1) to (4) above shall apply to each of those persons whether or not what any one of them is responsible for would by itself amount to a nuisance.

(6) Before instituting proceedings for an order under subsection (2) above against any person, the person aggrieved by the nuisance shall give to that person such notice in writing of his intention to bring the proceedings as is applicable to proceedings in respect of a nuisance of that description and the notice shall specify the matter complained of.

(7) The notice of the bringing of proceedings in respect of a statutory nuisance required by subsection (6) above which is applicable is—

(a) in the case of a nuisance falling within paragraph (g) of section 79(1) above, not less than three days' notice; and

(b) in the case of a nuisance of any other description, not less than twenty-one days' notice;

but the Secretary of State may, by order, provide that this subsection shall have effect as if such period as is specified in the order were the minimum period of notice applicable to any description of statutory nuisance specified in the order.

(8) A person who, without reasonable excuse, contravenes any requirement or prohibition imposed by an order under subsection (2) above shall be guilty of an offence and liable on summary conviction to a fine not exceeding level 5 on the standard scale together with a further fine of an amount equal to one-tenth of that level for each day on which the offence continues after the conviction.

(9) Subject to subsection (10) below, in any proceedings for an offence under subsection (8) above in respect of a statutory nuisance it shall be a defence to prove that the best practicable means were used to prevent, or to counteract the effects of, the nuisance.

(10) The defence under subsection (9) above is not available—

(a) in the case of a nuisance falling within paragraph (a), (d), (e), (f) or (g) of section 79(1) above except where the nuisance arises on industrial, trade or business premises;

(b) in the case of a nuisance falling within paragraph (b) of section 79(1) above except where the smoke is emitted from a chimney;

(c) in the case of a nuisance falling within paragraph (c) or (h) of section 79(1) above; and

(d) in the case of a nuisance which is such as to render the premises unfit for human habitation.

(11) If a person is convicted of an offence under subsection (8) above, a magistrates' court may, after giving the local authority in whose area the nuisance has occurred an opportunity of being heard, direct the authority to do anything which the person convicted was required to do by the order to which the conviction relates.

(12) Where on the hearing of proceedings for an order under subsection (2) above it is proved that the alleged nuisance existed at the date of the making of the complaint, then, whether or not at the date of the hearing it still exists or is likely to recur, the court shall order the defendant (or defendants in such proportions as appears fair and reasonable) to pay to the person bringing the proceedings such amount as the court considers reasonably sufficient to compensate him for any expenses properly incurred by him in the proceedings.

(13) If it appears to the magistrates' court that neither the person responsible for the nuisance nor the owner or occupier of the premises can be found the court may, after giving the local authority in whose area the nuisance has occurred an opportunity of being heard, direct the authority to do anything which the court would have ordered that person to do.

Statutory nuisances: Scotland

83 Statutory nuisances: Scotland

(1) Sections 79 to 82 above do not apply to Scotland.

(2) In section 16 of the Public Health (Scotland) Act 1897 (definition of nuisances), after paragraph (5) there shall be inserted the following paragraphs—

"(5A) Any fumes ("fumes" meaning airborne solid matter smaller than dust), gases or vapours emitted, so as to be a nuisance or injurious or dangerous to health, from any premises, or part thereof, used or intended to be used as a dwelling house.

(5B) Any dust caused by any trade, business, manufacture or process, being a nuisance or injurious or dangerous to health."

Termination of existing controls over offensive trades and businesses

84 Termination of Public Health Act controls over offensive trades etc

(1) Where a person carries on, in the area or part of the area of any local authority—

(a) in England or Wales, a trade which—

(i) is an offensive trade within the meaning of section 107 of the Public Health Act 1936 in that area or part of that area, and

(ii) constitutes a prescribed process designated for local control for the carrying on of which an authorisation is required under section 6 of this Act; or

(b) in Scotland, a business which—

(i) is mentioned in section 32(1) of the Public Health (Scotland) Act 1897 (or is an offensive business by virtue of that section) in that area or part of that area; and

(ii) constitutes a prescribed process designated for local control for the carrying on of which an authorisation is required under the said section 6,

subsection (2) below shall have effect in relation to that trade or business as from the date on which an authorisation is granted under section 6 of this Act or, if that person has not applied for such an authorisation within the period allowed under section 2(1) above for making applications under that section, as from the end of that period.

(2) Where this subsection applies in relation to the trade or business carried on by any person—

(a) nothing in section 107 of the Public Health Act 1936 or in section 32 of the Public Health (Scotland) Act 1897 shall apply in relation to it, and

(b) no byelaws or further byelaws made under section 108(2) of the said Act of 1936, or under subsection (2) of the said section 32, with respect to a trade or business of that description shall apply in relation to it;

but without prejudice to the continuance of, and imposition of any penalty in, any proceedings under the said section 107 or the said section 32 which were instituted before the date as from which this subsection has effect in relation to the trade or business.

(3) Subsection (2)(b) above shall apply in relation to the trade of fish frying as it applies in relation to an offensive trade.

(4) When the Secretary of State considers it expedient to do so, having regard to the operation of Part I and the preceding provisions of this Part of this Act in relation to offensive trades or businesses, he may by order repeal—

(a) sections 107 and 108 of the Public Health Act 1936; and

(b) section 32 of the Public Health (Scotland) Act 1897;

and different days may be so appointed in relation to trades or businesses which constitute prescribed processes and those which do not.

(5) In this section—

"prescribed process" has the same meaning as in Part I of this Act; and

"offensive trade" or "trade" has the same meaning as in section 107 of the Public Health Act 1936.

Application to gases of certain Clean Air Act provisions

85 Application to gases of certain Clean Air Act provisions

After section 7 of the Clean Air Act 1968 there shall be inserted the following section—

"7A Application to gases of certain provisions as to grit and dust

(1) The Minister may by regulations—

(a) apply all or any of the provisions of sections 2, 3, 4 and 5 of this Act and of sections 7, 18(2), 19(3), 20(4) and 22(1) of the principal Act (provisions relating to grit and dust or smoke) to prescribed gases as they apply to grit and dust; and

(b) apply all or any of the provisions of section 3 of the principal Act (requirement that new furnaces shall be so far as practicable smokeless) to prescribed gases as they apply to smoke;

subject, in either case, to such exceptions and modifications as the Minister thinks expedient.

(2) Regulations under this section may make different provision for different cases.

(3) No regulations shall be made under this section unless a draft of the regulations has been laid before Parliament and approved by each House of Parliament.

(4) In the application of any provision of the principal Act or this Act to prescribed gases by virtue of regulations under this section, any reference to the rate of emission of any substance shall be construed as a reference to the percentage by volume or by mass of the gas which may be emitted during a period specified in the regulations.

(5) In this section—

"gas" includes vapour and moisture precipitated from vapour; and "prescribed" means prescribed in regulations under this section."

PART IV

LITTER ETC

Provisions relating to litter

86 Preliminary

(1) The following provisions have effect for the purposes of this Part.

(2) In England and Wales the following are "principal litter authorities"—

(a) a county council,
(b) a district council,
(c) a London borough council,
(d) the Common Council of the City of London, and
(e) the Council of the Isles of Scilly;

but the Secretary of State may, by order, designate other descriptions of local authorities as litter authorities for the purposes of this Part; and any such authority shall also be a principal litter authority.

(3) In Scotland the following are "principal litter authorities"—

(a) a regional council;
(b) a district or islands council; and
(c) a joint board.

(4) Subject to subsection (8) below, land is "relevant land" of a principal litter authority if, not being relevant land falling within subsection (7) below, it is open to the air and is land (but not a highway or in Scotland a public road) which is under the direct control of such an authority to which the public are entitled or permitted to have access with or without payment.

(5) Land is "Crown land" if it is land—

(a) occupied by the Crown Estate Commissioners as part of the Crown Estate,
(b) occupied by or for the purposes of a government department or for naval, military or air force purposes, or
(c) occupied or managed by any body acting on behalf of the Crown;

is "relevant Crown land" if it is Crown land which is open to the air and is land (but not a highway or in Scotland a public road) to which the public are entitled or permitted to have access with or without payment; and "the appropriate Crown authority" for any Crown land is the Crown Estate Commissioners, the Minister in charge of the government department or the body which occupies or manages the land on the Crown's behalf, as the case may be.

(6) Subject to subsection (8) below, land is "relevant land" of a designated statutory undertaker if it is land which is under the direct control of any statutory undertaker or statutory undertaker of any description which may be designated by the Secretary of State, by order, for the purposes of this Part, being land to which the public are entitled or permitted to have access with or without payment or, in such cases as may

be prescribed in the designation order, land in relation to which the public have no such right or permission.

(7) Subject to subsection (8) below, land is "relevant land" of a designated educational institution if it is open to the air and is land which is under the direct control of the governing body of or, in Scotland, of such body or of the education authority responsible for the management of, any educational institution or educational institution of any description which may be designated by the Secretary of State, by order, for the purposes of this Part.

(8) The Secretary of State may, by order, designate descriptions of land which are not to be treated as relevant Crown land or as relevant land of principal litter authorities, of designated statutory undertakers or of designated educational institutions or of any description of any of them.

(9) Every highway maintainable at the public expense other than a trunk road which is a special road is a "relevant highway" and the local authority which is, for the purposes of this Part, "responsible" for so much of it as lies within its area is, subject to any order under subsection (11) below—

- (a) in Greater London, the council of the London borough or the Common Council of the City of London;
- (b) outside Greater London, the council of the district; and
- (c) the Council of the Isles of Scilly.

(10) In Scotland, every public road other than a trunk road which is a special road is a "relevant road" and the local authority which is, for the purposes of this Part, "responsible" for so much of it as lies within its area is, subject to any order under subsection (11) below, the district or islands council or (in the case of a special road) the regional or islands council.

(11) The Secretary of State may, by order, as respects relevant highways or relevant roads, relevant highways or relevant roads of any class or any part of a relevant highway or relevant road specified in the order, transfer the responsibility for the discharge of the duties imposed by section 89 below from the local authority to the highway or roads authority; but he shall not make an order under this subsection unless—

- (a) (except where he is the highway or roads authority) he is requested to do so by the highway or roads authority;
- (b) he consults the local authority; and
- (c) it appears to him to be necessary or expedient to do so in order to prevent or minimise interference with the passage or with the safety of traffic along the highway or, in Scotland, road in question;

and where, by an order under this subsection, responsibility for the discharge of those duties is transferred, the authority to which the transfer is made is, for the purposes of this Part, "responsible" for the highway, road or part specified in the order.

(12) Land is "relevant land within a litter control area of a local authority" if it is land included in an area designated by the local authority under section 90 below to which the public are entitled or permitted to have access with or without payment.

(13) A place on land shall be treated as "open to the air" notwithstanding that it is covered if it is open to the air on at least one side.

(14) The Secretary of State may, by order, apply the provisions of this Part which apply to refuse to any description of animal droppings in all or any prescribed circumstances subject to such modifications as appear to him to be necessary.

(15) Any power under this section may be exercised differently as respects different areas, different descriptions of land or for different circumstances.

87 Offence of leaving litter

(1) If any person throws down, drops or otherwise deposits in, into or from any place to which this section applies, and leaves, any thing whatsoever in such circumstances as to cause, or contribute to, or tend to lead to, the defacement by litter of any place to which this section applies, he shall, subject to subsection (2) below, be guilty of an offence.

(2) No offence is committed under this section where the depositing and leaving of the thing was—

- (a) authorised by law, or
- (b) done with the consent of the owner, occupier or other person or authority having control of the place in or into which that thing was deposited.

(3) This section applies to any public open place and, in so far as the place is not a public open place, also to the following places—

- (a) any relevant highway or relevant road and any trunk road which is a special road;
- (b) any place on relevant land of a principal litter authority;
- (c) any place on relevant Crown land;
- (d) any place on relevant land of any designated statutory undertaker;
- (e) any place on relevant land of any designated educational institution;
- (f) any place on relevant land within a litter control area of a local authority.

(4) In this section "public open place" means a place in the open air to which the public are entitled or permitted to have access without payment; and any covered place open to the air on at least one side and available for public use shall be treated as a public open place.

(5) A person who is guilty of an offence under this section shall be liable on summary conviction to a fine not exceeding level 4 on the standard scale.

(6) A local authority, with a view to promoting the abatement of litter, may take such steps as the authority think appropriate for making the effect of subsection (5) above known to the public in their area.

(7) In any proceedings in Scotland for an offence under this section it shall be lawful to convict the accused on the evidence of one witness.

88 Fixed penalty notices for leaving litter

(1) Where on any occasion an authorised officer of a litter authority finds a person who he has reason to believe has on that occasion committed an offence under section 87 above in the area of that authority, he may give that person a notice offering him the opportunity of discharging any liability to conviction for that offence by payment of a fixed penalty.

(2) Where a person is given a notice under this section in respect of an offence—

(a) no proceedings shall be instituted for that offence before the expiration of fourteen days following the date of the notice; and

(b) he shall not be convicted of that offence if he pays the fixed penalty before the expiration of that period.

(3) A notice under this section shall give such particulars of the circumstances alleged to constitute the offence as are necessary for giving reasonable information of the offence and shall state—

(a) the period during which, by virtue of subsection (2) above, proceedings will not be taken for the offence;

(b) the amount of the fixed penalty; and

(c) the person to whom and the address at which the fixed penalty may be paid;

and, without prejudice to payment by any other method, payment of the fixed penalty may be made by pre-paying and posting to that person at that address a letter containing the amount of the penalty (in cash or otherwise).

(4) Where a letter is sent in accordance with subsection (3) above payment shall be regarded as having been made at the time at which that letter would be delivered in the ordinary course of post.

(5) The form of notices under this section shall be such as the Secretary of State may by order prescribe.

(6) The fixed penalty payable to a litter authority in pursuance of a notice under this section shall, subject to subsection (7) below, be £10; and as respects the sums received by the authority, those sums—

(a) if received by an authority in England and Wales, shall be paid to the Secretary of State;

(b) if received by an authority in Scotland, shall be treated as if the penalty were a fine imposed by a district court.

(7) The Secretary of State may by order substitute a different amount for the amount for the time being specified as the amount of the fixed penalty in subsection (6) above.

(8) In any proceedings a certificate which—

(a) purports to be signed by or on behalf of—

(i) in England and Wales, the chief finance officer of the litter authority; or

(ii) in Scotland, the proper officer; and

(b) states that payment of a fixed penalty was or was not received by a date specified in the certificate,

shall be evidence of the facts stated.

(9) For the purposes of this section the following are "litter authorities"—

(a) any principal litter authority, other than a county council, a regional council or a joint board;

(b) any county council , regional council or joint board designated by the Secretary of State, by order, in relation to such area as is specified in the order (not being an area in a National Park);

(c) any National Park Committee;

(d) any Park board for any area in a National Park; and

(e) the Broads Authority.

(10) In this section—

"authorised officer" means an officer of, or in the case of any Park board or National Park Committee, an officer acting on behalf of, a litter authority who is authorised in writing by the authority for the purpose of issuing notices under this section;

"chief finance officer", in relation to a litter authority, means the person having responsibility for the financial affairs of the authority;

"National Park Committee" means a committee appointed to perform functions under paragraph 5 of Schedule 17 to the Local Government Act 1972;

"Park board", in relation to a National Park, means—

(a) a joint planning board reconstituted under paragraph 1 of Schedule 17 to the Local Government Act 1972; or

(b) a board reconstituted as a special planning board under paragraph 3 of that Schedule;

"proper officer" means the officer who has, as respects the authority, the responsibility mentioned in section 95 of the Local Government (Scotland) Act 1973 (financial administration).

89 Duty to keep land and highways clear of litter etc

(1) It shall be the duty of—

(a) each local authority, as respects any relevant highway or, in Scotland, relevant road for which it is responsible,

(b) the Secretary of State, as respects any trunk road which is a special road and any relevant highway or relevant road for which he is responsible,

(c) each principal litter authority, as respects its relevant land,

(d) the appropriate Crown authority, as respects its relevant Crown land,

(e) each designated statutory undertaker, as respects its relevant land,

(f) the governing body of each designated educational institution or in Scotland such body or, as the case may be, the education authority responsible for the management of the institution, as respects its relevant land, and

(g) the occupier of any relevant land within a litter control area of a local authority,

to ensure that the land is, so far as is practicable, kept clear of litter and refuse.

(2) Subject to subsection (6) below, it shall also be the duty of—

(a) each local authority, as respects any relevant highway or relevant road for which it is responsible,

(b) the Secretary of State, as respects any trunk road which is a special road and any relevant highway or relevant road for which he is responsible,

to ensure that the highway or road is, so far as is practicable, kept clean.

(3) In determining what standard is required, as respects any description of land, highway or road, for compliance with subsections (1) and (2) above, regard shall be had to the character and use of the land, highway or road as well as the measures which are practicable in the circumstances.

(4) Matter of any description prescribed by regulations made by the Secretary of State for the purposes of subsections (1)(a) and (2) above shall be litter or refuse to which the duties imposed by those subsections apply as respects relevant highways or relevant roads whether or not it would be litter or refuse apart from this subsection.

(5) It shall be the duty of a local authority, when discharging its duty under subsection (1)(a) or (2) above as respects any relevant highway or relevant road, to place and maintain on the highway or road such traffic signs and barriers as may be necessary for giving warning and preventing danger to traffic or for regulating it and afterwards to remove them as soon as they cease to be necessary for those purposes; but this subsection has effect subject to any directions given under subsection (6) below.

(6) In discharging its duty under subsection (1)(a) or (2) above to keep clear of litter and refuse or to clean any relevant highway or relevant road for which it is responsible, the local authority shall comply with any directions given to it by the highway or roads authority with respect to—

(a) the placing and maintenance of any traffic signs or barriers;

(b) the days or periods during which clearing or cleaning shall not be undertaken or undertaken to any extent specified in the direction;

and for the purpose of enabling it to discharge its duty under subsection (1)(a) or (2) above as respects any relevant highway or relevant road the local authority may apply to the highway authority or roads authority for that authority to exercise its powers under section 14(1) or (3) of the Road Traffic Regulation Act 1984 (temporary prohibition or restriction of traffic).

(7) The Secretary of State shall prepare and issue a code of practice for the purpose of providing practical guidance on the discharge of the duties imposed by subsections (1) and (2) above.

(8) Different codes of practice may be prepared and issued under subsection (7) above for different areas.

(9) The Secretary of State may issue modifications of, or withdraw, a code issued under subsection (7) above; but where a code is withdrawn, he shall prepare and issue a new code under that subsection in substitution for it.

(10) Any person subject to any duty imposed by subsection (1) or (2) above shall have regard to the code of practice in force under subsection (7) above in discharging that duty.

(11) A draft code prepared under subsection (7) above shall be laid before both Houses of Parliament and shall not be issued until after the end of the period of 40 days beginning with the day on which the code was so laid, or if the draft is laid on different days, the later of the two days.

(12) If, within the period mentioned in subsection (11) above, either House resolves that the code the draft of which was laid before it should not be issued, the Secretary of State shall not issue that code.

(13) No account shall be taken in reckoning any period of 40 days for the purposes of this section of any time during which Parliament is dissolved or prorogued or during which both Houses are adjourned for more than four days.

(14) In this section "traffic sign" has the meaning given in section 64(1) of the Road Traffic Regulation Act 1984.

90 Litter control areas

(1) The Secretary of State may, by order, prescribe descriptions of land which may be designated under subsection (3) below as, or as part of, a litter control area.

(2) The power of the Secretary of State to prescribe descriptions of land under subsection (1) above includes power to describe land by reference to the ownership or occupation of the land or the activities carried on on it.

(3) Any principal litter authority other than a county council, regional council or joint board may, in accordance with the following provisions of this section, by order designate any land in their area as, or as part of, a litter control area.

(4) No order under subsection (3) above designating any land shall be made unless the authority is of the opinion that, by reason of the presence of litter or refuse, the condition of the land is, and unless they make a designation order is likely to continue to be, such as to be detrimental to the amenities of the locality.

(5) The power to make a designation order under subsection (3) above shall be excluded from the functions to which section 101 of the Local Government Act 1972 (functions capable of delegation) applies.

(6) An authority proposing to make a designation order in relation to any land shall—

- (a) notify persons who appear to the authority to be persons who will be affected by the proposed order;
- (b) give them an opportunity to make representations about it within the period of twenty-one days beginning with the service of the notice; and
- (c) take any representations so made into account in making their decision.

(7) A designation order under subsection (3) above shall identify the land to which it applies and shall be in such form as the Secretary of State may by order prescribe.

91 Summary proceedings by persons aggrieved by litter

(1) A magistrates' court may act under this section on a complaint made by any person on the ground that he is aggrieved by the defacement, by litter or refuse, of—

- (a) any relevant highway;
- (b) any trunk road which is a special road;
- (c) any relevant land of a principal litter authority;
- (d) any relevant Crown land;
- (e) any relevant land of a designated statutory undertaker;
- (f) any relevant land of a designated educational institution; or
- (g) any relevant land within a litter control area of a local authority.

(2) A magistrates' court may also act under this section on a complaint made by any person on the ground that he is aggrieved by the want of cleanliness of any relevant highway or any trunk road which is a special road.

(3) A principal litter authority shall not be treated as a person aggrieved for the purposes of proceedings under this section.

(4) Proceedings under this section shall be brought against the person who has the duty to keep the land clear under section 89(1) above or to keep the highway clean under section 89(2) above, as the case may be.

(5) Before instituting proceedings under this section against any person, the complainant shall give to the person not less than five days written notice of his intention to make the complaint and the notice shall specify the matter complained of.

(6) If the magistrates' court is satisfied that the highway or land in question is defaced by litter or refuse or, in the case of a highway, is wanting in cleanliness, the court may, subject to subsections (7) and (8) below, make an order ("a litter abatement order") requiring the defendant to clear the litter or refuse away or, as the case may be, clean the highway within a time specified in the order.

(7) The magistrates' court shall not make a litter abatement order if the defendant proves that he has complied, as respects the highway or land in question, with his duty under section 89(1) and (2) above.

(8) The magistrates' court shall not make a litter abatement order where it appears that the matter complained of is the result of directions given to the local authority under section 89(6) above by the highway authority.

(9) A person who, without reasonable excuse, fails to comply with a litter abatement order shall be guilty of an offence and liable on summary conviction to a fine not exceeding level 4 on the standard scale together with a further fine of an amount equal to one-twentieth of that level for each day on which the offence continues after the conviction.

(10) In any proceedings for an offence under subsection (9) above it shall be a defence for the defendant to prove that he has complied, as respects the highway or land in question, with his duty under section 89(1) and (2) above.

(11) A code of practice under section 89(7) shall be admissible in evidence in any proceedings under this section and if any provision of such a code appears to the court to be relevant to any question in the proceedings it shall be taken into account in determining that question.

(12) Where a magistrates' court is satisfied on the hearing of a complaint under this section—

(a) that, when the complaint was made to it, the highway or land in question was defaced by litter or refuse or, as the case may be, was wanting in cleanliness, and

(b) that there were reasonable grounds for bringing the complaint,

the court shall order the defendant to pay such reasonable sum to the complainant as the court may determine in respect of the expenses incurred by the complainant in bringing the complaint and the proceedings before the court.

(13) In the application of this section to Scotland—

(a) for any reference to a magistrates' court there shall be substituted a reference to the sheriff;

(b) for any reference to a complaint there shall be substituted a reference to a summary application, and "complainant" shall be construed accordingly;

(c) for any reference to the defendant there shall be substituted a reference to the person against whom the proceedings are taken;

(d) for any reference to a highway and a relevant highway there shall be substituted a reference to a road and a relevant road; and

(e) for any reference to a highway authority there shall be substituted a reference to a roads authority, and any person against whom proceedings are brought may appeal on a point of law to the Court of Session against the making of a litter abatement order.

92 Summary proceedings by litter authorities

(1) Where a principal litter authority other than a county council, regional council or joint board are satisfied as respects—

- (a) any relevant Crown land,
- (b) any relevant land of a designated statutory undertaker,
- (c) any relevant land of a designated educational institution, or
- (d) any relevant land within a litter control area of a local authority,

that it is defaced by litter or refuse or that defacement of it by litter or refuse is likely to recur, the authority shall serve a notice (a "litter abatement notice") imposing either the requirement or the prohibition or both the requirement and the prohibition specified in subsection (2) below.

(2) The requirement and prohibition referred to in subsection (1) above are as follows, namely—

- (a) a requirement that the litter or refuse be cleared within a time specified in the notice;
- (b) a prohibition on permitting the land to become defaced by litter or refuse.

(3) The litter abatement notice shall be served—

- (a) as respects relevant Crown land, on the appropriate Crown authority;
- (b) as respects relevant land of a designated statutory undertaker, on the undertaker;
- (c) as respects relevant land of a designated educational institution, on the governing body of the institution or in Scotland on such body or, as the case may be, on the education authority responsible for the management of the institution;
- (d) in any other case, on the occupier of the land or, if it is unoccupied, on the owner of the land.

(4) The person served with the notice may appeal against the notice to a magistrates' court or, in Scotland, to the sheriff by way of summary application within the period of twenty-one days beginning with the date on which the notice was served.

(5) If, on any appeal under subsection (4) above, the appellant proves that, as respects the land in question, he has complied with his duty under section 89(1) above, the court shall allow the appeal.

(6) If a person on whom a litter abatement notice is served, without reasonable excuse, fails to comply with or contravenes the requirement or prohibition imposed by the notice, he shall be guilty of an offence and liable on summary conviction to a fine not exceeding level 4 on the standard scale together with a further fine of an amount equal to one-twentieth of that level for each day on which the offence continues after the conviction.

(7) In any proceedings for an offence under subsection (6) above it shall be a defence for the person charged to prove that he has complied, as respects the land in question, with his duty under section 89(1) above.

(8) A code of practice under section 89(7) above shall be admissible in evidence in any proceedings under this section and if any provision of such a code appears to the court to be relevant to any question in the proceedings it shall be taken into account in determining that question.

(9) If a person on whom a litter abatement notice is served fails to comply with the requirement imposed by the notice in respect of any land, the authority may, subject to subsection (10) below—

(a) enter on the land and clear the litter or refuse; and

(b) recover from that person the expenditure attributable to their having done so, except such of the expenditure as that person shows was unnecessary in the circumstances.

(10) Subsection (9) above does not apply in relation to relevant Crown land or relevant land of statutory undertakers.

93 Street litter control notices

(1) A principal litter authority other than a county council, regional council or a joint board may, with a view to the prevention of accumulations of litter or refuse in and around any street or open land adjacent to any street, issue notices ("street litter control notices") imposing requirements on occupiers of premises in relation to such litter or refuse, in accordance with this section and section 94 below.

(2) If the authority is satisfied, in respect of any premises which are of a description prescribed under section 94(1)(a) below and have a frontage on a street in their area, that—

(a) there is recurrent defacement by litter or refuse of any land, being part of the street or open land adjacent to the street, which is in the vicinity of the premises, or

(b) the condition of any part of the premises which is open land in the vicinity of the frontage is, and if no notice is served is likely to continue to be, detrimental to the amenities of the locality by reason of the presence of litter or refuse, or

(c) there is produced, as a result of the activities carried on on the premises, quantities of litter or refuse of such nature and in such amounts as are likely to cause the defacement of any part of the street, or of open land adjacent to the street, which is in the vicinity of the premises,

the authority may serve a street litter control notice on the occupier or, if the premises are unoccupied, on the owner of the premises.

(3) A notice shall, subject to section 94(2), (3) and (4) below—

(a) identify the premises and state the grounds under subsection (2) above on which it is issued;

(b) specify an area of open land which adjoins or is in the vicinity of the frontage of the premises on the street;

(c) specify, in relation to that area or any part of it, such reasonable requirements as the authority considers appropriate in the circumstances;

and, for the purposes of paragraph (b) above, an area which includes land on both sides of the frontage of the premises shall be treated as an area adjoining that frontage.

(4) In this section and section 94 below—

"notice" means a street litter control notice;

"open land" means land in the open air;

"the premises", in relation to a notice, means the premises in respect of which the notice is issued;

"specified area" means the area specified in a notice under subsection (3)(b) above; and

"street" means a relevant highway, a relevant road or any other highway or road over which there is a right of way on foot.

94 Street litter: supplementary provisions

(1) The Secretary of State may by order prescribe—

- (a) the descriptions of commercial or retail premises in respect of which a street litter control notice may be issued;
- (b) the descriptions of land which may be included in a specified area; and
- (c) the maximum area of land which may be included in a specified area;

and different descriptions or maximum dimensions may be prescribed under paragraph (b) or (c) above for different cases or circumstances.

(2) The power to describe premises or land under subsection (1)(a) or (b) above includes power to describe the premises or land by reference to occupation or ownership or to the activities carried on there.

(3) The land comprised in a specified area—

- (a) shall include only land of one or more of the descriptions prescribed under subsection (1)(b) above;
- (b) shall not include any land which is not—
  - (i) part of the premises,
  - (ii) part of a street,
  - (iii) relevant land of a principal litter authority, or
  - (iv) land under the direct control of any other local authority; and
- (c) shall not exceed any applicable maximum area prescribed under subsection (1)(c) above;

but a specified area shall not include any part of the premises which is or is part of a litter control area.

(4) The requirements which may be imposed by a notice shall relate to the clearing of litter or refuse from the specified area and may in particular require—

- (a) the provision or emptying of receptacles for litter or refuse;
- (b) the doing within a period specified in the notice of any such thing as may be so specified; or
- (c) the doing (while the notice remains in force) at such times or intervals, or within such periods, of any such thing as may be so specified;

but a notice may not require the clearing of litter or refuse from any carriageway, except at a time when the carriageway is closed to all vehicular traffic.

(5) In relation to so much of the specified area as is not part of the premises the authority shall take account, in determining what requirements to impose, of their own duties under this Part or otherwise, and of any similar duties of any other local authority, in relation to that land.

(6) An authority proposing to serve a notice shall—

(a) inform the person on whom the notice is to be served;
(b) give him the opportunity to make representations about the notice within the period of twenty-one days beginning with the day on which he is so informed; and
(c) take any representations so made into account in making their decision.

(7) A person on whom a notice is served may appeal against the notice to a magistrate's court or, in Scotland, to the sheriff by way of summary application; and the court may quash the notice or may quash, vary or add to any requirement imposed by the notice.

(8) If it appears to the authority that a person has failed or is failing to comply with any requirement imposed by a notice the authority may apply to a magistrate's court or, in Scotland, to the sheriff by way of summary application for an order requiring the person to comply with the requirement within such time as may be specified in the order.

(9) A person who, without reasonable excuse, fails to comply with an order under subsection (8) above shall be guilty of an offence and liable on summary conviction to a fine not exceeding level 4 on the standard scale.

95 Public registers

(1) It shall be the duty of each principal litter authority other than a county council, regional council or joint board to maintain, in accordance with this section, a register containing copies of—
(a) all orders made by the authority under section 90(3) above; and
(b) all street litter control notices issued under section 93(1) above.

(2) Where the requirements of a street litter control notice are varied or added to on an appeal under section 94(7) above a copy of the order making the variation or addition shall be included in the register.

(3) Copies of the orders and notices required to be kept in the register shall be so kept for so long as the order or notice is in force.

(4) It shall be the duty of each authority maintaining a register under this section—
(a) to secure that the register is available, at all reasonable times, for inspection by the public free of charge; and
(b) to afford to members of the public facilities for obtaining copies of the documents kept in the register, on payment of reasonable charges.

(5) A register under this section need not be kept in documentary form.

96 Application of Part II

(1) This section applies to litter and refuse collected—
(a) by any authority or person in pursuance of section 89(1) above;
(b) by a principal litter authority in pursuance of section 92(9) above; or
(c) by any person in pursuance of section 93 above.

(2) The Secretary of State may make regulations providing that prescribed provisions of Part II shall have effect, with such modifications (if any) as may be prescribed—

(a) as if references to controlled waste or controlled waste of a prescribed description included references to litter and refuse to which this section applies or any description of such litter and refuse;

(b) as if references to controlled waste or controlled waste of a prescribed description collected under section 45 above included references to litter and refuse collected as mentioned in subsection (1) above or any description of such litter and refuse.

(3) The powers conferred by this section are exercisable in relation to litter and refuse to which it applies whether or not the circumstances are such that the litter or refuse would be treated as controlled waste apart from this section and this section is not to affect the interpretation of the expressions defined in section 75 above.

97 Transitional provision relating to section 89

(1) The Secretary of State may, for the purposes of the transition to the duties imposed by section 89 above on local authorities and educational bodies, by regulations, make provision—

(a) modifying that section, or

(b) modifying Part I of the Local Government Act 1988 (competition rules for functional work or works contracts).

(2) Regulations under this section may make different provision for different descriptions of authorities, different areas or other different circumstances or cases.

(3) In this section—

"educational bodies" means the governing bodies and education authorities mentioned in section 89(1)(f) above; and

"local authorities" means the local authorities mentioned in section 89(1)(a) and (c) and (2)(a) above.

98 Definitions

(1) The following definitions apply for the interpretation of this Part.

(2) "Educational institution", in relation to England and Wales, means—

(a) any university (within the meaning of the Education Reform Act 1988) funded by the Universities Funding Council under section 131 of that Act;

(b) the Open University;

(c) any institution which provides higher education or further education (or both) which is full-time education being an institution which—

(i) is maintained by grants made by the Secretary of State under section 100(1)(b) of the Education Act 1944;

(ii) is designated by or under regulations under section 218 of the Education Reform Act 1988 as an institution dependent for its maintenance on assistance from local education authorities; or

(iii) is maintained by a local education authority;

(d) any higher education institution funded by the Polytechnics and Colleges Funding Council under section 132 of the Education Reform Act 1988;

(e) any city technology college or city college for the technology of the arts (within the meaning of section 105 of the Education Reform Act 1988);

(f) any county school, voluntary school or maintained special school;
(g) any grant-maintained school.

(3) "Educational institution", in relation to Scotland, means—
(a) any university within the meaning of the Education Reform Act 1988 funded by the Universities Funding Council under section 131 of that Act;
(b) the Open University;
(c) a college of further education—
(i) as defined in section 80(1) of the Self Governing Schools (Scotland) Act 1989 ("the 1989 Act"); or
(ii) managed by a company by virtue of section 65(1) of the 1989 Act;
(d) a grant-aided college within the meaning of section 77(5) of the Education (Scotland) Act 1980 ("the 1980 Act");
(e) a technology academy within the meaning of section 68(1) of the 1989 Act;
(f) a public school as defined in section 135(1) of the 1980 Act;
(g) a grant-aided school as defined in section 135(1) of the 1980 Act;
(h) a self-governing school within the meaning of section 1(3) of the 1989 Act.

(4) "Joint board", in relation to Scotland, has the meaning given by section 235(1) of the Local Government (Scotland) Act 1973.

(5) "Highway" (and "highway maintainable at the public expense"), "special road" and "trunk road", in relation to England and Wales, have the same meaning as in the Highways Act 1980 and "public road", "special road" and "trunk road", in relation to Scotland, have the same meaning as in the Roads (Scotland) Act 1984.

(6) "Statutory undertaker" means—
(a) any person authorised by any enactment to carry on any railway, light railway, tramway or road transport undertaking;
(b) any person authorised by any enactment to carry on any canal, inland navigation, dock, harbour or pier undertaking; or
(c) any relevant airport operator (within the meaning of Part V of the Airports Act 1986).

Abandoned trolleys

99 Powers in relation to abandoned shopping and luggage trolleys

(1) A local authority may, subject to subsection (3) below, resolve that Schedule 4 to this Act is to apply in its area; and if a local authority does so resolve, that Schedule shall come into force in its area on the day specified in the resolution, which must not be before the expiration of the period of three months beginning with the day on which the resolution is passed.

(2) A local authority shall publish in at least one newspaper circulating in its area a notice that the authority has passed a resolution under this section and indicating the general effect of that Schedule.

(3) It shall be the duty of a local authority, before making any resolution for the application of Schedule 4 to this Act in its area, to consult with the persons or representatives of persons who appear to the authority to be persons who will be affected by the application of that Schedule.

(4) It shall be the duty of a local authority from time to time to consult about the operation of Schedule 4 to this Act with the persons or representatives of persons who appear to be affected by its operation.

(5) In this section "local authority" means—

- (a) the council of a district;
- (b) the council of a London borough;
- (c) the Common Council of the City of London;
- (d) the council of the Isles of Scilly; and
- (e) in Scotland, an islands or district council.

(6) In Schedule 4 to this Act "the local authority" means any local authority which has resolved that that Schedule is to apply in its area.

PART V

AMENDMENT OF THE RADIOACTIVE SUBSTANCES ACT 1960

100 Appointment of inspectors and chief inspector

(1) After section 11 of the Radioactive Substances Act 1960 (referred to in this Part as "the 1960 Act") there shall be inserted the following section—

> **"11A Appointment of inspectors and chief inspector**
>
> (1) The Secretary of State may appoint as inspectors, to assist him in the execution of this Act, such number of persons appearing to him to be qualified for the purpose as he may from time to time consider necessary or expedient.
>
> (2) For the purposes of this Act the Secretary of State shall appoint one of those inspectors to be chief inspector.
>
> (3) A person may be appointed both as an inspector or as chief inspector under the preceding subsections of this section and as an inspector or as chief inspector under section 16 of the Environmental Protection Act 1990.
>
> (4) The chief inspector may, to any extent, delegate his functions under this Act to any other inspector appointed under this section.
>
> (5) The Secretary of State may make to or in respect of any person appointed under this section such payments, whether by way of remuneration, allowances or otherwise as he may, with the approval of the Treasury, determine.".

(2) In section 1, 2(3) and (4), 3, 5, 8(1) to (3) and 9 of the 1960 Act (which concern functions to be exercisable by the chief inspector) for the word "Minister" wherever it appears (otherwise than when referring to the Minister of Agriculture, Fisheries and Food) there shall be substituted the words "chief inspector".

(3) In section 2(6), 4(2), 6(5), 10, 12(2) and (5), 13(3), 15 and 18(6) of the 1960 Act (which concern functions which will continue to be exercisable by the Secretary of State) for the word "Minister" wherever it appears there shall be substituted the words "Secretary of State".

101 Fees and charges under 1960 Act

After section 15 of the 1960 Act there shall be inserted the following section—

"15A Fees and charges

(1) The Secretary of State may, with the approval of the Treasury, make and from time to time revise, a scheme prescribing—

(a) fees payable in respect of applications for registration under section one or section three of this Act or an authorisation under section six or section seven of this Act;

(b) fees payable in respect of the variation of the registration under section five of this Act or, as the case may be, in respect of the variation of the authorisation under section eight of this Act;

(c) charges payable by a person to whom such a registration relates or to whom such an authorisation has been granted in respect of the subsistence of that registration or authorisation;

and it shall be a condition of any such registration or authorisation that any applicable prescribed charge is paid in accordance with that scheme.

(2) The power to make and revise a scheme under this section, so far as it relates to, or to applications for, authorisations under section six of this Act which may only be granted by the chief inspector and the Minister of Agriculture, Fisheries and Food shall not be exercisable without the consent of the Minister of Agriculture, Fisheries and Food.

(3) A scheme under this section may, in particular—

(a) provide for different fees or charges to be payable in different cases or circumstances; and

(b) provide for the times at which and the manner in which payments are to be made;

and a scheme may make such incidental, supplementary and transitional provision as appears to the Secretary of State to be appropriate and different schemes may be made and revised for different areas.

(4) The Secretary of State shall so frame a scheme under this section as to secure, so far as practicable, that the amounts payable under it are sufficient, taking one financial year with another, to cover the expenditure of the chief inspector and the Minister of Agriculture, Fisheries and Food in exercising or performing their functions under this Act in relation to registrations and authorisations.

(5) The Secretary of State shall, on making or revising a scheme under this section, lay a copy of the scheme or of the revisions before each House of Parliament."

102 Enforcement powers of chief inspector

After the section 11A of the 1960 Act inserted by section 100 above there shall be inserted the following sections—

"11B Enforcement notices

(1) Subject to the provisions of this section, if the chief inspector is of the opinion that a person to whom a registration under section one or section three of this

Act relates or to whom an authorisation was granted under section six or section seven of this Act—

(a) is failing to comply with any limitation or condition subject to which the registration or authorisation has effect, or

(b) is likely to fail to comply with any such limitation or condition,

he may serve a notice under this section on that person.

(2) A notice under this section shall—

(a) state that the chief inspector is of the said opinion;

(b) specify the matters constituting the failure to comply with the limitations or conditions in question or the matters making it likely that such a failure will occur, as the case may be; and

(c) specify the steps that must be taken to remedy those matters and the period within which those steps must be taken.

(3) Where a notice is served under this section the chief inspector shall—

(a) in the case of a registration, if a certificate relating to the registration was sent to a local authority under subsection (6) of section one or subsection (5) of section three of this Act, or

(b) in the case of an authorisation, if a copy of the authorisation was sent to a public or local authority under subsection (5)(b) of section eight of this Act,

send a copy of the notice to that authority.

(4) In the case of an authorisation granted by the chief inspector and the Minister of Agriculture, Fisheries and Food in accordance with subsection (1) of section eight of this Act, the power to issue notices under this section shall be exercisable by the chief inspector or by the Minister of Agriculture, Fisheries and Food as if references to the chief inspector were references to the chief inspector or that Minister.

11C Prohibition notices

(1) Subject to the provisions of this section, if the chief inspector is of the opinion, as respects the keeping or use of radioactive material or of mobile radioactive apparatus, or the disposal or accumulation of radioactive waste, by a person in pursuance of a registration or authorisation under this Act, that the continuing to carry on that activity (or the continuing to do so in a particular manner) involves an imminent risk of pollution of the environment or of harm to human health he may serve a notice under this section on that person.

(2) A notice under this section may be served whether or not the manner of carrying on the activity in question complies with any limitations or conditions to which the registration or authorisation in question is subject.

(3) A notice under this section shall—

(a) state the chief inspector's opinion;

(b) specify the matters giving rise to the risk involved in the activity, the steps that must be taken to remove the risk and the period within which those steps must be taken; and

(c) direct that the registration or authorisation shall, until the notice is withdrawn, wholly or to the extent specified in the notice cease to have effect.

(4) Where the registration or authorisation is not wholly suspended by the direction given under the preceding subsection, the direction may specify limitations or conditions to which the registration or authorisation is to be subject until the notice is withdrawn.

(5) Where a notice is served under this section the chief inspector shall—

(a) in the case of a registration, if a certificate relating to the registration was sent to a local authority under subsection (6) of section one or subsection (5) of section three of this Act, or

(b) in the case of an authorisation, if a copy of the authorisation was sent to a public or local authority under subsection (5)(b) of section eight of this Act,

send a copy of the notice to that authority.

(6) The chief inspector shall, by notice to the recipient, withdraw a notice under this section when he is satisfied that the risk specified in it has been removed; and on so doing the chief inspector shall send a copy of the withdrawal notice to any public or local authority to whom a copy of the notice under this section was sent.

(7) In the case of an authorisation granted by the chief inspector and the Minister of Agriculture, Fisheries and Food in accordance with subsection (1) of section eight of this Act, the power to issue and withdraw notices under this section shall be exercisable by the chief inspector or by the Minister of Agriculture, Fisheries and Food as if references to the chief inspector were references to the chief inspector or that Minister."

103 Withdrawal of UKAEA exemptions from requirements of 1960 Act

Sections 2(1), 4(1) and 7(3)(a) of the 1960 Act (which exempt the United Kingdom Atomic Energy Authority from certain requirements of that Act relating to registrations and authorisations) shall cease to have effect.

104 Application to Crown of 1960 Act

For section 14 of the 1960 Act there shall be substituted the following section—

"14 Application of Act to Crown

(1) Subject to the provisions of this section, the provisions of this Act shall bind the Crown.

(2) The last preceding subsection does not apply in relation to premises—

(a) occupied on behalf of the Crown for naval, military or air force purposes or for the purposes of the department of the Secretary of State having responsibility for defence; or

(b) occupied by or for the purposes of a visiting force.

(3) No contravention by the Crown of any provision of this Act shall make the Crown criminally liable; but the High Court or, in Scotland, the Court of Session may, on the application of any authority charged with enforcing that provision, declare unlawful any act or omission of the Crown which constitutes such a contravention.

(4) Notwithstanding anything in subsection (3) of this section, the provisions of this Act shall apply to persons in the public service of the Crown as they apply to other persons.

(5) If the Secretary of State certifies that it appears to him requisite or expedient in the interests of national security that the powers of entry conferred by section twelve of this Act should not be exercisable in relation to any Crown premises specified in the certificate those powers shall not be exercisable in relation to those premises, and in this subsection "Crown premises" means premises held or used by or on behalf of the Crown.

(6) Where, in the case of any such premises as are mentioned in subsection (2) of this section—

(a) arrangements are made whereby radioactive waste is not to be disposed of from those premises except with the approval of the chief inspector, and

(b) in pursuance of those arrangements the chief inspector proposes to approve, or approves, the removal of radioactive waste from those premises to a place provided by a local authority as a place for the deposit of refuse,

the provisions of subsections (3) to (5) of section nine of this Act shall apply as if the proposal to approve the removal of the waste were an application for an authorisation under section six of this Act to remove it, or (as the case may be) the approval were such an authorisation.

(7) Nothing in this section shall be taken as in any way affecting Her Majesty in her private capacity; and this subsection shall be construed as if section 38(3) of the Crown Proceedings Act 1947 (interpretation of references in that Act to Her Majesty in her private capacity) were contained in this Act.

(8) In subsection (2) of this section "visiting force" means any such body, contingent or detachment of the forces of any country as is a visiting force for the purposes of any of the provisions of the Visiting Forces Act 1952."

105 Consequential and further amendments of 1960 Act

The 1960 Act shall be amended in accordance with the provisions of Schedule 5 to this Act (which contains amendments consequential on sections 100 to 103 above and further miscellaneous amendments, including amendments relating to the application of the 1960 Act in Scotland and in Northern Ireland).

PART VI

GENETICALLY MODIFIED ORGANISMS

Preliminary

106 Purpose of Part VI and meaning of "genetically modified organisms" and related expressions

(1) This Part has effect for the purpose of preventing or minimising any damage to the environment which may arise from the escape or release from human control of genetically modified organisms.

(2) In this Part the term "organism" means any acellular, unicellular or multicellular entity (in any form), other than humans or human embryos; and, unless the context otherwise requires, the term also includes any article or substance consisting of or including biological matter.

(3) For the purpose of subsection (2) above "biological matter" means anything (other than an entity mentioned in that subsection) which consists of or includes—

(a) tissue or cells (including gametes or propagules) or subcellular entities, of any kind, capable of replication or of transferring genetic material, or

(b) genes or other genetic material, in any form, which are so capable,

and it is immaterial, in determining if something is or is not an organism or biological matter, whether it is the product of natural or artificial processes of reproduction and, in the case of biological matter, whether it has ever been part of a whole organism.

(4) For the purposes of this Part an organism is "genetically modified" if any of the genes or other genetic material in the organism—

(a) have been modified by means of an artificial technique prescribed in regulations by the Secretary of State; or

(b) are inherited or otherwise derived, through any number of replications, from genes or other genetic material (from any source) which were so modified.

(5) The techniques which may be prescribed for the purposes of subsection (4) above include—

(a) any technique for the modification of any genes or other genetic material by the recombination, insertion or deletion of, or of any component parts of, that material from its previously occurring state, and

(b) any other technique for modifying genes or other genetic material which in the opinion of the Secretary of State would produce organisms which should for the purposes of this Part be treated as having been genetically modified,

but do not include techniques which involve no more than, or no more than the assistance of, naturally occurring processes of reproduction (including selective breeding techniques or *in vitro* fertilisation).

(6) It is immaterial for the purposes of subsections (4) and (5) above whether the modifications of genes or other genetic material effected by a prescribed technique are produced by direct operations on that genetic material or are induced by indirect means (including in particular the use of viruses, microbial plasmids or other vector systems or of mutation inducing agents).

(7) In this Part, where the context permits, a reference to "reproduction", in relation to an organism, includes a reference to its replication or its transferring genetic material.

107 Meaning of "damage to the environment", "control" and related expressions in Part VI

(1) The following provisions have effect for the interpretation of this Part.

(2) The "environment" consists of land, air and water or any of those media.

(3) "Damage to the environment" is caused by the presence in the environment of genetically modified organisms which have (or of a single such organism which has) escaped or been released from a person's control and are (or is) capable of causing harm to the living organisms supported by the environment.

(4) An organism shall be regarded as present in the environment notwithstanding that it is present in or on any human or other organism, or any other thing, which is itself present in the environment.

(5) Genetically modified organisms present in the environment are capable of causing harm if—

(a) they are individually capable, or are present in numbers such that together they are capable, of causing harm; or

(b) they are able to produce descendants which will be capable, or which will be present in numbers such that together they will be capable, of causing harm;

and a single organism is capable of causing harm either if it is itself capable of causing harm or if it is able to produce descendants which will be so capable.

(6) "Harm" means harm to the health of humans or other living organisms or other interference with the ecological systems of which they form part and, in the case of man, includes offence caused to any of his senses or harm to his property.

(7) "Harmful" and "harmless" mean respectively, in relation to genetically modified organisms, their being capable or their being incapable of causing harm.

(8) The Secretary of State may by regulations provide, in relation to genetically modified organisms of any description specified in the regulations, that—

(a) the capacity of those organisms for causing harm of any description so specified, or

(b) harm of any description so specified,

shall be disregarded for such purposes of this Part as may be so specified.

(9) Organisms of any description are under the "control" of a person where he keeps them contained by any system of physical, chemical or biological barriers (or combination of such barriers) used for either or both of the following purposes, namely—

(a) for ensuring that the organisms do not enter the environment or produce descendants which are not so contained; or

(b) for ensuring that any of the organisms which do enter the environment, or any descendants of the organisms which are not so contained, are harmless.

(10) An organism under a person's control is "released" if he deliberately causes or permits it to cease to be under his control or the control of any other person and to enter the

environment; and such an organism "escapes" if, otherwise than by being released, it ceases to be under his control or that of any other person and enters the environment.

(11) Genetically modified organisms of any description are "marketed" when products consisting of or including such organisms are placed on the market.

General controls

108 Risk assessment and notification requirements

(1) Subject to subsections (2) and (7) below, no person shall import or acquire, release or market any genetically modified organisms unless, before doing that act—

(a) he has carried out an assessment of any risks there are (by reference to the nature of the organisms and the manner in which he intends to keep them after their importation or acquisition or, as the case may be, to release or market them) of damage to the environment being caused as a result of doing that act; and

(b) in such cases and circumstances as may be prescribed, he has given the Secretary of State such notice of his intention of doing that act and such information as may be prescribed.

(2) Subsection (1) above does not apply to a person proposing to do an act mentioned in that subsection who is required under section 111(1)(a) below to have a consent before doing that act.

(3) Subject to subsections (4) and (7) below, a person who is keeping genetically modified organisms shall, in such cases or circumstances and at such times or intervals as may be prescribed—

(a) carry out an assessment of any risks there are of damage to the environment being caused as a result of his continuing to keep them;

(b) give the Secretary of State notice of the fact that he is keeping the organisms and such information as may be prescribed.

(4) Subsection (3) above does not apply to a person who is keeping genetically modified organisms and is required under section 111(2) below to have a consent authorising him to continue to keep the organisms.

(5) It shall be the duty of a person who carries out an assessment under subsection (1)(a) or (3)(a) above to keep, for the prescribed period, such a record of the assessment as may be prescribed.

(6) A person required by subsection (1)(b) or (3)(b) above to give notice to the Secretary of State shall give the Secretary of State such further information as the Secretary of State may by notice in writing require.

(7) Regulations under this section may provide for exemptions, or for the granting by the Secretary of State of exemptions to particular persons or classes of person, from the requirements of subsection (1) or (3) above in such cases or circumstances, and to such extent, as may be prescribed.

(8) The Secretary of State may at any time—

(a) give directions to a person falling within subsection (1) above requiring that person to apply for a consent before doing the act in question; or

(b) give directions to a person falling within subsection (3) above requiring that person, before such date as may be specified in the direction, to apply for a consent authorising him to continue keeping the organisms in question;

and a person given directions under paragraph (a) above shall then, and a person given directions under paragraph (b) above shall from the specified date, be subject to section 111 below in place of the requirements of this section.

(9) Regulations under this section may—

(a) prescribe the manner in which assessments under subsection (1) or (3) above are to be carried out and the matters which must be investigated and assessed;

(b) prescribe minimum periods of notice between the giving of a notice under subsection (1)(b) above and the doing of the act in question;

(c) make provision allowing the Secretary of State to shorten or to extend any such period;

(d) prescribe maximum intervals at which assessments under subsection (3)(a) above must be carried out;

and the regulations may make different provision for different cases and different circumstances.

(10) In this section "prescribed" means prescribed by the Secretary of State in regulations under this section.

109 General duties relating to importation, acquisition, keeping, release or marketing of organisms

(1) A person who—

(a) is proposing to import or acquire any genetically modified organisms, or

(b) is keeping any such organisms, or

(c) is proposing to release or market any such organisms,

shall, subject to subsection (5) below, be subject to the duties specified in subsection (2), (3) or (4) below, as the case may be.

(2) A person who proposes to import or acquire genetically modified organisms—

(a) shall take all reasonable steps to identify, by reference to the nature of the organisms and the manner in which he intends to keep them (including any precautions to be taken against their escaping or causing damage to the environment), what risks there are of damage to the environment being caused as a result of their importation or acquisition; and

(b) shall not import or acquire the organisms if it appears that, despite any precautions which can be taken, there is a risk of damage to the environment being caused as a result of their importation or acquisition.

(3) A person who is keeping genetically modified organisms—

(a) shall take all reasonable steps to keep himself informed of any damage to the environment which may have been caused as a result of his keeping the organisms and to identify what risks there are of damage to the environment being caused as a result of his continuing to keep them;

(b) shall cease keeping the organisms if, despite any additional precautions which can be taken, it appears, at any time, that there is a risk of damage to the environment being caused as a result of his continuing to keep them; and

(c) shall use the best available techniques not entailing excessive cost for keeping the organisms under his control and for preventing any damage to the environment being caused as a result of his continuing to keep the organisms;

and where a person is required by paragraph (b) above to cease keeping the organisms he shall dispose of them as safely and as quickly as practicable and paragraph (c) above shall continue to apply until he has done so.

(4) A person who proposes to release genetically modified organisms—

(a) shall take all reasonable steps to keep himself informed, by reference to the nature of the organisms and the extent and manner of the release (including any precautions to be taken against their causing damage to the environment), what risks there are of damage to the environment being caused as a result of their being released;

(b) shall not release the organisms if it appears that, despite the precautions which can be taken, there is a risk of damage to the environment being caused as a result of their being released; and

(c) subject to paragraph (b) above, shall use the best available techniques not entailing excessive cost for preventing any damage to the environment being caused as a result of their being released;

and this subsection applies, with the necessary modifications, to a person proposing to market organisms as it applies to a person proposing to release organisms.

(5) This section does not apply—

(a) to persons proposing to import or acquire, to release or to market any genetically modified organisms, in cases or circumstances where, under section 108 above, they are not required to carry out a risk assessment before doing that act;

(b) to persons who are keeping any genetically modified organisms and who—

(i) were not required under section 108 above to carry out a risk assessment before importing or acquiring them;

(ii) have not been required under that section to carry out a risk assessment in respect of the keeping of those organisms since importing or acquiring them; or

(c) to holders of consents, in the case of acts authorised by those consents.

110 Prohibition notices

(1) The Secretary of State may serve a notice under this section (a "prohibition notice") on any person he has reason to believe—

(a) is proposing to import or acquire, release or market any genetically modified organisms; or

(b) is keeping any such organisms;

if he is of the opinion that doing any such act in relation to those organisms or continuing to keep them, as the case may be, would involve a risk of causing damage to the environment.

(2) A prohibition notice may prohibit a person from doing an act mentioned in subsection (1)(a) above in relation to any genetically modified organisms or from continuing to keep them; and the prohibition may apply in all cases or circumstances or in such cases or circumstances as may be specified in the notice.

(3) A prohibition notice shall—

(a) state that the Secretary of State is, in relation to the person on whom it is served, of the opinion mentioned in subsection (1) above;

(b) specify what is, or is to be, prohibited by the notice; and

(c) if the prohibition is not to be effective on being served, specify the date on which the prohibition is to take effect;

and a notice may be served on a person notwithstanding that he may have a consent authorising any act which is, or is to be, prohibited by the notice.

(4) Where a person is prohibited by a prohibition notice from continuing to keep any genetically modified organisms, he shall dispose of them as quickly and safely as practicable or, if the notice so provides, as may be specified in the notice.

(5) The Secretary of State may at any time withdraw a prohibition notice served on any person by notice given to that person.

Consents

111 Consents required by certain persons

(1) Subject to subsection (7) below, no person shall import or acquire, release or market any genetically modified organisms—

(a) in such cases or circumstances as may be prescribed in relation to that act, or

(b) in any case where he has been given directions under section 108(8)(a) above,

except in pursuance of a consent granted by the Secretary of State and in accordance with any limitations and conditions to which the consent is subject.

(2) Subject to subsection (7) below, no person who has imported or acquired any genetically modified organisms (whether under a consent or not) shall continue to keep the organisms—

(a) in such cases or circumstances as may be prescribed, after the end of the prescribed period, or

(b) if he has been given directions under section 108(8)(b) above, after the date specified in the directions,

except in pursuance of a consent granted by the Secretary of State and in accordance with any limitations or conditions to which the consent is subject.

(3) A person who is required under subsection (2) above to cease keeping any genetically modified organisms shall dispose of them as quickly and safely as practicable.

(4) An application for a consent must contain such information and be made and advertised in such manner as may be prescribed and shall be accompanied by the fee required under section 113 below.

(5) The applicant shall, in prescribed circumstances, give such notice of his application to such persons as may be prescribed.

(6) The Secretary of State may by notice to the applicant require him to furnish such further information specified in the notice, within such period as may be so specified, as he may require for the purpose of determining the application; and if the applicant fails to furnish the information within the specified period the Secretary of State may refuse to proceed with the application.

(7) Regulations under this section may provide for exemptions, or for the granting by the Secretary of State of exemptions to particular persons or classes of person, from—

(a) any requirement under subsection (1) or (2) above to have a consent, or

(b) any of the requirements to be fulfilled under the regulations by an applicant for a consent,

in such cases or circumstances as may be prescribed.

(8) Where an application for a consent is duly made to him, the Secretary of State may grant the consent subject to such limitations and conditions as may be imposed under section 112 below or he may refuse the application.

(9) The conditions attached to a consent may include conditions which are to continue to have effect notwithstanding that the holder has completed or ceased the act or acts authorised by the consent.

(10) The Secretary of State may at any time, by notice given to the holder of a consent, revoke the consent or vary the consent (whether by attaching new limitations and conditions or by revoking or varying any limitations and conditions to which it is at that time subject).

(11) Regulations under this section may make different provision for different cases and different circumstances; and in this section "prescribed" means prescribed in regulations under this section.

112 Consents: limitations and conditions

(1) The Secretary of State may include in a consent such limitations and conditions as he may think fit; but no limitations or conditions shall be imposed for the purpose only of securing the health of persons at work (within the meaning of Part I of the Health and Safety at Work etc. Act 1974 or, in relation to Northern Ireland, Part II of the Health and Safety at Work (Northern Ireland) Order 1978).

(2) Without prejudice to the generality of subsection (1) above, the conditions included in a consent may—

(a) require the giving of notice of any fact to the Secretary of State; or

(b) prohibit or restrict the keeping, releasing or marketing of genetically modified organisms under the consent in specified cases or circumstances;

and where, under any condition, the holder of a consent is required to cease keeping any genetically modified organisms, he shall dispose of them, if no manner is specified in the conditions, as quickly and safely as practicable.

(3) Subject to subsection (6) below, there is implied in every consent for the importation or acquisition of genetically modified organisms a general condition that the holder of the consent shall—

(a) take all reasonable steps to keep himself informed (by reference to the nature of the organisms and the manner in which he intends to keep them after their importation or acquisition) of any risks there are of damage to the environment being caused as a result of their importation or acquisition; and

(b) if at any time it appears that any such risks are more serious than were apparent when the consent was granted, notify the Secretary of State forthwith.

(4) Subject to subsection (6) below, there is implied in every consent for keeping genetically modified organisms a general condition that the holder of the consent shall—

(a) take all reasonable steps to keep himself informed of any damage to the environment which may have been caused as a result of his keeping the organisms and of any risks there are of such damage being caused as a result of his continuing to keep them;

(b) if at any time it appears that any such risks are more serious than were apparent when the consent was granted, notify the Secretary of State forthwith; and

(c) use the best available techniques not entailing excessive cost for keeping the organisms under his control and for preventing any damage to the environment being caused as a result of his continuing to keep them.

(5) Subject to subsection (6) below, there is implied in every consent for releasing or marketing genetically modified organisms a general condition that the holder of the consent shall—

(a) take all reasonable steps to keep himself informed (by reference to the nature of the organisms and the extent and manner of the release or marketing) of any risks there are of damage to the environment being caused as a result of their being released or, as the case may be, marketed;

(b) if any time it appears that any such risks are more serious than were apparent when the consent was granted, notify the Secretary of State forthwith; and

(c) use the best available techniques not entailing excessive cost for preventing any damage to the environment being caused as a result of their being released or, as the case may be, marketed.

(6) The general condition implied into a consent under subsection (3), (4) or (5) above has effect subject to any conditions imposed under subsection (1) above; and the obligations imposed by virtue of subsection (4)(c) or (5)(c) above shall not apply to any aspect of an act authorised by a consent which is regulated by such a condition.

(7) There shall be implied in every consent for keeping, releasing or marketing genetically modified organisms of any description a general condition that the holder of the consent—

(a) shall take all reasonable steps to keep himself informed of developments in the techniques which may be available in his case for preventing damage to the environment being caused as a result of the doing of the act authorised by the consent in relation to organisms of that description; and

(b) f it appears at any time that any better techniques are available to him than is required by any condition included in the consent under subsection (1) above, shall notify the Secretary of State of that fact forthwith.

But this general condition shall have effect subject to any conditions imposed under subsection (1) above.

113 Fees and charges

(1) The Secretary of State may, with the approval of the Treasury, make and from time to time revise a scheme prescribing—

(a) fees payable in respect of applications for consents; and

(b) charges payable by persons holding consents in respect of the subsistence of their consents;

and it shall be a condition of any such consent that any applicable prescribed charge is paid in accordance with that scheme.

(2) A scheme under this section may, in particular—

(a) provide for different fees or charges to be payable in different cases or circumstances;

(b) provide for the times at which and the manner in which payments are to be made; and

(c) make such incidental, supplementary and transitional provision as appears to the Secretary of State to be appropriate.

(3) The Secretary of State shall so frame a scheme under this section as to secure, so far as practicable, that the amounts payable under it will be sufficient, taking one financial year with another, to cover the expenditure of the Secretary of State in discharging his functions under this Part in relation to consents.

(4) The Secretary of State shall, on making or revising a scheme under this section, lay a copy of the scheme or of the scheme as revised before each House of Parliament.

Inspectors

114 Appointment etc of inspectors

(1) The Secretary of State may appoint as inspectors, for carrying this Part into effect, such number of persons appearing to him to be qualified for the purpose as he may consider necessary.

(2) The Secretary of State may make to or in respect of any person so appointed such payments by way of remuneration, allowances or otherwise as he may with the approval of the Treasury determine.

(3) An inspector shall not be personally liable in any civil or criminal proceedings for anything done in the purported exercise of any power under section 115 or 117 below if the court is satisfied that the act was done in good faith and that there were reasonable grounds for doing it.

(4) In England and Wales an inspector, if authorised to do so by the Secretary of State, may, although not of counsel or a solicitor, prosecute before a magistrates' court proceedings for an offence under section 118(1) below.

(5) In this Part "inspector" means, subject to section 125 below, a person appointed as an inspector under subsection (1) above.

115 Rights of entry and inspection

(1) An inspector may, on production (if so required) of his authority, exercise any of the powers specified in subsection (3) below for the purposes of the discharge of the functions of the Secretary of State under this Part.

(2) Those powers are exercisable—

(a) in relation to premises—

(i) on which the inspector has reason to believe a person is keeping or has kept any genetically modified organisms, or

(ii) from which he has reason to believe any such organisms have been released or have escaped; and

(b) in relation to premises on which the inspector has reason to believe there may be harmful genetically modified organisms or evidence of damage to the environment caused by genetically modified organisms;

but they are not exercisable in relation to premises used wholly or mainly for domestic purposes.

(3) The powers of an inspector are—

(a) at any reasonable time (or, in a situation in which in his opinion there is an immediate risk of damage to the environment, at any time)—

(i) to enter premises which he has reason to believe it is necessary for him to enter and to take with him any person duly authorised by the Secretary of State and, if the inspector has reasonable cause to apprehend any serious obstruction in the execution of his duty, a constable; and

(ii) to take with him any equipment or materials required for any purpose for which the power of entry is being exercised;

(b) to carry out such tests and inspections (and to make such recordings), as may in any circumstances be necessary;

(c) to direct that any, or any part of, premises which he has power to enter, or anything in or on such premises, shall be left undisturbed (whether generally or in particular respects) for so long as is reasonably necessary for the purpose of any test or inspection;

(d) to take samples of any organisms, articles or substances found in or on any premises which he has power to enter, and of the air, water or land in, on, or in the vicinity of, the premises;

(e) in the case of anything found in or on any premises which he has power to enter, which appears to him to contain or to have contained genetically modified organisms which have caused or are likely to cause damage to the environment, to cause it to be dismantled or subjected to any process or test (but not so as to damage or destroy it unless this is necessary);

(f) in the case of anything mentioned in paragraph (e) above or anything found on premises which he has power to enter which appears to be a genetically modified organism or to consist of or include genetically modified organisms, to take possession of it and detain it for so long as is necessary for all or any of the following purposes, namely—

(i) to examine it and do to it anything which he has power to do under that paragraph;

(ii) to ensure that it is not tampered with before his examination of it is completed; and

(iii) to ensure that it is available for use as evidence in any proceedings for an offence under section 118 below;

(g) to require any person whom he has reasonable cause to believe to be able to give any information relevant to any test or inspection under this subsection to answer (in the absence of persons other than a person nominated to be present and any persons whom the inspector may allow to be present) such questions as the inspector thinks fit to ask and to sign a declaration of the truth of his answers;

(h) to require the production of, or where the information is recorded in computerised form, the furnishing of extracts from, any records which are required to be kept under this Part or it is necessary for him to see for the purposes of any test or inspection under this subsection and to inspect, and take copies of, or of any entry in, the records;

(i) to require any person to afford him such facilities and assistance with respect to any matters or things within that person's control or in relation to which that person has responsibilities as are necessary to enable the inspector to exercise any of the powers conferred on him by this section;

(j) any other power for the purpose mentioned in subsection (1) above which is conferred by regulations made by the Secretary of State.

(4) The Secretary of State may by regulations make provision as to the procedure to be followed in connection with the taking of, and the dealing with, samples under subsection (3)(d) above.

(5) Where an inspector proposes to exercise the power conferred by subsection (3)(e) above, he shall, if so requested by a person who at the time is present on and has responsibilities in relation to those premises, cause anything which is to be done by virtue of that power to be done in the presence of that person.

(6) Before exercising the power conferred by subsection (3)(e) above, an inspector shall consult such persons as appear to him appropriate for the purpose of ascertaining what dangers, if any, there may be in doing anything which he proposes to do under the power.

(7) Where under the power conferred by subsection (3)(f) above an inspector takes possession of anything found on any premises, he shall leave there, either with a responsible person or, if that is impracticable, fixed in a conspicuous position, a notice giving particulars sufficient to identify what he has seized and stating that he has taken possession of it under that power; and before taking possession under that power of—

(a) any thing that forms part of a batch of similar things, or

(b) any substance,

an inspector shall, if it is practical and safe for him to do so, take a sample of it and give to a responsible person at the premises a portion of the sample marked in a manner sufficient to identify it.

(8) No answer given by a person in pursuance of a requirement imposed under subsection (3)(g) above shall be admissible in evidence—

(a) in any proceedings in England and Wales against that person; or

(b) in any criminal proceedings in Scotland against that person.

(9) The powers conferred by subsection (3)(a), (b), (c), (d), (e) and (h) above shall also be exercisable (subject to subsections (4), (5) and (6) above) by any person authorised for the purpose in writing by the Secretary of State.

(10) Nothing in this section shall be taken to compel the production by any person of a document of which he would on grounds of legal professional privilege be entitled to withhold production on an order for discovery in an action in the High Court or, in relation to Scotland, on an order for the production of documents in an action in the Court of Session.

Enforcement powers and offences

116 Obtaining of information from persons

(1) For the purposes of the discharge of his functions under this Part, the Secretary of State may, by notice in writing served on any person who appears to him—

(a) to be involved in the importation, acquisition, keeping, release or marketing of genetically modified organisms; or

(b) to be about to become, or to have been, involved in any of those activities;

require that person to furnish such relevant information available to him as is specified in the notice, in such form and within such period following service of the notice as is so specified.

(2) For the purposes of this section "relevant information" means information concerning any aspects of the activities in question, including any damage to the environment which may be or have been caused thereby; and the discharge by the Secretary of State of an obligation of the United Kingdom under the Community Treaties or any international agreement concerning the protection of the environment from harm caused by genetically modified organisms shall be treated as a function of his under this Part.

117 Power to deal with cause of imminent danger of damage to the environment

(1) Where, in the case of anything found by him on any premises which he has power to enter, an inspector has reason to believe that it is a genetically modified organism or that it consists of or includes genetically modified organisms and that, in the circumstances in which he finds it, it is a cause of imminent danger of damage to the environment, he may seize it and cause it to be rendered harmless (whether by destruction, by bringing it under proper control or otherwise).

(2) Before there is rendered harmless under this section—

(a) any thing that forms part of a batch of similar things, or

(b) any substance,

the inspector shall, if it is practicable and safe for him to do so, take a sample of it and give to a responsible person at the premises a portion of the sample marked in a manner sufficient to identify it.

(3) As soon as may be after anything has been seized and rendered harmless under this section, the inspector shall prepare and sign a written report giving particulars of the circumstances in which it was seized and so dealt with by him, and shall—

(a) give a signed copy of the report to a responsible person at the premises where it was found by him; and

(b) unless that person is the owner of it, also serve a signed copy of the report on the owner;

and if, where paragraph (b) above applies, the inspector cannot after reasonable inquiry ascertain the name or address of the owner, the copy may be served on him by giving it to the person to whom a copy was given under paragraph (a) above.

118 Offences

(1) It is an offence for a person—

(a) to do anything in contravention of section 108(1) above in relation to something which is, and which he knows or has reason to believe is, a genetically modified organism;

(b) to fail to comply with section 108(3) above when keeping something which is, and which he knows or has reason to believe is, a genetically modified organism;

(c) to do anything in contravention of section 111(1) or (2) above in relation to something which is, and which he knows or has reason to believe is, a genetically modified organism;

(d) to fail to comply with any requirement of subsection (2), (3)(a), (b) or (c) or (4) of section 109 above in relation to something which is, and which he knows or has reason to believe is, a genetically modified organism;

(e) to fail, without reasonable excuse, to comply with section 108(5) or (6) above;

(f) to contravene any prohibition imposed on him by a prohibition notice;

(g) without reasonable excuse, to fail to comply with any requirement imposed under section 115 above;

(h) to prevent any other person from appearing before or from answering any question to which an inspector may, by virtue of section 115(3) above, require an answer;

(i) intentionally to obstruct an inspector in the exercise or performance of his powers or duties, other than his powers or duties under section 117 above;

(j) intentionally to obstruct an inspector in the exercise of his powers or duties under section 117 above;

(k) to fail, without reasonable excuse, to comply with any requirement imposed by a notice under section 116 above;

(l) to make a statement which he knows to be false or misleading in a material particular, or recklessly to make a statement which is false or misleading in a material particular, where the statement is made—

  (i) in purported compliance with a requirement to furnish any information imposed by or under any provision of this Part; or

  (ii) for the purpose of obtaining the grant of a consent to himself or any other person or the variation of a consent;

(m) intentionally to make a false entry in any record required to be kept under section 108 or 111 above;

(n) with intent to deceive, to forge or use a document purporting to be issued under section 111 above or required for any purpose thereunder or to make or have in his possession a document so closely resembling any such document as to be likely to deceive;

(o) falsely to pretend to be an inspector.

(2) It shall be a defence for a person charged with an offence under paragraph (a), (b), (c), (d) or (f) of subsection (1) above to prove that he took all reasonable precautions and exercised all due diligence to avoid the commission of the offence.

(3) A person guilty of an offence under paragraph (c) or (d) of subsection (1) above shall be liable—

(a) on summary conviction, to a fine not exceeding £20,000 or to imprisonment for a term not exceeding six months, or to both;

(b) on conviction on indictment, to a fine or to imprisonment for a term not exceeding five years, or to both.

(4) A person guilty of an offence under paragraph (f) of subsection (1) above shall be liable—

(a) on summary conviction, to a fine not exceeding £20,000 or to imprisonment for a term not exceeding six months, or to both;

(b) on conviction on indictment, to a fine or to imprisonment for a term not exceeding two years, or to both.

(5) A person guilty of an offence under paragraph (a) or (b) of subsection (1) above shall be liable—

(a) on summary conviction, to a fine not exceeding the statutory maximum or to imprisonment for a term not exceeding six months, or to both;

(b) on conviction on indictment, to a fine or to imprisonment for a term not exceeding five years, or to both.

(6) A person guilty of an offence under paragraph (e), (j), (k), (l), (m) or (n) of subsection (1) above shall be liable—

(a) on summary conviction, to a fine not exceeding the statutory maximum or to imprisonment for a term not exceeding six months, or to both;

(b) on conviction on indictment, to a fine or to imprisonment for a term not exceeding two years, or to both.

(7) A person guilty of an offence under paragraph (g), (h) or (i) of subsection (1) above shall be liable on summary conviction to a fine not exceeding the statutory maximum or to imprisonment for a term not exceeding three months, or to both.

(8) A person guilty of an offence under paragraph (o) of subsection (1) above shall be liable on summary conviction to a fine not exceeding level 5 on the standard scale.

(9) Where a person is convicted of an offence under paragraph (b) of subsection (1) above in respect of his keeping any genetically modified organism, then, if the contravention in respect of which he was convicted is continued after he was convicted he shall be guilty of a further offence and liable on summary conviction to a fine of one-fifth of level 5 on the standard scale for each day on which the contravention is so continued.

(10) Proceedings in respect of an offence under this section shall not be instituted in England and Wales except by the Secretary of State or with the consent of the Director of Public Prosecutions or in Northern Ireland except with the consent of the Director of Public Prosecutions for Northern Ireland.

119 Onus of proof as regards techniques and evidence

(1) In any proceedings for either of the following offences, that is to say—

(a) an offence under section 118(1)(c) above consisting in a failure to comply with the general condition implied by section 112(4)(c) or (5)(c) above; or

(b) an offence under section 118(1)(d) above consisting in a failure to comply with section 109(3)(c) or (4)(c) above;

it shall be for the accused to prove that there was no better available technique not entailing excessive cost than was in fact used to satisfy the condition or to comply with that section.

(2) Where an entry is required by a condition in a consent to be made in any record as to the observance of any other condition and the entry has not been made, that fact shall be admissible as evidence that that other condition has not been observed.

120 Power of court to order cause of offence to be remedied

(1) Where a person is convicted of an offence under section 118(1)(a), (b), (c), (d), (e) or (f) above in respect of any matters which appear to the court to be matters which it is in his power to remedy, the court may, in addition to or instead of imposing any punishment, order him, within such time as may be fixed by the order, to take such steps as may be specified in the order for remedying those matters.

(2) The time fixed by an order under subsection (1) above may be extended or further extended by order of the court on an application made before the end of the time as originally fixed or as extended under this subsection, as the case may be.

(3) Where a person is ordered under subsection (1) above to remedy any matters, that person shall not be liable under section 118 above in respect of those matters, in so far as they continue during the time fixed by the order or any further time allowed under subsection (2) above.

121 Power of Secretary of State to remedy harm

(1) Where the commission of an offence under section 118(1)(a), (b), (c), (d), (e) or (f) above causes any harm which it is possible to remedy, the Secretary of State may, subject to subsection (2) below—

- (a) arrange for any reasonable steps to be taken towards remedying the harm; and
- (b) recover the cost of taking those steps from any person convicted of that offence.

(2) The Secretary of State shall not exercise his powers under this section, where any of the steps are to be taken on or will affect land in the occupation of any person other than a person convicted of the offence in question, except with the permission of that person.

Publicity

122 Public register of information

(1) The Secretary of State shall maintain a register ("the register") containing prescribed particulars of or relating to—

- (a) notices given or other information furnished under section 108 above;
- (b) directions given under section 108(8) above;
- (c) prohibition notices;
- (d) applications for consents (and any further information furnished in connection with them) and any advice given by the committee appointed under section 124 below in relation to such applications;
- (e) consents granted by the Secretary of State and any information furnished to him in pursuance of consent conditions;
- (f) any other information obtained or furnished under any provision of this Part;
- (g) convictions for such offences under section 118 above as may be prescribed;
- (h) such other matters relating to this Part as may be prescribed;

but that duty is subject to section 123 below.

(2) It shall be the duty of the Secretary of State—

(a) to secure that the register is open to inspection by members of the public free of charge at all reasonable hours; and

(b) to afford to members of the public facilities for obtaining copies of entries, on payment of reasonable charges.

(3) The register may be kept in any form.

(4) The Secretary of State may make regulations with respect to the keeping of the register; and in this section "prescribed" means prescribed in regulations made by the Secretary of State.

123 Exclusion from register of certain information

(1) No information shall be included in the register under section 122 above if and so long as, in the opinion of the Secretary of State, the inclusion of the information would be contrary to the interests of national security.

(2) No information shall be included in the register if and so long as, in the opinion of the Secretary of State, it ought to be excluded on the ground that its inclusion might result in damage to the environment.

(3) No information relating to the affairs of any individual or business shall be included in the register without the consent of that individual or the person for the time being carrying on that business, if the Secretary of State has determined that the information—

(a) is, in relation to him, commercially confidential; and

(b) is not information of a description to which subsection (7) below applies;

unless the Secretary of State is of the opinion that the information is no longer commercially confidential in relation to him.

(4) Nothing in subsection (3) above requires the Secretary of State to determine whether any information is or is not commercially confidential except where the person furnishing the information applies to have it excluded on the ground that it is (in relation to himself or another person) commercially confidential.

(5) Where an application has been made for information to be excluded under subsection (3) above, the Secretary of State shall make a determination and inform the applicant of it as soon as is practicable.

(6) Where it appears to the Secretary of State that any information (other than information furnished by the person to whom it relates) which has been obtained under or by virtue of any provision of this Part might be commercially confidential, the Secretary of State shall—

(a) give to the person to whom or to whose business it relates notice that the information is required to be included in the register unless excluded under subsection (3) above; and

(b) give him a reasonable opportunity—

(i) of objecting to the inclusion of the information on the ground that it is commercially confidential; and

(ii) of making representations to the Secretary of State for the purpose of justifying any such objection;

and the Secretary of State shall take any representations into account before determining whether the information is or is not commercially confidential.

(7) The prescribed particulars of or relating to the matters mentioned in section 122(1)(a), (d) and (e) above shall be included in the register notwithstanding that they may be commercially confidential if and so far as they are of any of the following descriptions, namely—

(a) the name and address of the person giving the notice or furnishing the information;

(b) the description of any genetically modified organisms to which the notice or other information relates;

(c) the location at any time of those organisms;

(d) the purpose for which those organisms are being imported, acquired, kept, released or marketed (according to whichever of those acts the notice or other information relates);

(e) results of any assessment of the risks of damage to the environment being caused by the doing of any of those acts;

(f) notices under section 112(3), (4), (5) or (7) above;

and the Secretary of State may by regulations prescribe any other description of information as information which the public interest requires to be included in the register notwithstanding that it may be commercially confidential.

(8) Information excluded from the register under subsection (3) above shall be treated as ceasing to be commercially confidential for the purposes of that subsection at the expiry of a period of four years beginning with the date of the determination by virtue of which it was excluded; but the person who furnished it or to whom or to whose business it relates may apply to the Secretary of State for the information to remain excluded on the ground that it is still commercially confidential.

(9) The Secretary of State may by order substitute for the period for the time being specified in subsection (8) above such other period as he considers appropriate.

Supplementary

124 Advisory committee for purposes of Part VI

(1) The Secretary of State shall appoint a committee to provide him with advice—

(a) on the exercise of his powers under sections 111, 112 and 113 above;

(b) on the exercise of any power under this Part to make regulations;

and on such other matters concerning his functions under this Part as he may from time to time direct.

(2) The chairman and other members of the committee shall hold and vacate office in accordance with the terms of their appointment.

(3) The Secretary of State shall pay to the members of the committee such remuneration (if any) and such allowances as he may, with the consent of the Treasury, determine.

125 Delegation of enforcement functions

(1) The Secretary of State may, by an agreement made with any public authority, delegate to that authority or to any officer appointed by an authority exercising functions on behalf of that authority any of his enforcement functions under this Part, subject to such restrictions and conditions as may be specified in the agreement.

(2) For the purposes of this section the following are "enforcement functions" of the Secretary of State, that is to say, his functions under—

section 110;

section 114(1) and (4);

section 116;

section 118(10); and

section 121;

and "inspector" in sections 115 and 117 includes, to the extent of the delegation, any inspector appointed by an authority other than the Secretary of State by virtue of an agreement under this section.

(3) The Secretary of State shall, if and so far as an agreement under this section so provides, make payments to the authority to reimburse the authority the expenses incurred in the performance of functions delegated under this section; but no such agreement shall be made without the approval of the Treasury.

126 Exercise of certain functions jointly by Secretary of State and Minister of Agriculture, Fisheries and Food

(1) Subject to subsection (2) below, any reference in this Part to a function exercisable by the Secretary of State shall, in any case where the function is to be exercised in relation to a matter with which the Minister of Agriculture, Fisheries and Food is concerned, be exercisable by the Secretary of State and that Minister acting jointly.

(2) The validity of anything purporting to be done in pursuance of the exercise of any such function shall not be affected by any question whether that thing fell, by virtue of this section, to be done by the Secretary of State and the Minister of Agriculture, Fisheries and Food.

127 Definitions

(1) In this Part—

"acquire", in relation to genetically modified organisms, includes any method by which such organisms may come to be in a person's possession, other than by their being imported;

"consent" means a consent granted under section 111 above, and a reference to the limitations or conditions to which a consent is subject is a reference to the limitations or conditions subject to which the consent for the time being has effect;

"descendant", in relation to a genetically modified organism, means any other organism whose genes or other genetic material is derived, through any number of generations, from that organism by any process of reproduction;

"import" means import into the United Kingdom;

"premises" includes any land;

"prohibition notice" means a notice under section 110 above.

(2) This Part, except in so far as it relates to importations of genetically modified organisms, applies to the territorial sea adjacent to Great Britain, and to any area for the time being designated under section 1(7) of the Continental Shelf Act 1964, as it applies in Great Britain.

PART VII

NATURE CONSERVATION IN GREAT BRITAIN AND COUNTRYSIDE MATTERS IN WALES

New Councils for England, Scotland and Wales

128 Creation and constitution of new Councils

(1) There shall be three councils, to be called the Nature Conservancy Council for England, the Nature Conservancy Council for Scotland, and the Countryside Council for Wales (in this Part referred to as "the Councils").

(2) The Councils shall have the following membership, that is to say—

(a) the Nature Conservancy Council for England shall have not less than 10 nor more than 14 members;

(b) the Nature Conservancy Council for Scotland shall have not less than 8 nor more than 12 members; and

(c) the Countryside Council for Wales shall have not less than 8 nor more than 12 members;

and those members shall be appointed by the Secretary of State.

(3) The Secretary of State may by order amend paragraph (a), (b) or (c) of subsection (2) above so as to substitute for the number for the time being specified as the maximum membership of a Council such other number as he thinks appropriate.

(4) The Councils shall establish a committee to be called the Joint Nature Conservation Committee (in this Part referred to as "the joint committee").

(5) Schedules 6 and 7 to this Act shall have effect with respect to the constitution and proceedings of the Councils and of the joint committee and related matters.

129 Grants by Secretary of State to new Councils

(1) The Secretary of State may with the approval of the Treasury make to the Councils grants of such amounts as the Secretary of State thinks fit.

(2) A grant under this section may be made subject to such conditions (including in particular conditions as to the use of the money for purposes of the joint committee) as the Secretary of State may with the approval of the Treasury think fit.

Countryside matters

130 Countryside functions of Welsh Council

(1) The Countryside Council for Wales shall, in place of the Commission established under section 1 of the National Parks and Access to the Countryside Act 1949 (so far as concerns Wales), have such of the functions under the Acts amended by Schedule 8 to this Act (which relates to countryside matters) as are assigned to them in accordance with the amendments effected by that Schedule.

(2) The Countryside Council for Wales shall discharge those functions—

(a) for the conservation and enhancement of natural beauty in Wales and of the natural beauty and amenity of the countryside in Wales, both in the areas designated under the National Parks and Access to the Countryside Act 1949 as National Parks or as areas of outstanding natural beauty and elsewhere;

(b) for encouraging the provision or improvement, for persons resorting to the countryside in Wales, of facilities for the enjoyment thereof and for the enjoyment of the opportunities for open-air recreation and the study of nature afforded thereby;

and shall have regard to the social and economic interests of rural areas in Wales.

(3) The reference in subsection (2) above to the conservation of the natural beauty of the countryside includes the conservation of its flora, fauna and geological and physiographical features.

(4) The Countryside Council for Wales and the Countryside Commission shall discharge their respective functions under those Acts (as amended by Schedule 8) on and after a day to be appointed by an order made by the Secretary of State.

Nature conservation in Great Britain

131 Nature conservation functions: preliminary

(1) For the purposes of nature conservation, and fostering the understanding thereof, the Councils shall, in place of the Nature Conservancy Council established under the Nature Conservancy Council Act 1973, have the functions conferred on them by sections 132 to 134 below (which are in this Part referred to as "nature conservation functions").

(2) It shall be the duty of the Councils in discharging their nature conservation functions to take appropriate account of actual or possible ecological changes.

(3) The Councils shall discharge their nature conservation functions on and after a day to be appointed by an order made by the Secretary of State.

(4) The Secretary of State may give the Councils, or any of them, directions of a general or specific character with regard to the discharge of any of their nature conservation functions other than those conferred on them by section 132(1)(a) below.

(5) Any reference in this section to the Councils includes a reference to the joint committee and, accordingly, directions under subsection (4) above may be given to the joint committee as respects any of the functions dischargeable by them (other than under section 133(2)(a)).

(6) In this Part "nature conservation" means the conservation of flora, fauna or geological or physiographical features.

132 General functions of the Councils

(1) The Councils shall each have the following functions, namely—

(a) such of the functions previously discharged by the Nature Conservancy Council under the Acts amended by Schedule 9 to this Act as are assigned to them in accordance with the amendments effected by that Schedule;

(b) the establishment, maintenance and management of nature reserves (within the meaning of section 15 of the National Parks and Access to the Countryside Act 1949) in their area;

(c) the provision of advice for the Secretary of State or any other Minister on the development and implementation of policies for or affecting nature conservation in their area;

(d) the provision of advice and the dissemination of knowledge to any persons about nature conservation in their area or about matters arising from the discharge of their functions under this section or section 134 below;

(e) the commissioning or support (whether by financial means or otherwise) of research which in their opinion is relevant to any of their functions under this section or section 134 below;

and the Councils shall, in discharging their functions under this section, have regard to any advice given to them by the joint committee under section 133(3) below.

(2) The Councils shall each have power—

(a) to accept any gift or contribution made to them for the purposes of any of the functions conferred on them by subsection (1) above or section 134 below and, subject to the terms of the gift or contribution, to apply it to those purposes;

(b) to initiate and carry out such research directly related to those functions as it is appropriate that they should carry out instead of commissioning or supporting other persons under paragraph (e) of that subsection;

and they may do all such other things as are incidental or conducive to those functions including (without prejudice to the generality of this provision) making charges and holding land or any interest in or right over land.

(3) Nothing in this section shall be taken as preventing any of the Councils—

(a) if consulted by another of the Councils about a matter relating to the functions of that other Council, from giving that other Council any advice or information which they are able to give; or

(b) from giving advice or information to the joint committee about any matter relating to any of the functions conferred by section 133(2) and (3) below.

133 Special functions of Councils

(1) The Councils shall jointly have the following functions which may, however, be discharged only through the joint committee; and in this section the functions so dischargeable are referred to as "special functions".

(2) The special functions of the Councils are—

(a) such of the functions previously discharged by the Nature Conservancy Council under the Wildlife and Countryside Act 1981 as are assigned to the Councils jointly as special functions in accordance with the amendments to that Act effected by Schedule 9 to this Act;

(b) the provision of advice for the Secretary of State or any other Minister on the development and implementation of policies for or affecting nature conservation for Great Britain as a whole or nature conservation outside Great Britain;

(c) the provision of advice and the dissemination of knowledge to any persons about nature conservation for Great Britain as a whole or nature conservation outside Great Britain;

(d) the establishment of common standards throughout Great Britain for the monitoring of nature conservation and for research into nature conservation and the analysis of the resulting information;

(e) the commissioning or support (whether by financial means or otherwise) of research which in the opinion of the joint committee is relevant to any matter mentioned in paragraphs (a) to (d) above;

and section 132(2) above shall apply to the special functions as it applies to the functions conferred by subsection (1) of that section.

(3) The joint committee may give advice or information to any of the Councils on any matter arising in connection with the functions of that Council under section 132 above which, in the opinion of the committee, concerns nature conservation for Great Britain as a whole or nature conservation outside Great Britain.

(4) For the purposes of this section, references to nature conservation for Great Britain as a whole are references to—

(a) any nature conservation matter of national or international importance or which otherwise affects the interests of Great Britain as a whole; or

(b) any nature conservation matter which arises throughout Great Britain and raises issues common to England, Scotland and Wales,

and it is immaterial for the purposes of paragraph (a) above that a matter arises only in relation to England, to Scotland or to Wales.

(5) The Secretary of State may, as respects any matter arising in connection with—

(a) any special function of the Councils, or

(b) the function of the joint committee under subsection (3) above,

give directions to any of the Councils requiring that Council (instead of the joint committee) to discharge that function in relation to that matter.

134 Grants and loans by the Councils

(1) The Councils may each, with the consent of or in accordance with a general authorisation given by the Secretary of State, give financial assistance by way of grant or loan (or partly in one way and partly in the other) to any person in respect of expenditure incurred or to be incurred by him in doing anything which in their opinion is conducive to nature conservation or fostering the understanding of nature conservation.

(2) No consent or general authorisation shall be given by the Secretary of State under subsection (1) above without the approval of the Treasury.

(3) On making a grant or loan a Council may impose such conditions as they think fit, including (in the case of a grant) conditions for repayment in specified circumstances.

(4) The Councils shall exercise their powers under subsection (3) above so as to ensure that any person receiving a grant or loan under this section in respect of premises to which the public are to be admitted (on payment or otherwise) shall, in the means of access both to and within the premises, and in the parking facilities and sanitary conveniences to be available (if any), make provision, so far as it is in the circumstances both practicable and reasonable, for the needs of members of the public visiting the premises who are disabled.

Transfer of property, rights and liabilities to new Councils

135 Schemes for the transfer of property etc. of the Nature Conservancy Council

(1) The Nature Conservancy Council shall make one or more schemes ("transfer schemes") for the division of all their property, rights and liabilities (other than rights and liabilities under the contracts of employment of their staff and in respect of the provision of pensions, allowances or gratuities) between the Councils.

(2) On the date appointed by a transfer scheme, the property, rights and liabilities of the Nature Conservancy Council which are the subject of the scheme shall, by virtue of this subsection, become property, rights and liabilities of the Councils to which they are allocated by the scheme.

(3) Part I of Schedule 10 to this Act shall have effect in relation to transfer schemes under this section.

(4) The rights and liabilities of the Nature Conservancy Council in respect of the provision of pensions, allowances and gratuities for or in respect of their members and employees or their former members or employees shall, on the date appointed under section 131(3) above, by virtue of this subsection, become rights and liabilities of the Secretary of State.

136 Transfer to Welsh Council of certain property etc. of Countryside Commission

(1) The Countryside Commission shall make one or more schemes ("transfer schemes") for allocating to the Countryside Council for Wales so much of their property, rights and liabilities (other than rights and liabilities under the contracts of employment of their staff) as the Commission consider appropriate having regard to the countryside functions conferred on the Council by section 130 above.

(2) On the date appointed by a transfer scheme, the property, rights and liabilities of the Countryside Commission which are the subject of the scheme shall, by virtue of this subsection, become property, rights and liabilities of the Countryside Council for Wales.

(3) Part II of Schedule 10 to this Act shall have effect in relation to transfer schemes under this section.

Employment by new Councils of staff of existing bodies

137 Offers of employment to employees of Nature Conservancy Council and certain employees of Countryside Commission

(1) Any person who immediately before the date appointed under section 131(3) above is employed by the Nature Conservancy Council shall be entitled to receive an offer of employment from one of the Councils (to be determined in accordance with proposals made by the Nature Conservancy Council).

(2) Subsection (1) above does not apply to a person whose contract of employment with the Nature Conservancy Council terminates on the day immediately preceding the date appointed under section 131(3) above.

(3) The Countryside Council for Wales shall also make an offer of employment to any person who—

(a) is, immediately before the date appointed under section 130(4) above, employed by the Countryside Commission; and

(b) is a person the Commission has proposed should receive such an offer.

(4) Part III of Schedule 10 to this Act shall have effect with respect to offers and proposals under this section.

Dissolution of Nature Conservancy Council

138 Winding up and dissolution of Nature Conservancy Council

(1) On the date appointed under section 131(3) above the chairman and other members of the Nature Conservancy Council shall cease to hold office and after that date—

(a) the Council shall consist only of a chairman appointed by the Secretary of State and such one or more other persons as may be so appointed; and

(b) the Council shall have only the following functions, namely—

(i) anything which falls to be done by the Council under any transfer scheme under section 135 above;

(ii) the preparation of such accounts and reports as the Secretary of State may direct;

and such other functions as are necessary for winding up their affairs.

(2) The Secretary of State may, by order, after consultation with the Nature Conservancy Council and the Councils, dissolve the Nature Conservancy Council on a day specified in the order as soon as he is satisfied that nothing remains to be done by that Council.

(3) The Secretary of State may pay to persons who cease to hold office by virtue of subsection (1) above such sums by way of compensation for loss of office, or loss or diminution of pension rights, as the Secretary of State may, with the approval of the Treasury, determine.

Transitional provisions and savings

139 Transitional provisions and savings

Schedule 11 to this Act (which contains transitional provisions and savings relating to this Part) shall have effect.

PART VIII

MISCELLANEOUS

Other controls on substances, articles or waste

140 Power to prohibit or restrict the importation, use, supply or storage of injurious substances or articles

(1) The Secretary of State may by regulations prohibit or restrict—

(a) the importation into and the landing and unloading in the United Kingdom,

(b) the use for any purpose,

(c) the supply for any purpose, and

(d) the storage,

of any specified substance or article if he considers it appropriate to do so for the purpose of preventing the substance or article from causing pollution of the environment or harm to human health or to the health of animals or plants.

(2) Any such prohibition or restriction may apply—

(a) in all, or only in specified, areas;

(b) in all, or only in specified, circumstances or if conditions imposed by the regulations are not complied with; and

(c) to all, or only to specified descriptions of, persons.

(3) Regulations under this section may—

(a) confer on the Secretary of State power to direct that any substance or article whose use, supply or storage is prohibited or restricted is to be treated as waste or controlled waste of any description and in relation to any such substance or article—

(i) to apply, with or without modification, specified provisions of Part II; or

(ii) to direct that it be disposed of or treated in accordance with the direction;

(b) confer on the Secretary of State power, where a substance or article has been imported, landed or unloaded in contravention of a prohibition or restriction imposed under subsection (1)(a) above, to require that the substance or article be disposed of or treated in or removed from the United Kingdom;

(c) confer powers corresponding to those conferred by section 17 above on persons authorised for any purpose of the regulations by the Secretary of State or any local or other authority; and

(d) include such other incidental and supplemental, and such transitional provisions, as the Secretary of State considers appropriate.

(4) The Secretary of State may, by regulations under this section, direct that, for the purposes of any power conferred on him under subsection (3)(b) above, any prohibition or restriction on the importation into or the landing and unloading in the United Kingdom imposed—

(a) by or under any Community instrument, or

(b) by or under any enactment,

shall be treated as imposed under subsection (1)(a) above and any power conferred on him under subsection (3)(b) above shall be exercisable accordingly.

(5) The Secretary of State may by order establish a committee to give him advice in relation to the exercise of the power to make regulations under this section and Schedule 12 to this Act shall have effect in relation to it.

(6) Subject to subsection (7) below, it shall be the duty of the Secretary of State before he makes any regulations under this section other than regulations under subsection (4) above—

(a) to consult the committee constituted under subsection (5) above about the proposed regulations;

(b) having consulted the committee, to publish in the London Gazette and, if the regulations apply in Scotland or Northern Ireland, the Edinburgh Gazette or, as the case may be, Belfast Gazette and in any other publication which he considers appropriate, a notice indicating the effect of the proposed regulations and specifying—

(i) the date on which it is proposed that the regulations will come into force;

(ii) a place where a draft of the proposed regulations may be inspected free of charge by members of the public during office hours; and

(iii) a period of not less than fourteen days, beginning with the date on which the notice is first published, during which representations in writing may be made to the Secretary of State about the proposed regulations; and

(c) to consider any representations which are made to him in accordance with the notice.

(7) The Secretary of State may make regulations under this section in relation to any substance or article without observing the requirements of subsection (6) above where it appears to him that there is an imminent risk, if those requirements are observed, that serious pollution of the environment will be caused.

(8) The Secretary of State may, after performing the duty imposed on him by subsection (6) above with respect to any proposed regulations, make the regulations either—

(a) in the form of the draft mentioned in subsection (6)(b) above, or

(b) in that form with such modifications as he considers appropriate;

but the Secretary of State shall not make any regulations incorporating modifications unless he is of opinion that it is appropriate for the requirements of subsection (6) above to be disregarded.

(9) Regulations under this section may provide that a person who contravenes or fails to comply with a specified provision of the regulations or causes or permits another person to contravene or fail to comply with a specified provision of the regulations commits an offence and may prescribe the maximum penalty for the offence.

(10) No offence under the regulations shall be made punishable with imprisonment for more than two years or punishable on summary conviction with a fine exceeding level 5 on the standard scale (if not calculated on a daily basis) or, in the case of a continuing offence, exceeding one-tenth of the level on the standard scale specified as the maximum penalty for the original offence.

(11) In this section—

"the environment" means the air, water and land, or any of those media, and the medium of air includes the air within buildings and the air within other natural or man-made structures above or below ground;

"specified" means specified in the regulations; and

"substance" means any natural or artificial substance, whether in solid or liquid form or in the form of a gas or vapour and it includes mixtures of substances.

141 Power to prohibit or restrict the importation or exportation of waste

(1) The Secretary of State may, for the purpose of preventing any risk of pollution of the environment or of harm to human health arising from waste being imported or exported or of conserving the facilities or resources for dealing with waste, make regulations prohibiting or restricting, or providing for the prohibition or restriction of—

(a) the importation into and the landing and unloading in the United Kingdom, or

(b) the exportation, or the loading for exportation, from the United Kingdom,

of waste of any description.

(2) Regulations under this section may make different provision for different descriptions of waste or waste of any description in different circumstances.

(3) Regulations under this section may, as respects any description of waste, confer or impose on waste regulation authorities or any of them such functions in relation to the importation of waste as appear to be appropriate to the Secretary of State, subject to such limitations and conditions as are specified in the regulations.

(4) Regulations under this section may confer or impose on waste regulation authorities or any of them functions of enforcing any of the regulations on behalf of the Secretary of State whether or not the functions fall within subsection (3) above.

(5) Regulations under this section may—

(a) as respects functions conferred or imposed on waste regulation authorities—

(i) make them exercisable in relation to individual consignments or consignments in a series by the same person but not in relation to consignments or descriptions of consignments generally; and

(ii) confer on the Secretary of State power, by direction to the authorities or any of them, to make the functions or any of them exercisable instead by him whether indefinitely or for any period;

(b) impose or provide for the imposition of prohibitions either absolutely or only if conditions or procedures prescribed in or under the regulations are not complied with;

(c) impose duties to be complied with before, on or after any importation or exportation of waste by persons who are, or are to be, consignors, consignees, carriers or holders of the waste or any waste derived from it;

(d) confer powers corresponding to those conferred by section 69(3) above;

(e) provide for appeals to the Secretary of State from determinations made by authorities under the regulations;

(f) provide for the keeping by the Secretary of State, waste regulation authorities and waste collection authorities of public registers of information relating to the importation and exportation of waste and for the transmission of such information between any of those persons;

(g) create offences, subject to the limitation that no offence shall be punishable with imprisonment for more than two years or punishable on summary conviction with imprisonment for more than six months or a fine exceeding level 5 on the standard scale (if not calculated on a daily basis) or, in the case of a continuing offence, exceeding one-tenth of the level on the standard scale specified as the maximum penalty for the original offence.

(6) In this section—

"the environment" means land, water and air or any of them;

"harm" includes offence to any of man's senses;

"waste", "waste collection authority", and "waste regulation authority" have the same meaning as in Part II; and

"the United Kingdom" includes its territorial sea.

(7) In the application of this section to Northern Ireland and the territorial sea of the United Kingdom adjacent to Northern Ireland "waste regulation authority" means a district council established under the Local Government Act (Northern Ireland) 1972.

142 Powers to obtain information about potentially hazardous substances

(1) The Secretary of State may, for the purpose of assessing their potential for causing pollution of the environment or harm to human health, by regulations make provision for and in connection with the obtaining of relevant information relating to substances which may be specified by him by order for the purposes of this section.

(2) The Secretary of State shall not make an order under subsection (1) above specifying any substance—

(a) which was first supplied in any member State on or after 18th September 1981; or

(b) in so far as it is a regulated substance for the purposes of any relevant enactment.

(3) The Secretary of State shall not make an order under subsection (1) above specifying any substance without consulting the committee established under section 140(5) except where it appears to him that information about the substance needs to be obtained urgently under this section.

(4) Regulations under this section may—

(a) prescribe the descriptions of relevant information which are to be furnished under this section in relation to specified substances;

(b) impose requirements on manufacturers, importers or suppliers generally to furnish information prescribed under paragraph (a) above;

(c) provide for the imposition of requirements on manufacturers, importers or suppliers generally to furnish relevant information relating to products or articles containing specified substances in relation to which information has been furnished in pursuance of paragraph (b) above;

(d) provide for the imposition of requirements on particular manufacturers, importers or suppliers to furnish further information relating to specified substances in relation to which information has been furnished in pursuance of paragraph (b) above;

(e) provide for the imposition of requirements on particular manufacturers or importers to carry out tests of specified substances and to furnish information of the results of the tests;

(f) authorise persons to comply with requirements to furnish information imposed on them by or under the regulations by means of representative persons or bodies;

(g) impose restrictions on the disclosure of information obtained under this section and provide for determining what information is, and what information is not, to be treated as furnished in confidence;

(h) create offences, subject to the limitation that no offence shall be punishable with imprisonment or punishable on summary conviction with a fine exceeding level 5 on the standard scale;

(i) make any public authority designated by the regulations responsible for the enforcement of the regulations to such extent as may be specified in the regulations;

(j) include such other incidental and supplemental, and such transitional, provisions as the Secretary of State considers appropriate.

(5) The Secretary of State shall have regard, in imposing or providing for the imposition of any requirement under subsection (4)(b), (c), (d) or (e) above, to the cost likely to be involved in complying with the requirement.

(6) In this section—

"the environment" means the air, water and land or any of them;

"relevant information", in relation to substances, products or articles, means information relating to their properties, production, distribution, importation or use or intended use and, in relation to products or articles, to their disposal as waste;

"substance" means any natural or artificial substance, whether in solid or liquid form or in the form of a gas or vapour and it includes mixtures of substances.

(7) The enactments which are relevant for the purposes of subsection (2)(b) above are the following—

the Explosive Substances Act 1875;

the Radioactive Substances Act 1960;

Parts II, III and VIII of the Medicines Act 1968;

Part IV of the Agriculture Act 1970;

the Misuse of Drugs Act 1971;

Part III of the Food and Environment Protection Act 1985; and the Food Safety Act 1990;

and a substance is a regulated substance for the purposes of any such enactment in so far as any prohibition, restriction or requirement is imposed in relation to it by or under the enactment for the purposes of that enactment.

143 Public registers of land which may be contaminated

(1) For the purposes of the registers to be maintained under this section, the Secretary of State may, by regulations—

(a) specify contaminative uses of land;

(b) prescribe the form of the registers and the particulars to be included in them; and

(c) make such other provision as appears to him to be appropriate in connection with the maintenance of the registers.

(2) It shall be the duty of a local authority, as respects land in its area subject to contamination, to maintain, in accordance with the regulations, a register in the prescribed form and containing the prescribed particulars.

(3) The duty imposed by subsection (2) above on a local authority is a duty to compile and maintain the register from the information available to the authority from time to time.

(4) A local authority shall secure that the register is open to inspection at its principal office by members of the public free of charge at all reasonable hours and shall afford to members of the public reasonable facilities for obtaining, on payment of reasonable charges, copies of entries in the register.

(5) Regulations under subsection (1)(c) above may prescribe the measures to be taken by local authorities for informing persons whose land is the subject of entries in a register about the entries or for enabling them to inform themselves about them.

(6) In this section—

"contaminative use" means any use of land which may cause it to be contaminated with noxious substances;

"land subject to contamination" means land which is being or has been put to a contaminative use;

"local authority" means—

(a) in Greater London, a London borough council or the Common Council of the City of London;

(b) in England and Wales outside Greater London, a district council;

(c) in Scotland, a planning authority; and

(d) the Council of the Isles of Scilly; and

"substance" means any natural or artificial substance, whether in solid or liquid form or in the form of a gas or vapour.

144 Amendments of hazardous substances legislation

Schedule 13 to this Act (which contains miscellaneous amendments to the legislation relating to hazardous substances) shall have effect.

145 Penalties for offences of polluting controlled waters etc

(1) In section 107(6) of the Water Act 1989 (penalties for offences of polluting controlled waters or contravening consent conditions), in paragraph (a), for the words "the statutory maximum" there shall be substituted "£20,000".

(2) In sections 31(7)(a), 31A(2)(c)(i) and 32(7)(a) of the Control of Pollution Act 1974 (corresponding penalties for Scotland), for the words "the statutory maximum" there shall be substituted "£20,000".

Pollution at sea

146 Deposits of substances and articles in the sea, etc

(1) Part II of the Food and Environment Protection Act 1985 (under which licences are required for deposits by British vessels etc at sea anywhere or by foreign vessels etc in United Kingdom waters or, in certain circumstances, within British fishery limits) shall be amended as follows.

(2) In section 5 (licences for depositing at sea)—

(a) in paragraph (a), after the words "United Kingdom waters" there shall be inserted the words "or United Kingdom controlled waters";

(b) paragraphs (c) and (d) shall be omitted;

(c) in paragraph (e)—

(i) in sub-paragraph (i), after the words "United Kingdom waters" there shall be inserted the words "or United Kingdom controlled waters" and at the end there shall be inserted the word "or"; and

(ii) sub-paragraph (iii) shall be omitted.

(3) In section 6 (licences for incineration at sea), in subsection (1)(a)—

(a) in sub-paragraph (i), after the words "United Kingdom waters" there shall be inserted the words "or United Kingdom controlled waters" and at the end there shall be inserted the word "or"; and

(b) sub-paragraph (iii) shall be omitted.

(4) In section 9(5) (Convention State defence to offence of acting without or in contravention of a licence), in paragraph (b), for the word "waters" there shall be substituted the words "controlled waters (and not within United Kingdom waters)".

(5) In section 11 (powers of officers)—

(a) in subsection (2)(b), for the words "British fishery limits" there shall be substituted the words "United Kingdom waters or United Kingdom controlled waters;"; and

(b) in subsection (3)(a), for the words "British fishery limits" there shall be substituted the words "United Kingdom waters or United Kingdom controlled waters;".

(6) In section 21 (penalties for offences)—

(a) in subsection (2), for the words "2(4) and 9(1)" there shall be substituted the words "and 2(4)"; and

(b) after that subsection, there shall be inserted the following subsection—

"(2A) A person guilty of an offence under section 9(1) shall be liable—

(a) on summary conviction, to a fine of an amount not exceeding £50,000; and

(b) on conviction on indictment, to a fine or to imprisonment for a term not exceeding two years or to both."

(7) In section 24(1) (definitions) at the end of the definition of "United Kingdom waters" there shall be inserted the words "and "United Kingdom controlled waters" means any part of the sea within the limits of an area designated under section 1(7) of the Continental Shelf Act 1964".

(8) In Schedule 2 (powers in relation to vessels, aircraft, etc. for the purposes of Part I or Part II or both Parts of the Act), in paragraph 3(3) (removal to United Kingdom), after the words "Part I" there shall be inserted the words "or II".

147 Public registers relating to deposits in the sea and incineration at sea

In Part II of the Food and Environment Protection Act 1985, for section 14 (registers of licences) there shall be substituted the following section—

"14 Duty of licensing authority to keep public registers of information

(1) It shall be the duty of each licensing authority, as respects licences for which it is the licensing authority, to maintain, in accordance with regulations, a register containing prescribed particulars of or relating to—

(a) applications for licences made to that authority;

(b) the licences issued by that authority;

(c) variations of licences effected by that authority;

(d) revocations of licences effected by that authority;

(e) convictions for any offences under section 9 above;

(f) information obtained or furnished in pursuance of section 8(3), (4) or (5) above;

(g) the occasions on which either of the Ministers has carried out any operation under section 10 above; and

(h) such other matters relating to operations for which licences are needed under this Part of this Act as may be prescribed.

(2) No information shall be included in any register which, in the opinion of either of the Ministers, is such that its disclosure on the register—

(a) would be contrary to the interests of national security, or

(b) would prejudice to an unreasonable degree some person's commercial interests.

(3) Information excluded from a register by virtue of subsection (2)(b) above shall be treated as ceasing to prejudice a person's commercial interests at the expiry of the period of four years beginning with the date on which the Minister made his decision under that subsection; but, on the application of any person to whom it relates, the Minister shall decide whether the information should be included or continue to be excluded from the register.

(4) Where information of any description is excluded from a register by virtue of subsection (2)(b) above, a statement shall be entered in the register indicating the existence of information of that description.

(5) It shall be the duty of each licensing authority—

(a) to secure that the register maintained by the authority under this section is available, at all reasonable times, for inspection by the public free of charge; and

(b) to afford to members of the public facilities for obtaining copies of entries, on payment of reasonable charges.

(6) Registers under this section may be kept in any form.

(7) In this section "prescribed" means prescribed in regulations.

(8) Either of the Ministers may exercise any power to make regulations under this section and any such power shall be exercisable by statutory instrument, subject to annulment in pursuance of a resolution of either House of Parliament."

148 Oil pollution from ships

(1) Schedule 14 to this Act (which amends the provisions of the Prevention of Oil Pollution Act 1971) shall have effect.

(2) Without prejudice to the generality of subsections (1), (3) and (4) of section 20 of the Merchant Shipping Act 1979, an Order under subsection (1) of that section may make in connection with offences created by or under any such Order provision corresponding to that made in connection with offences under section 2(2A) of the Prevention of Oil Pollution Act 1971 by any provision of—

(a) section 19(4A) of that Act, and

(b) sections 19A and 20 of that Act,

and may do so whether by applying (or making provision for the application of) any of those provisions, subject to such modifications as may be specified by or under the Order, or otherwise.

(3) This section (and Schedule 14) shall not apply in relation to any offence committed before this section comes into force.

Control of Dogs

149 Seizure of stray dogs

(1) Every local authority shall appoint an officer (under whatever title the authority may determine) for the purpose of discharging the functions imposed or conferred by this section for dealing with stray dogs found in the area of the authority.

(2) The officer may delegate the discharge of his functions to another person but he shall remain responsible for securing that the functions are properly discharged.

(3) Where the officer has reason to believe that any dog found in a public place or on any other land or premises is a stray dog, he shall (if practicable) seize the dog and detain it, but, where he finds it on land or premises which is not a public place, only with the consent of the owner or occupier of the land or premises.

(4) Where any dog seized under this section wears a collar having inscribed thereon or attached thereto the address of any person, or the owner of the dog is known, the officer shall serve on the person whose address is given on the collar, or on the owner, a notice in writing stating that the dog has been seized and where it is being kept and stating that the dog will be liable to be disposed of if it is not claimed within seven clear days after the service of the notice and the amounts for which he would be liable under subsection (5) below are not paid.

(5) A person claiming to be the owner of a dog seized under this section shall not be entitled to have the dog returned to him unless he pays all the expenses incurred by reason of its detention and such further amount as is for the time being prescribed.

(6) Where any dog seized under this section has been detained for seven clear days after the seizure or, where a notice has been served under subsection (4) above, the service of the notice and the owner has not claimed the dog and paid the amounts due under subsection (5) above the officer may dispose of the dog—

(a) by selling it or giving it to a person who will, in his opinion, care properly for the dog;

(b) by selling it or giving it to an establishment for the reception of stray dogs; or

(c) by destroying it in a manner to cause as little pain as possible;

but no dog seized under this section shall be sold or given for the purposes of vivisection.

(7) Where a dog is disposed of under subsection (6)(a) or (b) above to a person acting in good faith, the ownership of the dog shall be vested in the recipient.

(8) The officer shall keep a register containing the prescribed particulars of or relating to dogs seized under this section and the register shall be available, at all reasonable times, for inspection by the public free of charge.

(9) The officer shall cause any dog detained under this section to be properly fed and maintained.

(10) Notwithstanding anything in this section, the officer may cause a dog detained under this section to be destroyed before the expiration of the period mentioned in subsection (6) above where he is of the opinion that this should be done to avoid suffering.

(11) In this section—

"local authority", in relation to England and Wales, means a district council, a London borough council, the Common Council of the City of London or the Council of the Isles of Scilly and, in relation to Scotland, means an islands or district council;

"officer" means an officer appointed under subsection (1) above;

"prescribed" means prescribed in regulations made by the Secretary of State; and

"public place" means—

(i) as respects England and Wales, any highway and any other place to which the public are entitled or permitted to have access;

(ii) as respects Scotland, any road (within the meaning of the Roads (Scotland) Act 1984) and any other place to which the public are entitled or permitted to have access;

and, for the purposes of section 160 below in its application to this section, the proper address of the owner of a dog which wears a collar includes the address given on the collar.

150 Delivery of stray dogs to police or local authority officer

(1) Any person (in this section referred to as "the finder") who takes possession of a stray dog shall forthwith either—

(a) return the dog to its owner; or

(b) take the dog—

(i) to the officer of the local authority for the area in which the dog was found; or

(ii) to the police station which is nearest to the place where the dog was found;

and shall inform the officer of the local authority or the police officer in charge of the police station, as the case may be, where the dog was found.

(2) Where a dog has been taken under subsection (1) above to the officer of a local authority, then—

(a) if the finder desires to keep the dog, he shall inform the officer of this fact and shall furnish his name and address and the officer shall, having complied with the procedure (if any) prescribed under subsection (6) below, allow the finder to remove the dog;

(b) if the finder does not desire to keep the dog, the officer shall, unless he has reason to believe it is not a stray, treat it as if it had been seized by him under section 149 above.

(3) Where the finder of a dog keeps the dog by virtue of this section he must keep it for not less than one month.

(4) In Scotland a person who keeps a dog by virtue of this section for a period of two months without its being claimed by the person who has right to it shall at the end of that period become the owner of the dog.

(5) If the finder of a dog fails to comply with the requirements of subsection (1) or (3) above he shall be liable on summary conviction to a fine not exceeding level 2 on the standard scale.

(6) The Secretary of State may, by regulations, prescribe the procedure to be followed under subsection (2)(a) above.

(7) In this section "local authority" and "officer" have the same meaning as in section 149 above.

151 Enforcement of orders about collars and tags for dogs

(1) Section 13 of the Animal Health Act 1981 (orders for control, etc. of dogs) shall be amended by the insertion, after subsection (2), of the following subsections—

"(3) An order under subsection (2)(a) above may include provision for the execution and enforcement of the order by the officers of local authorities (and not by the police force for any area).

(4) In subsection (3) above "local authority" and "officer" have the same meaning as in section 149 of the Environmental Protection Act 1990."

(2) In section 50(1) of that Act (meaning of "local authority") at the end there shall be inserted the words "and to section 13(3) above".

(3) In section 60(1) of that Act (enforcement), at the end, there shall be inserted the words "but subject, in the case of orders under section 13, to any provision made under subsection (3) of that section."

Straw and stubble burning

152 Burning of straw and stubble etc

(1) The appropriate Minister may by regulations prohibit or restrict the burning of crop residues on agricultural land by persons engaged in agriculture and he may (by the same or other regulations) provide exemptions from any prohibition or restriction so imposed.

(2) Regulations providing an exemption from any prohibition or restriction may make the exemption applicable—

(a) in all, or only in specified, areas;

(b) to all, or only to specified, crop residues; or

(c) in all, or only in specified, circumstances.

(3) Any power to make regulations under this section includes power—

(a) to make different provision for different areas or circumstances;

(b) where burning of a crop residue is restricted, to impose requirements to be complied with before or after the burning;

(c) to create offences subject to the limitation that no offence shall be made punishable otherwise than on summary conviction and the fine prescribed for the offence shall not exceed level 5 on the standard scale; and

(d) to make such incidental, supplemental and transitional provision as the appropriate Minister considers appropriate.

(4) Where it appears to the appropriate Minister appropriate to do so in consequence of any regulations made under the foregoing provisions of this section, the appropriate Minister may, by order, repeal any byelaws of local authorities dealing with the burning of crop residues on agricultural land.

(5) In this section—

"agriculture" and "agricultural land" have, as respects England or as respects Wales, the same meaning as in the Agriculture Act 1947 and, as respects Scotland, the same meaning as in the Agriculture (Scotland) Act 1948;

"crop residue" means straw or stubble or any other crop residue;

"the appropriate Minister" means the Minister of Agriculture, Fisheries and Food or the Secretary of State or both of them.

Environmental expenditure

153 Financial assistance for environmental purposes

(1) The Secretary of State may, with the consent of the Treasury, give financial assistance to, or for the purposes of, any of the following—

(a) the United Nations Environment Programme;

(b) the European Environmental Bureau;

(c) the chemicals programme of the Organisation for Economic Co-operation and Development;

(d) the joint inter-Governmental panel on Climate Change of the United Nations Environment Programme and the World Meteorological Organisation;

(e) the International Union for the Conservation of Nature and Natural Resources;
(f) the Convention on International Trade in Endangered Species of Wild Fauna and Flora;
(g) the Convention on Wetlands of International Importance Especially as Waterfowl Habitat;
(h) the Convention on Long-range Transboundary Air Pollution and any protocol to that Convention;
(i) the Convention and Protocol for the Protection of the Ozone Layer;
(j) the Convention on the Conservation of Migratory Species of Wild Animals;
(k) the Groundwork Foundation and Trusts;
(l) the environmental protection technology scheme for research and development in the United Kingdom in relation to such technology;
(m) the programme known as the special grants programme so far as it relates to the protection, improvement or better understanding of the environment of, or of any part of, Great Britain.

(2) Financial assistance may be given in respect of particular activities or generally in respect of all or some part of the activities carried on or supported by the recipient.

(3) Financial assistance shall be given in such form and on such terms as the Secretary of State may think fit and, in particular, assistance may be given by making grants (whether or not repayable), loans or guarantees to, or by incurring expenditure, or providing services, staff or equipment for the benefit of, the recipient.

(4) The Secretary of State may, by order, vary subsection (1) above by adding to or deleting from it any description of organisation, scheme, programme or international agreement whose purposes relate to the protection, improvement or better understanding of the environment.

(5) Subject to any Order made after the passing of this Act by virtue of subsection (1)(a) of section 3 of the Northern Ireland Constitution Act 1973, the environmental protection technology scheme for research and development in the United Kingdom in relation to such technology shall not be a transferred matter for the purposes of that Act but shall for the purposes of subsection (2) of that section be treated as specified in Schedule 3 to that Act.

154 The Groundwork Foundation: superannuation

Employment with the Groundwork Foundation shall be and shall be deemed always to have been included among the kinds of employment to which a superannuation scheme under section 1 of the Superannuation Act 1972 can apply, and accordingly in Schedule 1 to that Act (in which those kinds of employment are listed) the words "Groundwork Foundation" shall be inserted after the words "Gaming Board for Great Britain".

155 Remuneration of chairman of Inland Waterways Amenity Advisory Council

In section 110 of the Transport Act 1968 (Inland Waterways Amenity Advisory Council) at the end there shall be inserted—

"(7) The Secretary of State may, with the consent of the Treasury, pay the chairman of the Council out of money provided by Parliament such remuneration as the Secretary of State may determine; and where the chairman is in receipt of such remuneration he shall not be paid any allowance under subsection (6) of this section in respect of loss of remunerative time."

PART IX

GENERAL

156 Power to give effect to Community and other international obligations etc

(1) The Secretary of State may by regulations provide that the provisions to which this section applies shall have effect with such modifications as may be prescribed for the purpose of enabling Her Majesty's Government in the United Kingdom—

(a) to give effect to any Community obligation or exercise any related right; or

(b) to give effect to any obligation or exercise any related right under any international agreement to which the United Kingdom is for the time being a party.

(2) This section applies to the following provisions of this Act—

(a) Part I;

(b) Part II;

(c) Part VI; and

(d) in Part VIII, sections 140, 141 or 142;

and the provisions of the Radioactive Substances Act 1960.

(3) In this section—

"modifications" includes additions, alterations and omissions;

"prescribed" means prescribed in regulations under this section; and

"related right", in relation to an obligation, includes any derogation or other right to make more onerous provisions available in respect of that obligation.

(4) This section, in its application to Northern Ireland, has effect subject to the following modifications, that is to say—

(a) in its application in relation to Part VI and sections 140, 141, and 142, the reference to Her Majesty's Government in the United Kingdom includes a reference to Her Majesty's Government in Northern Ireland; and

(b) in its application in relation to the Radioactive Substances Act 1960, the reference to the Secretary of State shall be construed as a reference to the Department of the Environment for Northern Ireland and the reference to Her Majesty's Government in the United Kingdom shall be construed as a reference to Her Majesty's Government in Northern Ireland;

and regulations under it made by that Department shall be a statutory rule for the purposes of the Statutory Rules (Northern Ireland) Order 1979 and shall be subject to negative resolution within the meaning of section 41(6) of the Interpretation Act (Northern Ireland) 1954.

157 Offences by bodies corporate

(1) Where an offence under any provision of this Act committed by a body corporate is proved to have been committed with the consent or connivance of, or to have been attributable to any neglect on the part of, any director, manager, secretary or other

similar officer of the body corporate or a person who was purporting to act in any such capacity, he as well as the body corporate shall be guilty of that offence and shall be liable to be proceeded against and punished accordingly.

(2) Where the affairs of a body corporate are managed by its members, subsection (1) above shall apply in relation to the acts or defaults of a member in connection with his functions of management as if he were a director of the body corporate.

158 Offences under Parts I, II, IV, VI, etc. due to fault of others

Where the commission by any person of an offence under Part I, II, IV, or VI, or section 140, 141 or 142 above is due to the act or default of some other person, that other person may be charged with and convicted of the offence by virtue of this section whether or not proceedings for the offence are taken against the first-mentioned person.

159 Application to Crown

(1) Subject to the provisions of this section, the provisions of this Act and of regulations and orders made under it shall bind the Crown.

(2) No contravention by the Crown of any provision of this Act or of any regulations or order made under it shall make the Crown criminally liable; but the High Court or, in Scotland, the Court of Session may, on the application of any public or local authority charged with enforcing that provision, declare unlawful any act or omission of the Crown which constitutes such a contravention.

(3) Notwithstanding anything in subsection (2) above, the provisions of this Act and of regulations and orders made under it shall apply to persons in the public service of the Crown as they apply to other persons.

(4) If the Secretary of State certifies that it appears to him, as respects any Crown premises and any powers of entry exercisable in relation to them specified in the certificate that it is requisite or expedient that, in the interests of national security, the powers should not be exercisable in relation to the premises, those powers shall not be exercisable in relation to those premises; and in this subsection "Crown premises" means premises held or used by or on behalf of the Crown.

(5) Nothing in this section shall be taken as in any way affecting Her Majesty in her private capacity; and this subsection shall be construed as if section 38(3) of the Crown Proceedings Act 1947 (interpretation of references in that Act to Her Majesty in her private capacity) were contained in this Act.

(6) References in this section to regulations or orders are references to regulations or orders made by statutory instrument.

(7) For the purposes of this section in its application to Part II and Part IV the authority charged with enforcing the provisions of those Parts in its area is—

- (a) in the case of Part II, any waste regulation authority, and
- (b) in the case of Part IV, any principal litter authority.

160 Service of notices

(1) Any notice required or authorised by or under this Act to be served on or given to an inspector may be served or given by delivering it to him or by leaving it at, or sending it by post to, his office.

(2) Any such notice required or authorised to be served on or given to a person other than an inspector may be served or given by delivering it to him, or by leaving it at his proper address, or by sending it by post to him at that address.

(3) Any such notice may—

(a) in the case of a body corporate, be served on or given to the secretary or clerk of that body;

(b) in the case of a partnership, be served on or given to a partner or a person having the control or management of the partnership business.

(4) For the purposes of this section and of section 7 of the Interpretation Act 1978 (service of documents by post) in its application to this section, the proper address of any person on or to whom any such notice is to be served or given shall be his last known address, except that—

(a) in the case of a body corporate or their secretary or clerk, it shall be the address of the registered or principal office of that body;

(b) in the case of a partnership or person having the control or the management of the partnership business, it shall be the principal office of the partnership;

and for the purposes of this subsection the principal office of a company registered outside the United Kingdom or of a partnership carrying on business outside the United Kingdom shall be their principal office within the United Kingdom.

(5) If the person to be served with or given any such notice has specified an address in the United Kingdom other than his proper address within the meaning of subsection (4) above as the one at which he or someone on his behalf will accept notices of the same description as that notice, that address shall also be treated for the purposes of this section and section 7 of the Interpretation Act 1978 as his proper address.

(6) The preceding provisions of this section shall apply to the sending or giving of a document as they apply to the giving of a notice.

161 Regulations, orders and directions

(1) Any power of the Secretary of State or the Minister of Agriculture, Fisheries and Food under this Act to make regulations or orders shall be exercisable by statutory instrument; but this subsection does not apply to orders under section 72 above or paragraph 4 of Schedule 3.

(2) A statutory instrument containing regulations under this Act shall be subject to annulment in pursuance of a resolution of either House of Parliament.

(3) Except in the cases specified in subsection (4) below, a statutory instrument containing an order under this Act shall be subject to annulment in pursuance of a resolution of either House of Parliament.

(4) Subsection (3) above does not apply to an order under section 130(4), 131(3) or 138(2) above or section 164(3) below.

(5) Any power conferred by this Act to give a direction shall include power to vary or revoke the direction.

(6) Any direction given under this Act shall be in writing.

162 Consequential and minor amendments and repeals

(1) The enactments specified in Schedule 15 to this Act shall have effect subject to the amendments specified in that Schedule.

(2) The enactments specified in Schedule 16 to this Act are hereby repealed subject to section 77 above, Schedule 11 to this Act and any provision made by way of a note in Schedule 16.

(3) The repeal of section 124 of the Civic Government (Scotland) Act 1982 shall not affect a compulsory purchase order made for the purposes of that section under the Local Government (Scotland) Act 1973 before the coming into force of the repeal and such compulsory purchase order may be proceeded with and shall have effect as if the said section 124 had not been repealed.

(4) The Secretary of State may by order repeal or amend any provision of any local Act passed before this Act (including an Act confirming a provisional order) or of any order or other instrument made under an Act so passed if it appears to him that the provision is inconsistent with, or has become unnecessary or requires alteration in consequence of, any provision of this Act or corresponds to any provision repealed by this Act.

(5) Any regulations made under section 100 of the Control of Pollution Act 1974 shall have effect after the repeal of that section by subsection (2) above as if made under section 140 of this Act.

163 Financial provisions

(1) There shall be paid out of money provided by Parliament—

(a) any administrative or other expenses incurred by any Minister of the Crown in consequence of the provisions of this Act; and

(b) any increase attributable to this Act in the sums payable out of money so provided under any other Act.

(2) Any fees or other sums received by any Minister of the Crown by virtue of any provisions of this Act shall be paid into the Consolidated Fund.

164 Short title, commencement and extent

(1) This Act may be cited as the Environmental Protection Act 1990.

(2) The following provisions of the Act shall come into force at the end of the period of two months beginning with the day on which it is passed, namely—

sections 79 to 85;

section 97;

section 99;

section 105 in so far as it relates to paragraphs 7, 13, 14 and 15 of Schedule 5;

section 140;

section 141;

section 142;

section 145;

section 146;

section 148;

section 153;

section 154;

section 155;

section 157;

section 160;

section 161;

section 162(1) in so far as it relates to paragraphs 4, 5, 7, 8, 9, 18, 22, 24 and 31(4)(b) of Schedule 15; but, in the case of paragraph 22, in so far only as that paragraph inserts a paragraph (m) into section 7(4) of the Act of 1984;

section 162(2) in so far as it relates to Part III of Schedule 16 and, in Part IX of that Schedule, the repeal of section 100 of the Control of Pollution Act 1974;

section 162(5);

section 163.

(3) The remainder of this Act (except this section) shall come into force on such day as the Secretary of State may by order appoint and different days may be appointed for different provisions or different purposes.

(4) Only the following provisions of this Act (together with this section) extend to Northern Ireland, namely—

section 3(5) to (8);

section 62(2)(e) in so far as it relates to importation;

Part V;

Part VI in so far as it relates to importation and, without that restriction, section 127(2) in so far as it relates to the continental shelf;

section 140 in so far as it relates to importation;

section 141;

section 142 in so far as it relates to importation;

section 146;

section 147;

section 148;

section 153 except subsection (1)(k) and (m);

section 156 in so far as it relates to Part VI and sections 140, 141 and 142 in so far as they extend to Northern Ireland and in so far as it relates to the Radioactive Substances Act 1960;

section 158 in so far as it relates to Part VI and sections 140, 141 and 142 in so far as they extend to Northern Ireland.

(5) Where any enactment amended or repealed by this Act extends to any part of the United Kingdom, the amendment or repeal extends to that part, subject, however, to any express provision in Schedule 15 or 16.

SCHEDULES

SCHEDULE 1

Section 6.

AUTHORISATIONS FOR PROCESSES: SUPPLEMENTARY PROVISIONS

PART I

GRANT OF AUTHORISATIONS

Applications for authorisations

1 (1) An application to the enforcing authority for an authorisation must contain such information, and be made in such manner, as may be prescribed in regulations made by the Secretary of State.

(2) An application to the enforcing authority for an authorisation must also, unless regulations made by the Secretary of State exempt applications of that class, be advertised in such manner as may be prescribed in regulations so made.

(3) The enforcing authority may, by notice in writing to the applicant, require him to furnish such further information specified in the notice, within the period so specified, as the authority may require for the purpose of determining the application.

(4) If a person fails to furnish any information required under sub-paragraph (3) above within the period specified thereunder the enforcing authority may refuse to proceed with the application.

(5) Regulations under this paragraph may make different provision for different classes of applications.

Determination of applications

2 (1) Subject to sub-paragraph (2) below, the enforcing authority shall give notice of any application for an authorisation, enclosing a copy of the application, to the persons who are prescribed or directed to be consulted under this paragraph and shall do so within the specified period for notification.

(2) The Secretary of State may, by regulations, exempt any class of application from the requirements of this paragraph or exclude any class of information contained in applications for authorisations from those requirements, in all cases or as respects specified classes only of persons to be consulted.

(3) Any representations made by the persons so consulted within the period allowed shall be considered by the enforcing authority in determining the application.

(4) For the purposes of sub-paragraph (1) above—

(a) persons are prescribed to be consulted on any description of application for an authorisation if they are persons specified for the purposes of applications of that description in regulations made by the Secretary of State;

(b) persons are directed to be consulted on any particular application if the Secretary of State specifies them in a direction given to the enforcing authority;

and the "specified period for notification" is the period specified in the regulations or in the direction.

(5) Any representations made by any other persons within the period allowed shall also be considered by the enforcing authority in determining the application.

(6) Subject to sub-paragraph (7) below, the period allowed for making representations is—

(a) in the case of persons prescribed or directed to be consulted, the period of twenty-eight days beginning with the date on which notice of the application was given under sub-paragraph (1) above, and

(b) in the case of other persons, the period of twenty-eight days beginning with the date on which the making of the application was advertised in pursuance of paragraph 1(2) above.

(7) The Secretary of State may, by order, substitute for the period for the time being specified in sub-paragraph (6)(a) or (b) above, such other period as he considers appropriate.

3 (1) The Secretary of State may give directions to the enforcing authority requiring that any particular application or any class of applications for an authorisation shall be transmitted to him for determination pending a further direction under sub-paragraph (5) below.

(2) The enforcing authority shall inform the applicant of the fact that his application is being transmitted to the Secretary of State.

(3) Where an application for an authorisation is referred to him under sub-paragraph (1) above the Secretary of State may—

(a) cause a local inquiry to be held in relation to the application; or

(b) afford the applicant and the authority concerned an opportunity of appearing before and being heard by a person appointed by the Secretary of State;

and he shall exercise one of the powers under this sub-paragraph in any case where, in the manner prescribed by regulations made by the Secretary of State, a request is made to be heard with respect to the application by the applicant or the local enforcing authority concerned.

(4) Subsections (2) to (5) of section 250 of the Local Government Act 1972 (supplementary provisions about local inquiries under that section) or, in relation to Scotland, subsections (2) to (8) of section 210 of the Local Government (Scotland) Act 1973 (which make similar provision) shall, without prejudice to the generality of subsection (1) of either of those sections, apply to inquiries in pursuance of sub-paragraph (3) above as they apply to inquiries in pursuance of either of those sections and, in relation to England and Wales, as if the reference to a local authority in subsection (4) of the said section 250 included a reference to the enforcing authority.

(5) The Secretary of State shall, on determining any application transferred to him under this paragraph, give to the enforcing authority such a direction as he thinks fit as to

whether it is to grant the application and, if so, as to the conditions that are to be attached to the authorisation.

4 The Secretary of State may give the enforcing authority a direction with respect to any particular application or any class of applications for an authorisation requiring the authority not to determine or not to proceed with the application or applications of that class until the expiry of any such period as may be specified in the direction, or until directed by the Secretary of State that they may do so, as the case may be.

5 (1) Except in a case where an application has been referred to the Secretary of State under paragraph 3 above and subject to sub-paragraph (3) below, the enforcing authority shall determine an application for an authorisation within the period of four months beginning with the day on which it received the application or within such longer period as may be agreed with the applicant.

(2) If the enforcing authority fails to determine an application for an authorisation within the period allowed by or under this paragraph the application shall, if the applicant notifies the authority in writing that he treats the failure as such, be deemed to have been refused at the end of that period.

(3) The Secretary of State may, by order, substitute for the period for the time being specified in sub-paragraph (1) above such other period as he considers appropriate and different periods may be substituted for different classes of application.

PART II

VARIATION OF AUTHORISATIONS

Variations by the enforcing authority

6 (1) The requirements of this paragraph apply where an enforcing authority has decided to vary an authorisation under section 10 and is of the opinion that any action to be taken by the holder of the authorisation in consequence of the variation will involve a substantial change in the manner in which the process is being carried on.

(2) Subject to sub-paragraph (3) below, the enforcing authority shall give notice of the action to be taken by the holder of the authorisation to the persons who are prescribed or directed to be consulted under this paragraph and shall do so within the specified period for notification; and the holder shall advertise the action in the manner prescribed in regulations made by the Secretary of State.

(3) The Secretary of State may, by regulations, exempt any class of variation from all or any of the requirements of this paragraph or exclude any class of information relating to action to be taken by holders of authorisations from all or any of those requirements, in all cases or as respects specified classes only of persons to be consulted.

(4) Any representations made by the persons so consulted within the period allowed shall be considered by the enforcing authority in taking its decision.

(5) For the purposes of sub-paragraph (2) above—

(a) persons are prescribed to be consulted on any description of variation if they are persons specified for the purposes of variations of that description in regulations made by the Secretary of State;

(b) persons are directed to be consulted on any particular variation if the Secretary of State specifies them in a direction given to the enforcing authority;

and the "specified period for notification" is the period specified in the regulations or in the direction.

(6) Any representations made by any other persons within the period allowed shall also be considered by the enforcing authority in taking its decision.

(7) Subject to sub-paragraph (8) below, the period allowed for making representations is—

(a) in the case of persons prescribed or directed to be consulted, the period of twenty-eight days beginning with the date on which notice was given under sub-paragraph (2) above, and

(b) in the case of other persons, the period of twenty-eight days beginning with the date of the advertisement under sub-paragraph (2) above.

(8) The Secretary of State may, by order, substitute for the period for the time being specified in sub-paragraph (7)(a) or (b) above, such other period as he considers appropriate.

Applications for variation

7 (1) The requirements of this paragraph apply where an application is made to an enforcing authority under section 11(4) for the variation of an authorisation.

(2) Subject to sub-paragraph (3) below, the enforcing authority shall give notice of any such application for a variation of an authorisation, enclosing a copy of the application, to the persons who are prescribed or directed to be consulted under this paragraph and shall do so within the specified period for notification; and the holder of the authorisation shall advertise the application in the manner prescribed in regulations made by the Secretary of State.

(3) The Secretary of State may, by regulations, exempt any class of application from all or any of the requirements of this paragraph or exclude any class of information furnished with applications for variations of authorisations from all or any of those requirements, in all cases or as respects specified classes only of persons to be consulted.

(4) Any representations made by the persons so consulted within the period allowed shall be considered by the enforcing authority in determining the application.

(5) For the purposes of sub-paragraph (2) above—

(a) persons are prescribed to be consulted on any description of application for a variation if they are persons specified for the purposes of applications of that description in regulations made by the Secretary of State;

(b) persons are directed to be consulted on any particular application if the Secretary of State specifies them in a direction given to the enforcing authority;

and the "specified period for notification" is the period specified in the regulations or in the direction.

(6) Any representation made by any other persons within the period allowed shall also be considered by the enforcing authority in determining the application.

(7) Subject to sub-paragraph (8) below, the period allowed for making representations is—

(a) in the case of persons prescribed or directed to be consulted, the period of twenty-eight days beginning with the date on which notice of the application was given under sub-paragraph (2) above; and

(b) in the case of other persons, the period of twenty-eight days beginning with the date on which the making of the application was advertised in pursuance of sub-paragraph (2) above.

(8) The Secretary of State may, by order, substitute for the period for the time being specified in sub-paragraph (7)(a) or (b) above, such other period as he considers appropriate.

SCHEDULE 2

Section 32.

Waste Disposal Authorities and Companies

Part I

Transition to Companies

Preliminary

1 In this Part of this Schedule—

"authority" means an existing disposal authority as defined in section 32(1);

"company" means a waste disposal contractor formed under the Companies Act 1985 by a waste disposal authority as mentioned in section 30(5);

"direction" means a direction under section 32(2);

"joint company" means a company in which more than one authority holds securities;

"securities", in relation to a company includes shares, debentures, bonds or other securities of the company, whether or not constituting a charge on the assets of the company; and

"the vesting date" means the date on which property, rights and liabilities vest in a company by virtue of a transfer scheme under paragraph 6 below.

Notice of direction

2 (1) The Secretary of State, before giving any directions to any authority or constituent authority, shall give notice of his intention to do so to that authority.

(2) A notice under this paragraph shall give a general indication of the provisions to be included in the direction, indicating in particular whether the proposed direction will require the formation of one or more than one company and the authority or authorities who are to form or control the company or companies and whether any existing disposal authority will be abolished.

(3) A notice under this paragraph shall state that the authority to whom it is given is entitled, within a period specified in the notice, to make to the Secretary of State applications or representations with respect to the proposed direction under paragraph 3 below.

Applications for exemption from and representations about directions

3 (1) An authority which has been given notice under paragraph 2 above of a proposed direction may, within the period specified in the notice, make to the Secretary of State either an application under sub-paragraph (2) below or representations under sub-paragraph (3) below.

(2) An authority may, under this sub-paragraph, apply to the Secretary of State requesting him not to make a direction in its case on the ground that the authority falls within any of paragraphs (a), (b), (c) or (d) of section 32(3).

(3) An authority may, under this sub-paragraph, make representations to the Secretary of State requesting him to make, in the direction, other provision than that proposed in the notice.

(4) It shall be the duty of the Secretary of State to consider any application duly made under sub-paragraph (2) above and to notify the authority of his decision.

(5) It shall be the duty of the Secretary of State to consider any representations duly made under sub-paragraph (3) above before he gives a direction.

Directions

4 (1) A direction may require the authority or authorities to whom it is given to form or participate in forming one or more than one company or to form or participate in forming one or more than one joint company and it shall specify the date before which the company or companies is or are to be formed.

(2) Where a direction is to require a joint company to be formed the direction may be given to such of the authorities as the Secretary of State considers appropriate (the "representative authority").

(3) Where a direction is given to an authority as the representative authority it shall be the duty of that representative authority to consult the other authorities concerned before forming a company in accordance with the direction.

(4) The Secretary of State may exercise his powers to vary or revoke a direction and give a further direction at any time before the vesting date, whether before or after a company has been formed in accordance with the direction or previous direction, as the case may be.

Formation and status of companies

5 (1) An authority which has been directed to form a company shall do so by forming it under the Companies Act 1985 as a company which—

(a) is limited by shares, and

(b) is a wholly-owned subsidiary of the authority or authorities forming it;

and it shall do so before such date as the Secretary of State specifies in the direction.

(2) The authority shall so exercise its control of the company as to secure that, at some time before the vesting date, the conditions specified in section 68(6)(a) to (h) of the Local Government and Housing Act 1989 (conditions for "arm's length companies") apply in relation to the company and shall, at some time before the vesting date, resolve that the company shall be an arm's length company for the purposes of Part V of that Act.

(3) In this paragraph "wholly-owned subsidiary", in relation to a company and an authority, is to be construed in accordance with section 736 of the Companies Act 1985.

Transfer schemes

6 (1) Where an authority has formed a company or companies in pursuance of a direction, the authority shall, before such date as the Secretary of State may specify in a direction given to the authority under this sub-paragraph, submit to the Secretary of State a scheme providing for the transfer to the company or companies of any property, rights or liabilities of that or that and any other authority, or of any subsidiary of its or theirs, which appear to be appropriate to transfer as representing the relevant part of the undertaking of that authority or of that authority and the other authorities.

(2) In preparing a scheme in pursuance of sub-paragraph (1) above the authority shall take into account any advice given by the Secretary of State as to the provisions he regards as appropriate for inclusion in the scheme (and in particular any advice as to the description of property, rights and liabilities which it is in his view appropriate to transfer to the company).

(3) A scheme under this paragraph shall not come into force until it has been approved by the Secretary of State and the date on which it is to come into force shall be such date as the Secretary of State may, either in giving his approval or subsequently, specify in writing to the authority; and the Secretary of State may approve a scheme either without modifications or with such modifications as he thinks fit after consulting the authority who submitted the scheme.

(4) If it appears to the Secretary of State that a scheme submitted under sub-paragraph (1) above does not accord with any advice given by him, he may do one or other of the following things, as he thinks fit, namely—

(a) approve the scheme under sub-paragraph (3) above with modifications; or

(b) after consulting the authority who submitted the scheme, substitute for it a scheme of his own, to come into force on such date as may be specified in the scheme.

(5) In the case of a scheme for the transfer to a company or joint company of the relevant part of the undertaking of two or more authorities, the representative authority shall consult the other authority or authorities before submitting the scheme under sub-paragraph (1) above; and the Secretary of State shall not approve the scheme (whether with or without modifications), or substitute a scheme of his own unless—

(a) he has given that other authority or (as the case may be) those other authorities an opportunity of making, within such time as he may allow for the purpose, written representations with respect to the scheme; and

(b) he has considered any such representations made to him within that time.

(6) The Secretary of State shall not specify the date on which the scheme is to come into force without consulting the authority which submitted the scheme and, where the scheme was submitted by a representative authority, the other authorities concerned.

(7) On the coming into force of a scheme under this paragraph the property, rights and liabilities affected by the scheme shall be transferred and vest in accordance with the scheme.

(8) As a consequence of the vesting by virtue of the scheme of property, rights and liabilities of an authority in a company, that company shall issue to the authority such securities of the company as are specified in the transfer scheme.

Transfer schemes: supplementary provisions

7 A scheme under paragraph 6 above may define the property, rights and liabilities to be transferred by the scheme—

(a) by specifying the property, rights and liabilities in question; or

(b) by referring to all the property, rights and liabilities comprised in any specified part of the undertaking or undertakings to be transferred; or

(c) partly in the one way and partly in the other;

and may make such supplemental, incidental and consequential provision as the authority making the scheme considers appropriate.

8 (1) The provisions of this paragraph apply to the transfer to a company of the property, rights and liabilities representing the relevant part of an authority's undertaking.

(2) Any property, rights or liabilities held or subsisting partly for the purpose of the relevant part of the authority's undertaking and partly for the purpose of another part shall, where the nature of the property, rights or liabilities permits, be divided or apportioned between the authority and the company in such proportions as may be appropriate; and where any estate or interest in land falls to be so divided, any rent payable under a lease in respect of that estate or interest, and any rent charged on that estate or interest, shall be correspondingly apportioned or divided so that the one part is payable in respect of, or charged on, only one part of the estate or interest and the other part is payable in respect of, or charged on, only the other part of the estate or interest.

(3) Any property, rights or liabilities held or subsisting as mentioned in sub-paragraph (2) above the nature of which does not permit their division or apportionment as so mentioned shall be transferred to the company or retained by the authority according to which of them appear at the vesting date likely to make use of the property, or, as the case may be, to be affected by the right or liability, to the greater extent, subject to such arrangements for the protection of the other of them as may be agreed between them.

(4) It shall be the duty of the authority and the company, before or after the vesting date, so far as practicable to enter into such written agreements, and to execute such other instruments, as are necessary or expedient to identify or define the property, rights and liabilities transferred to the company or retained by the authority and as will—

(a) afford to the authority and the company as against one another such rights and safeguards as they may require for the proper discharge of the authority's functions and the proper carrying on of the company's undertaking; and

(b) make, as from such date (not being earlier than the vesting date) as may be specified in that agreement or instrument, such clarifications and modifications of the division of the authority's undertaking as will best serve the proper discharge of the authority's functions and the proper carrying on of the company's undertaking.

(5) Any such agreement shall provide so far as it is expedient—

(a) for the granting of leases and for the creation of other liabilities and rights over land whether amounting in law to interests in land or not, and whether involving the surrender of any existing interest or the creation of a new interest or not;

(b) for the granting of indemnities in connection with the severance of leases and other matters;

(c) for responsibility for complying with any statutory requirements as respects matters to be registered and any licences, authorisations or permissions which need to be obtained.

(6) If the authority or the company represents to the Secretary of State, or if it appears to him without such a representation, that it is unlikely in the case of any matter on which agreement is required under sub-paragraph (4) above that such agreement will be reached, the Secretary of State may, whether before or after the vesting date, give a direction determining the manner in which the property, rights or liabilities in question are to be divided between the authority and the company, and may include in the direction any provision which might have been included in an agreement under that sub-paragraph; and any property, rights or liabilities required by the direction to be transferred to the company shall be regarded as having been transferred to, and by virtue of the transfer scheme vested in, the company accordingly.

Tax and company provisions

9 (1) Any shares in a company which are issued as a consequence of the vesting by a transfer scheme of property, rights and liabilities in the company shall—

(a) be issued as fully paid; and

(b) treated for the purposes of the application of the Companies Act 1985 in relation to that company as if they had been paid up by virtue of the payment to the company of their nominal value in cash.

(2) For the purposes of Chapter I of Part II of the Capital Allowances Act 1990 (capital allowance in respect of machinery and plant) property which is vested in a company by virtue of a transfer scheme shall be treated as if—

(a) it had been acquired by the company on the transfer date for the purposes for which it is used by the company on and after that date; and

(b) capital expenditure of an amount equal to the price which the property would have fetched if sold in the open market had been incurred on that date by the company on the acquisition of the property for the purposes mentioned in paragraph (a) above.

Benefit of certain planning permission

10 (1) This paragraph applies in relation to planning permission deemed to have been granted to the authority under regulation 4 of the Town and Country Planning

General Regulations 1976 (deemed planning permission for development by local authorities) which subsists at the vesting date.

(2) Any planning permission to which this paragraph applies which authorises the use of land by the authority for the treatment, keeping or disposal of waste shall, on the transfer of the land to the company by the scheme, enure for the benefit of the land.

Right to production of documents of title

11 Where on any transfer by virtue of a transfer scheme the authority is entitled to retain possession of any documents relating to the title to, or to the management of, any land or other property transferred to the company, the authority shall be deemed to have given to the company an acknowledgement in writing of the right of the company to production of that document and to delivery of copies thereof; and, in England and Wales, section 64 of the Law of Property Act 1925 shall have effect accordingly, and on the basis that the acknowledgement did not contain any such expression of contrary intention as is mentioned in that section.

Proof of title by certificate

12 (1) A joint certificate by or on behalf of the authority and the company that any property specified in the certificate, or any such interest in or right over any such property as may be specified in the certificate, is by virtue of the transfer scheme for the time being vested in the authority or in the company shall be conclusive evidence for all purposes of that fact.

(2) If on the expiration of one month after a request from the authority or the company for the preparation of such a joint certificate the authority and the company have failed to agree on the terms of the certificate, they shall refer the matter to the Secretary of State and issue the certificate in such terms as the Secretary of State may direct.

Construction of agreements

13 Where any of the rights or liabilities transferred by a transfer scheme are rights or liabilities under an agreement to which the authority was a party immediately before the vesting date, whether in writing or not, and whether or not of such a nature that rights and liabilities thereunder could be assigned by the authority, that agreement shall have effect on and after the vesting date as if—

(a) the company had been a party to the agreement; and

(b) for any reference (however worded and whether express or implied) to the authority there were substituted a reference, as respects anything falling to be done on or after the vesting date, to the company; and

(c) any reference (however worded and whether express or implied) to any officer or servant of the authority were, as respects anything falling to be done on or after the vesting date, a reference to such person as the company may appoint or, in default of appointment, to the officer or servant of the company who corresponds as nearly as may be to that officer or servant of the authority; and

(d) where the agreement refers to property, rights or liabilities which fall to be apportioned or divided between the authority and the company, as if the agreement constituted two separate agreements separately enforceable by and against the authority and the company respectively as regards the part of the property, rights and liabilities retained by the authority or, as the case may be, the part of the property, rights and liabilities vesting in the company and not as regards the other part;

and sub-paragraph (d) above shall apply in particular to the covenants, stipulations and conditions of any lease by or to the authority.

14 Without prejudice to the generality of the provisions of paragraph 13 above, the company and any other person shall, as from the vesting date, have the same rights, powers and remedies (and in particular the same rights and powers as to the taking or resisting of legal proceedings or the making or resisting of applications to any authority) for ascertaining, perfecting or enforcing any right or liability transferred to and vested in the company by a transfer scheme as he would have had if that right or liability had at all times been a right or liability of the company, and any legal proceedings or applications to any authority pending on the vesting date by or against the authority, in so far as they relate to any property, right or liability transferred to the company by the scheme, or to any agreement to any such property, right or liability, shall be continued by or against the company to the exclusion of the authority.

Third parties affected by vesting provisions

15 (1) Without prejudice to the provisions of paragraphs 13 and 14 above, any transaction effected between the authority and the company in pursuance of paragraph 8(4) above or of a direction under paragraph 8(6) above shall be binding on all other persons, and notwithstanding that it would, apart from this sub-paragraph, have required the consent or concurrence of any other person.

(2) It shall be the duty of the authority and the company, if they effect any transaction in pursuance of paragraph 8(4) above or of a direction under paragraph 8(6) above, to notify any person who has rights or liabilities which thereby become enforceable as to part by or against the authority and as to part by or against the company; and if such a person applies to the Secretary of State and satisfies him that the transaction operated unfairly against him the Secretary of State may give such directions to the authority and the company as appear to him to be appropriate for varying the transaction.

(3) If in consequence of a transfer by a transfer scheme or of anything done in pursuance of paragraphs 8 to 14 above the rights or liabilities of any person other than the authority which were enforceable against or by the authority become enforceable as to part against or by the authority and as to part against or by the company, and the value of any property or interest of that person is thereby diminished, such compensation as may be just shall be paid to that person by the authority, the company or both, and any dispute as to whether and if so how much compensation is payable, or as to the person by whom it shall be paid, shall be referred to, and determined by, the Lands Tribunal.

Transfer of staff

16 (1) The Transfer of Undertakings (Protection of Employment) Regulations 1981 shall apply in relation to the relevant employees of an authority in accordance with sub-paragraph (2) below.

(2) For the purposes of the application of those Regulations in relation to any of the relevant employees of an authority, the relevant part of the undertaking of the authority shall (whether or not it would otherwise be so regarded) be regarded—

(a) as a part of an undertaking within the meaning of those Regulations which is transferred from the authority to the company on the vesting date, and

(b) as being so transferred by a transfer to which those Regulations apply and which is completed on that date.

(3) Where a person is, in pursuance of section 32, to cease to be employed by an authority and to become employed by a company, none of the agreed redundancy procedures applicable to persons employed by waste disposal authorities shall apply to him.

(4) For the purposes of this paragraph persons are "relevant employees" of an authority if they are to become, in pursuance of section 32, employees of a company to which the relevant part of the undertaking of the authority is to be transferred.

Information for purposes of transfer scheme

17 (1) The Secretary of State may, by directions, prescribe descriptions of information which are to be furnished for purposes connected with the transfer by authorities to companies of the relevant part of the undertakings of authorities.

(2) It shall be the duty of a waste regulation authority or a waste disposal authority, on being requested to do so by a written notice served on it by the Secretary of State, to furnish to the Secretary of State such information of a description prescribed under sub-paragraph (1) above as may be specified in the notice.

PART II

PROVISIONS REGULATING WASTE DISPOSAL AUTHORITIES AND COMPANIES

Terms of waste disposal contracts

18 A waste disposal authority shall, in determining the terms and conditions of any contract which the authority proposes to enter into for the keeping, treatment or disposal of waste, so frame the terms and conditions as to avoid undue discrimination in favour of one description of waste disposal contractor as against other descriptions of waste disposal contractors.

19 (1) A waste disposal authority shall have regard to the desirability of including in any contract which the authority proposes to enter into for the keeping, treatment or disposal of waste terms or conditions designed to—

(a) minimize pollution of the environment or harm to human health due to the disposal or treatment of the waste under the contract; and

(b) maximize the recycling of waste under the contract.

(2) A waste disposal authority shall be entitled—

(a) to invite tenders for any such contract, and

(b) to accept or refuse to accept any tender for such a contract and accordingly to enter or not to enter into a contract,

by reference to acceptance or refusal of acceptance by persons tendering for the contract of any terms or conditions included in the draft contract in pursuance of sub-paragraph (1) above.

Procedure for putting waste disposal contracts out to tender

20 (1) A waste disposal authority which proposes to enter into a contract for the keeping, treatment or disposal of controlled waste shall comply with the following requirements before making the contract and if it does not any contract which is made shall be void.

(2) The authority shall publish, in at least two publications circulating among waste disposal contractors, a notice containing—

(a) a brief description of the contract work;

(b) a statement that during a specified period any person may inspect a detailed specification of the contract work free of charge at a specified place and time;

(c) a statement that during that period any person will be supplied with a copy of the detailed specification on request and on payment of the specified charge;

(d) a statement that any person who wishes to submit a tender for the contract must notify the authority of his wish within a specified period; and

(e) a statement that the authority intend to invite tenders for the contract, in accordance with sub-paragraph (4) below.

(3) The authority shall—

(a) ensure that the periods, place and time and the charge specified in the notice are such as are reasonable;

(b) make the detailed specification available for inspection in accordance with the notice; and

(c) make copies of the detailed specification available for supply in accordance with the notice.

(4) If any persons notified the authority, in accordance with the notice, of their wish to submit tenders for the contract, the authority shall—

(a) if more than four persons did so, invite at least four of them to tender for the contract;

(b) if less than four persons did so, invite each of them to tender for the contract.

(5) In this paragraph—

"the contract work", in relation to a contract for the keeping, treatment or disposal of waste, means the work comprising the services involved in the keeping, treatment or disposal of the waste under the contract; and

"specified" means specified in the notice under sub-paragraph (2) above.

21 A waste disposal authority, in taking any of the following decisions, namely—

(a) who to invite to tender for the contract under paragraph 20(4)(a) above, and

(b) who to enter into the contract with,

shall disregard the fact that any waste disposal contractor tendering for the contract is, or is not, controlled by the authority.

Variation of waste disposal contracts

22 Where a waste disposal authority has entered into a contract with a waste disposal contractor under the authority's control, paragraph 18 above shall, with the necessary modifications, apply on any proposed variation of the contract during the subsistence of that control, in relation to the terms and conditions that would result from the variation as it applies to the original contract.

Avoidance of restrictions on transfer of securities of companies

23 (1) Subject to sub-paragraph (3) below, any provision to which this paragraph applies shall be void in so far as it operates—

(a) to preclude the holder of any securities of a waste disposal contractor from disposing of those securities; or

(b) to require the holder of any such securities to dispose, or offer to dispose, of those securities to particular persons or to particular classes of persons; or

(c) to preclude the holder of any securities from disposing of those securities except—

(i) at a particular time or at particular times; or

(ii) on the fulfilment of particular conditions or in other particular circumstances.

(2) This paragraph applies to any provision relating to any securities of a waste disposal contractor which is controlled by a waste disposal authority or to which the authority has transferred the relevant part of its undertaking and contained in—

(a) the memorandum or articles of association of the company or any other instrument purporting to regulate to any extent the respective rights and liabilities of the members of the company;

(b) any resolution of the company; or

(c) any instrument issued by the company and embodying terms and conditions on which any such securities are to be held by persons for the time being holding them.

(3) No provision shall be void by reason of its operating as mentioned in sub-paragraph (1) above if the Secretary of State has given his approval in writing to that provision.

SCHEDULE 3

Section 81.

STATUTORY NUISANCES: SUPPLEMENTARY PROVISIONS

Appeals to magistrates' court

1 (1) This paragraph applies in relation to appeals under section 80(3) against an abatement notice to a magistrates' court.

(2) An appeal to which this paragraph applies shall be by way of complaint for an order and the Magistrates' Courts Act 1980 shall apply to the proceedings.

(3) An appeal against any decision of a magistrates' court in pursuance of an appeal to which this paragraph applies shall lie to the Crown Court at the instance of any party to the proceedings in which the decision was given.

(4) The Secretary of State may make regulations as to appeals to which this paragraph applies and the regulations may in particular—

(a) include provisions comparable to those in section 290 of the Public Health Act 1936 (appeals against notices requiring the execution of works);

(b) prescribe the cases in which an abatement notice is , or is not, to be suspended until the appeal is decided, or until some other stage in the proceedings;

(c) prescribe the cases in which the decision on appeal may in some respects be less favourable to the appellant than the decision from which he is appealing;

(d) prescribe the cases in which the appellant may claim that an abatement notice should have been served on some other person and prescribe the procedure to be followed in those cases.

Powers of entry etc

2 (1) Subject to sub-paragraph (2) below, any person authorised by a local authority may, on production (if so required) of his authority, enter any premises at any reasonable time—

(a) for the purpose of ascertaining whether or not a statutory nuisance exists; or

(b) for the purpose of taking any action, or executing any work, authorised or required by Part III.

(2) Admission by virtue of sub-paragraph (1) above to any premises used wholly or mainly for residential purposes shall not except in an emergency be demanded as of right unless twenty-four hours notice of the intended entry has been given to the occupier.

(3) If it is shown to the satisfaction of a justice of the peace on sworn information in writing—

(a) that admission to any premises has been refused, or that refusal is apprehended, or that the premises are unoccupied or the occupier is temporarily absent, or that the case is one of emergency, or that an application for admission would defeat the object of the entry; and

(b) that there is reasonable ground for entry into the premises for the purpose for which entry is required,

the justice may by warrant under his hand authorise the local authority by any authorised person to enter the premises, if need be by force.

(4) An authorised person entering any premises by virtue of sub-paragraph (1) or a warrant under sub-paragraph (3) above may—

(a) take with him such other persons and such equipment as may be necessary;

(b) carry out such inspections, measurements and tests as he considers necessary for the discharge of any of the local authority's functions under Part III; and

(c) take away such samples or articles as he considers necessary for that purpose.

(5) On leaving any unoccupied premises which he has entered by virtue of sub-paragraph (1) above or a warrant under sub-paragraph (3) above the authorised person shall leave them as effectually secured against trespassers as he found them.

(6) A warrant issued in pursuance of sub-paragraph (3) above shall continue in force until the purpose for which the entry is required has been satisfied.

(7) Any reference in this paragraph to an emergency is a reference to a case where the person requiring entry has reasonable cause to believe that circumstances exist which are likely to endanger life or health and that immediate entry is necessary to verify the existence of those circumstances or to ascertain their cause and to effect a remedy.

Offences relating to entry

3 (1) A person who wilfully obstructs any person acting in the exercise of any powers conferred by paragraph 2 above shall be liable, on summary conviction, to a fine not exceeding level 3 on the standard scale.

(2) If a person discloses any information relating to any trade secret obtained in the exercise of any powers conferred by paragraph 2 above he shall, unless the disclosure was made in the performance of his duty or with the consent of the person having the right to disclose the information, be liable, on summary conviction, to a fine not exceeding level 5 on the standard scale.

Default powers

4 (1) This paragraph applies to the following function of a local authority, that is to say its duty under section 79 to cause its area to be inspected to detect any statutory nuisance which ought to be dealt with under section 80 and its powers under paragraph 2 above.

(2) If the Secretary of State is satisfied that any local authority has failed, in any respect, to discharge the function to which this paragraph applies which it ought to have discharged, he may make an order declaring the authority to be in default.

(3) An order made under sub-paragraph (2) above which declares an authority to be in default may, for the purpose of remedying the default, direct the authority ("the defaulting authority") to perform the function specified in the order and may specify the manner in which and the time or times within which the function is to be performed by the authority.

(4) If the defaulting authority fails to comply with any direction contained in such an order the Secretary of State may, instead of enforcing the order by mandamus, make an order transferring to himself the function of the authority specified in the order.

(5) Where the function of a defaulting authority is transferred under sub-paragraph (4) above, the amount of any expenses which the Secretary of State certifies were incurred by him in performing the function shall on demand be paid to him by the defaulting authority.

(6) Any expenses required to be paid by a defaulting authority under sub-paragraph (5) above shall be defrayed by the authority in like manner, and shall be debited to the like account, as if the function had not been transferred and the expenses had been incurred by the authority in performing them.

(7) The Secretary of State may by order vary or revoke any order previously made by him under this paragraph.

(8) Any order under this paragraph may include such incidental, supplemental and transitional provisions as the Secretary of State considers appropriate.

Protection from personal liability

5 Nothing done by, or by a member of, a local authority or by any officer of or other person authorised by a local authority shall, if done in good faith for the purpose of executing Part III, subject them or any of them personally to any action, liability, claim or demand whatsoever (other than any liability under section 19 or 20 of the Local Government Finance Act 1982 (powers of district auditor and court)).

Statement of right of appeal in notices

6 Where an appeal against a notice served by a local authority lies to a magistrates' court by virtue of section 80, it shall be the duty of the authority to include in such a notice a statement indicating that such an appeal lies as aforesaid and specifying the time within which it must be brought.

SCHEDULE 4

Section 99.

ABANDONED SHOPPING AND LUGGAGE TROLLEYS

Application

1 (1) Subject to sub-paragraph (2) below, this Schedule applies where any shopping or luggage trolley is found by an authorised officer of the local authority on any land in the open air and appears to him to be abandoned.

(2) This Schedule does not apply in relation to a shopping or luggage trolley found on the following descriptions of land, that is to say—

(a) land in which the owner of the trolley has a legal estate or, in Scotland, of which the owner of the trolley is the owner or occupier;

(b) where an off-street parking place affords facilities to the customers of shops for leaving there shopping trolleys used by them, land on which those facilities are afforded;

(c) where any other place designated by the local authority for the purposes of this Schedule affords like facilities, land on which those facilities are afforded; and

(d) as respects luggage trolleys, land which is used for the purposes of their undertaking by persons authorised by an enactment to carry on any railway, light railway, tramway or road transport undertaking or by a relevant airport operator (within the meaning of Part V of the Airports Act 1986).

Power to seize and remove trolleys

2 (1) Where this Schedule applies in relation to a shopping or luggage trolley, the local authority may, subject to sub-paragraph (2) below,—

(a) seize the trolley; and

(b) remove it to such place under its control as the authority thinks fit.

(2) When a shopping or luggage trolley is found on any land appearing to the authorised officer to be occupied by any person, the trolley shall not be removed without the consent of that person unless—

(a) the local authority has served on that person a notice stating that the authority proposes to remove the trolley; and

(b) no notice objecting to its removal is served by that person on the local authority within the period of fourteen days beginning with the day on which the local authority served the notice of the proposed removal on him.

Retention, return and disposal of trolleys

3 (1) Subject to the following sub-paragraphs, the local authority, as respects any shopping or luggage trolley it has seized and removed,—

(a) shall keep the trolley for a period of six weeks; and

(b) may sell or otherwise dispose of the trolley at any time after the end of that period.

(2) The local authority shall, as respects any trolley it has seized or removed, as soon as reasonably practicable (but not later than fourteen days) after its removal, serve on the person (if any) who appears to the authority to be the owner of the trolley a notice stating—

(a) that the authority has removed the trolley and is keeping it;

(b) the place where it is being kept; and

(c) that, if it is not claimed, the authority may dispose of it.

(3) Subject to sub-paragraph (4) below, if, within the period mentioned in sub-paragraph (1)(a) above, any person claims to be the owner of a shopping or luggage trolley being kept by the authority under that sub-paragraph, the local authority shall, if it appears that the claimant is the owner, deliver the trolley to him.

(4) A person claiming to be the owner of a shopping or luggage trolley shall not be entitled to have the trolley delivered to him unless he pays the local authority, on demand, such charge as the authority requires.

(5) No shopping or luggage trolley shall be disposed of by the local authority unless (where it has not been claimed) the authority has made reasonable enquiries to ascertain who owns it.

Charges

4 (1) The local authority, in fixing the charge to be paid under paragraph 3 above by the claimant of a shopping or luggage trolley, shall secure that the charges so payable by claimants shall be such as are sufficient, taking one financial year with another, to cover the cost of removing, storing and disposing of such trolleys under this Schedule.

(2) The local authority may agree with persons who own shopping or luggage trolleys and make them available for use in its area a scheme for the collection by them of trolleys they make available for use; and where such an agreement is in force with any person, no charge may be demanded under paragraph 3 above by the local authority in respect of any trolley within the scheme in relation to which the provisions of the scheme are complied with.

Definitions

5 In this Schedule—

"luggage trolley" means a trolley provided by a person carrying on an undertaking mentioned in paragraph 1(2)(d) above to travellers for use by them for carrying their luggage to, from or within the premises used for the purposes of his undertaking, not being a trolley which is power-assisted; and

"shopping trolley", means a trolley provided by the owner of a shop to customers for use by them for carrying goods purchased at the shop, not being a trolley which is power-assisted.

SCHEDULE 5

Section 105.

FURTHER AMENDMENTS OF THE RADIOACTIVE SUBSTANCES ACT 1960

PART I

MISCELLANEOUS AND CONSEQUENTIAL AMENDMENTS

Amendments relating to appointment of chief inspector

1 (1) Section 8 of the 1960 Act (requirement for disposal etc. of radioactive waste to be authorised by both chief inspector and Minister of Agriculture, Fisheries and Food) shall be amended as follows.

(2) In subsection (1) for the words "those Ministers" there shall be substituted the words "the chief inspector and the Minister".

(3) In subsection (4) for the words "Minister or Ministers granting the authorisation" there shall be substituted the words "chief inspector or, as the case may be, the chief inspector and the Minister".

(4) In subsection (5) for the words "Minister or Ministers concerned" where they first appear, there shall be substituted the words "chief inspector or, as the case may be, the chief inspector and the Minister".

(5) In subsections (6) and (8) for the words "Minister or Ministers concerned", and in subsection (7) for the words "Minister or Ministers", there shall be substituted the words "chief inspector or, as the case may be, the chief inspector and the Minister".

2 (1) In section 9 (functions of public and local authorities) in subsection (3) and (4) for the words "of those Ministers" there shall be substituted the words "the chief inspector or the Minister".

(2) In section 12(2), for the words "the preceding subsection" there shall be substituted the words "section 11A of this Act".

3 In section 19 (general interpretation), after the definition of "the Authority" there shall be inserted the following definition—

""the chief inspector" means the chief inspector appointed under subsection (2) of section 11A of this Act;".

Amendments consequential on the introduction of fees and charges

4 (1) In section 1(2) (applications for registration of users of radioactive material) after the words "shall be" there shall be inserted the words "accompanied by the prescribed fee and".

(2) In section 8 (authorisation for disposal and accumulation of radioactive waste), after subsection (3) there shall be inserted the following subsection—

"(3A) Any application for an authorisation shall be accompanied by the prescribed fee."

5 In section 19 (interpretation), in the definition of "prescribed" after the word "Act" there shall be inserted the words "or, in relation to fees or charges payable in

accordance with a scheme under section 15A of this Act, prescribed under that scheme".

Documents to be sent to local authorities

6 (1) In section 1 of the 1960 Act (registration for users of radioactive material)—

(a) in subsection (2) (applications for registration), at the end there shall be inserted the following words "; and on any such application being made the chief inspector shall, subject to directions under this section, send a copy of the application to each local authority in whose area the premises are situated.";

(b) in subsection (6), for the words from "(unless" to "restricted)" there shall be substituted the words "(subject to directions under this section)";

(c) after subsection (6) there shall be inserted the following subsection—

"(7) The Secretary of State may direct the chief inspector that in his opinion, on grounds of national security, it is necessary that knowledge of—

(a) any particular application for registration under this section or applications of any description specified in the directions, or

(b) any particular registration or registrations of any description so specified,

should be restricted; and where it appears to the chief inspector that an application or registration is the subject of any such directions, the chief inspector shall not send a copy of the application or the certificate of registration, as the case may be, to any local authority under any provision of this section."

(2) In section 3 of the 1960 Act (registration of mobile radioactive apparatus)—

(a) after subsection (4) there shall be inserted the following subsection—

"(4A) On any application being made the chief inspector shall, subject to any directions under this section, send a copy of the application to each local authority in whose area it appears to him the apparatus will be kept or will be used for releasing radioactive material into the environment.";

(b) in subsection (5) at the end, there shall be inserted the words "and (subject to directions under this section) shall send a copy of the certificate to each local authority in whose area it appears to him the apparatus will be kept or will be used for releasing radioactive material into the environment.";

(c) after subsection (5) there shall be inserted the following subsection—

"(6) The Secretary of State may direct the chief inspector that, in his opinion, on grounds of national security, it is necessary that knowledge of—

(a) any particular application for registration under this section or applications of any description specified in the directions, or

(b) any particular registration or registrations of any description so specified, should be restricted; and where it appears to the chief inspector that an application or registration is the subject of any such directions, the chief inspector shall not send a copy of the application or the certificate of registration, as the case may be, to any local authority under any provision of this section."

(3) In section 5(2) of the 1960 Act (notice of cancellation or variation of registration), after the words "section one" there shall be inserted the words "or subsection (5) of section three".

(4) In section 8 of the 1960 Act (supplementary provisions as to authorisations)—

(a) after subsection (4) there shall be inserted the following subsection—

"(4A) On any application being made the chief inspector shall, subject to any directions under this section, send a copy of the application to each local authority in whose area, in accordance with the authorisation applied for, radioactive waste is to be disposed of or accumulated.";

(b) in subsection (5)(b), for the words from "(unless" to "restricted)" there shall be substituted the words ", subject to any directions under this section,";

(c) after subsection (5) there shall be inserted the following subsection—

"(5A) The Secretary of State or, as the case may be the Secretary of State and the Minister of Agriculture, Fisheries and Food may direct the chief inspector that in his or their opinion, on grounds of national security, it is necessary that knowledge of—

(a) any particular application for authorisation under section six or section seven of this Act or applications of any description specified in the directions, or

(b) any particular authorisation under section six or section seven of this Act or authorisations of any description so specified,

should be restricted; and where it appears to the chief inspector that an application or authorisation is the subject of any such directions, the chief inspector shall not send a copy of the application or the certificate of authorisation, as the case may be, to any public or local authority under any provision of this section.";

(d) in subsection (6), for the words "the last preceding subsection" there shall be substituted the words "subsection (5) of this section".

Mobile radioactive apparatus

7 (1) In section 3 of the 1960 Act (registration of mobile radioactive apparatus) for subsections (1) to (3) there shall be substituted the following subsections—

"(1) No person shall, for the purpose of any activities to which this section applies—

(a) keep, use, lend or let on hire mobile radioactive apparatus of any description, or

(b) cause or permit mobile radioactive apparatus of any description to be kept, used, lent or let on hire, unless he is registered under this section in respect of that apparatus or is exempted from registration under this section in respect of mobile radioactive apparatus of that description.

(2) This section applies to activities involving the use of the apparatus concerned for—

(a) testing, measuring or otherwise investigating any of the characteristics of substances or articles; or

(b) releasing quantities of radioactive material into the environment or introducing such material into organisms.

(3) Any application for registration under this section shall be accompanied by the prescribed fee and shall be made to the chief inspector, specifying—

(a) the apparatus to which the application relates, and

(b) the manner in which it is proposed to use the apparatus,

and containing such other information as may be prescribed."

(2) In section 18 of the 1960 Act, for subsection (5) (meaning of "mobile radioactive apparatus") there shall be substituted the following subsection—

"(5) In this Act "mobile radioactive apparatus" means any apparatus, equipment, appliance or other thing which is radioactive material and—

(a) is constructed or adapted for being transported from place to place; or

(b) is portable and designed or intended to be used for releasing radioactive material into the environment or introducing it into organisms."

(3) In section 6(2) of the 1960 Act (disposal of waste from use of mobile radioactive apparatus), for the words "the provision by him of services" there shall be substituted the word "activities".

Site and disposal records

8 After section 8 of the 1960 Act there shall be inserted the following section—

"8A Retention and production of site or disposal records

"8A "8A Retention and production of site or disposal records

(1) The chief inspector may, by notice served on him, impose on any person to whom a registration under section one or section three of this Act relates or an authorisation under section six or section seven of this Act has been granted such requirements authorised by this section in relation to site or disposal records kept by that person as the chief inspector may specify in the notice.

(2) The requirements that may be imposed on a person under this section in relation to site or disposal records are—

(a) to retain copies of the records for a specified period after he ceases to carry on the activities regulated by his registration or authorisation; or

(b) to furnish the chief inspector with copies of the records in the event of his registration being cancelled or his authorisation being revoked or in the event of his ceasing to carry on the activities regulated by his registration or authorisation.

(3) In relation to authorisations under section six of this Act in so far as the power to grant or revoke such authorisations is exercisable by the chief inspector and the Minister of Agriculture, Fisheries and Food, references in the preceding subsections to the chief inspector shall be construed as references to the chief inspector and that Minister.

(4) In this section, in relation to a registration and the person registered or an authorisation and the person authorised—

"the activities regulated" by his registration or authorisation means—

(a) in the case of registration under section one of this Act, the keeping or use of radioactive material;

(b) in the case of registration under section three of this Act, the keeping, using, lending or hiring of the mobile radioactive apparatus;

(c) in the case of an authorisation under section six of this Act, the disposal of radioactive waste; and

(d) in the case of an authorisation under section seven of this Act, the accumulation of radioactive waste;

"records" means records required to be kept by virtue of the conditions attached to the registration or authorisation relating to the activities regulated by the registration or authorisation; and "site records" means records relating to the condition of the premises on which those activities are carried on or, in the case of registration in respect of mobile radioactive apparatus, of any place where the apparatus is kept and "disposal records" means records relating to the disposal of radioactive waste on or from the premises on which the activities are carried on; and

"specified" means specified in a notice under this section."

Hearings in connection with certain authorisations

9 (1) In section 11 of the 1960 Act (procedure in connection with applications and authorisations), for subsections (1) and (2) there shall be substituted the following subsection—

"(1) Before the chief inspector and the Minister of Agriculture, Fisheries and Food—

(a) refuse an application for an authorisation under section six of this Act, or

(b) attach any limitations or conditions to such an authorisation, or

(c) vary such an authorisation, otherwise than by revoking a limitation or condition subject to which it has effect, or

(d) revoke such an authorisation,

the person directly concerned shall, and such local authorities or other persons whom the Secretary of State and the Minister consider appropriate may, be afforded the opportunity of appearing before, and being heard by, a person appointed for the purpose by the Secretary of State and the Minister."

(2) In subsection (4) of that section—

(a) for the words from "a registration" where they first appear to "Act," in the second place it appears, there shall be substituted the words "an authorisation under section six of this Act,";

(b) for the words from "a registration" (in the second place they appear) to the end there shall be substituted the words "such an authorisation is a reference to attaching limitations or conditions thereto either in granting the authorisation or in the exercise of any power to vary it."

Appeals against certain other decisions of the chief inspector

10 After the section 11C of the 1960 Act inserted by section 102 of this Act there shall be inserted the following sections—

"11D Registrations, authorisations and notices: appeals from decisions of chief inspector

"11D "11D Registrations, authorisations and notices: appeals from decisions of chief inspector

(1) Where the chief inspector—

(a) refuses an application for registration under section one or section three of this Act, or refuses an application for an authorisation under section six or section seven of this Act;

(b) attaches any limitations or conditions to such a registration or to such an authorisation, or

(c) varies such a registration or such an authorisation, otherwise than by revoking a limitation or condition subject to which it has effect, or

(d) cancels such a registration or revokes such an authorisation,

the person directly concerned may, subject to subsection (3) below, appeal to the Secretary of State.

(2) A person on whom a notice under section 11B or section 11C of this Act is served may, subject to subsections (3) and (4) below, appeal against the notice to the Secretary of State.

(3) No appeal shall lie—

(a) under subsection (1) above in relation to authorisations which are subject to subsection (1) of section eight of this Act;

(b) under subsection (1) or (2) above in respect of any decision taken by the chief inspector in pursuance of a direction of the Secretary of State under section 12A or 12B of this Act.

(4) No appeal shall lie under subsection (2) above in respect of any notice served in exercise of the power under section 11B or 11C of this Act by the Minister of Agriculture, Fisheries and Food.

(5) The Secretary of State may refer any matter involved in an appeal to a person appointed by him for the purpose.

(6) An appeal under this section shall, if and to the extent required by regulations under subsection (11) of this section, be advertised in such manner as may be prescribed.

(7) If either party to the appeal so requests, an appeal shall be in the form of a hearing (which may, if the person hearing the appeal so decides, be held, or held to any extent, in private).

(8) On determining an appeal from a decision of the chief inspector under subsection (1) of this section the Secretary of State—

(a) may affirm the decision, or

(b) where that decision was the refusal of an application, may direct the chief inspector to grant the application,

(c) where that decision involved limitations or conditions attached to a registration or authorisation, may quash those limitations or conditions wholly or in part,

(d) where that decision was a cancellation or revocation of a registration or authorisation, may quash the decision,

and where the Secretary of State does any of the things mentioned in paragraph (b), (c) or (d) of this subsection he may give directions to the chief inspector as to the limitations and conditions to be attached to the registration or authorisation in question.

(9) On the determination of an appeal in respect of a notice under subsection (2) of this section, the Secretary of State may either cancel or affirm the notice and, if he affirms it, may do so either in its original form or with such modifications as he may think fit.

(10) The bringing of an appeal against a cancellation or revocation of a registration or authorisation shall, unless the Secretary of State otherwise directs, have the effect of suspending the operation of the cancellation or revocation pending the determination of the appeal; but otherwise the bringing of an appeal shall not, unless the Secretary of State so directs, affect the validity of the decision or notice in question during that period.

(11) The Secretary of State may by regulations make provision with respect to appeals under this section (including in particular provision as to the period within which appeals are to be brought).

(12) In this section "the person directly concerned" means—

(a) in relation to a registration under section one or section three of this Act, the person applying for the registration or to whom the registration relates;

(b) in relation to an authorisation under section six or section seven of this Act, the person applying for the authorisation or to whom it was granted;

and any reference to attaching limitations or conditions to a registration or authorisation is a reference to attaching limitations or conditions thereto either in effecting or granting the registration or authorisation or in exercising any power to vary it.

11E Enforcement and prohibition notices by the Minister of Agriculture, Fisheries and Food: representations

11E 11E Enforcement and prohibition notices by the Minister of Agriculture, Fisheries and Food: representations

The Minister of Agriculture, Fisheries and Food shall afford to any person—

(a) on whom he has served a notice under section 11B or section 11C of this Act; and

(b) who requests a hearing within the prescribed period,

an opportunity to appear before and be heard by a person appointed by him for the purpose."

Period within which applications under Act to be determined

11 (1) In section 1 of the 1960 Act (registration for users of radioactive material), after subsection (3) there shall be inserted the following subsection—

"(3A) An application for registration under this section which is duly made to the chief inspector may be treated by the applicant as having been refused if it is not determined within the prescribed period for determinations or within such longer period as may be agreed with the applicant."

(2) In section 3 of that Act (registration for mobile apparatus), after the subsection (4A) inserted by paragraph 6(2) above there shall be inserted the following subsection—

"(4B) An application for registration under this section which is duly made to the chief inspector may be treated by the applicant as having been refused if it is not determined within the prescribed period for determinations or within such longer period as may be agreed with the applicant."

(3) In section 8 of that Act (supplementary provisions relating to authorisations) after the subsection (3A) inserted by paragraph 4(2) above there shall be inserted the following subsection—

"(3B) An application for an authorisation under section six or section seven of this Act (other than an application to which subsection (1) of this section applies) which is duly made to the chief inspector may be treated by the applicant as having been refused if it is not determined within the prescribed period for determinations or such longer period as may be agreed with the applicant."

(4) In section 19 of that Act (interpretation)—

(a) in subsection (1), after the definition of "prescribed", there shall be inserted the following definition—

""the prescribed period for determinations", in relation to any applications under this Act, means, subject to subsection (1A) below, the period of four months beginning with the day on which the application was received;" and

(b) after subsection (1), there shall be inserted the following subsection—

"(1A) The Secretary of State may by order substitute for the period for the time being specified in the last preceding subsection as the prescribed period for determinations such other period as he considers appropriate."

Directions to chief inspector

12 After section 12 of the 1960 Act there shall be inserted the following sections—

"12A Power of Secretary of State to give directions to chief inspector

"12A "12A Power of Secretary of State to give directions to chief inspector

(1) The Secretary of State may, if he thinks fit in relation to—

(a) an application for registration under section one or section three of this Act,

(b) an application for an authorisation under section six or section seven of this Act,

(c) any such registration or authorisation,

give directions to the chief inspector requiring him to take any of the steps mentioned in the following subsections in accordance with the directions.

(2) A direction under the preceding subsection may require the chief inspector so to exercise his powers under this Act as—

(a) to refuse an application for registration or authorisation, or

(b) to effect or grant a registration or authorisation, attaching such limitations or conditions (if any) as may be specified in the direction, or

(c) to vary a registration or authorisation, as may be so specified, or

(d) to cancel or revoke (or not to cancel or revoke) a registration or authorisation.

(3) The Secretary of State may give directions to the chief inspector, as respects any registration or authorisation, requiring him to serve a notice under section 11B or section 11C of this Act in such terms as may be specified in the directions.

(4) The Secretary of State may give directions requiring the chief inspector to send such written particulars relating to, or to activities carried on in pursuance of, registrations effected or authorisations granted under any provision of this Act as may be specified in the directions to such local authorities as may be so specified.

12B Power of Secretary of State to require certain applications to be determined by him

12B 12B Power of Secretary of State to require certain applications to be determined by him

(1) The Secretary of State may—

(a) give general directions to the chief inspector requiring him to refer applications under this Act for registrations or authorisations of any description specified in the directions to the Secretary of State for his determination; and

(b) give directions to the chief inspector in respect of any particular application requiring him to refer the application to the Secretary of State for his determination.

(2) Where an application is referred to the Secretary of State in pursuance of directions given under this section the Secretary of State may cause a local inquiry to be held in relation to the application.

(3) Subsections (2) to (5) of section 250 of the Local Government Act 1972 (supplementary provisions about local enquiries under that section) shall apply to inquiries in pursuance of subsection (2) above as if, in subsection (4) of that section, the words "such local authority or" were omitted.

(4) In Scotland, subsections (2) to (8) of section 210 of the Local Government (Scotland) Act 1973 (power to direct inquiries) shall apply to inquiries in pursuance of subsection (2) above.

(5) After determining any application so referred, the Secretary of State may give the chief inspector directions under section 12A of this Act as to the steps to be taken by him in respect of the application."

Inspectors: powers and protection

13 (1) Section 12 of the 1960 Act (rights of entry and inspection) shall be amended as follows.

(2) In subsection (2)—

(a) in paragraph (a), after the words "reasonable time" there shall be inserted the words "or, in an emergency, at any time";

(b) in paragraph (b)—

(i) after the word "tests" there shall be inserted the words "(including dismantling and subjecting to any process)";

(ii) after the word "inspections" there shall be inserted the words "and take such photographs"; and

(iii) the words "of waste" shall be omitted;

(c) after paragraph (b), there shall be inserted the following paragraph—

"(bb) give directions that the whole or any part of such premises, or anything in them, be left undisturbed for so long as is reasonably necessary for the purpose of any tests or inspections; and"; and

(d) in paragraph (c)—

(i) after the words "inspector with" there shall be inserted the words "such facilities and assistance and"; and

(ii) for the word "specify" there shall be substituted the words "require, and in the case of answers to his questions, to sign a declaration of the truth of the answers".

(3) After subsection (6) there shall be inserted the following subsection—

"(6A) The last preceding subsection does not apply in respect of premises in respect of which—

(a) a person has been (but is no longer) registered under section one of this Act;

or

(b) an authorisation has been (but is no longer) in force under subsection (1) of section six or under section seven of this Act; or

in respect of premises on which there are reasonable grounds for believing that mobile radioactive apparatus has been or is being kept or used.";

and at the beginning of subsection (6) there shall be inserted the words "Subject to the next following subsection".

(4) After subsection (7) there shall be inserted the following subsections—

"(7A) An inspector appointed under section 11A of this Act or under subsection (7) (a) of this section shall not be liable in any civil or criminal proceedings for anything done in the purported exercise of his powers under this section if the court is satisfied that the act was done in good faith and that there were reasonable grounds for doing it.

(7B) In England and Wales, an inspector appointed under section 11A of this Act, if authorised to do so by the chief inspector, may, although not of counsel or a solicitor, prosecute before a magistrates' court proceedings for an offence under section 13 of this Act."

Offences under 1960 Act

14 (1) Section 13 of the 1960 Act (offences) shall be amended as follows.

(2) In subsection (1) after paragraph (c) there shall be inserted the following paragraph ", or

(d) being a person who is registered under section one or section three of this Act or to whom an authorisation under section six or section seven of this Act has been granted, fails to comply with any requirement of a notice served on him under section 11B or 11C of this Act".

(3) In subsection (2) (penalties for offence under subsection (1)) in paragraph (a), for the words after "summary conviction" there shall be substituted the words "to a fine not exceeding £20,000, or to imprisonment for a term not exceeding six months or both".

(4) In subsection (4) (penalties for offence under subsection (3)) in paragraph (a), for the words from "exceeding" where it first appears to "or to", there shall be substituted the words "exceeding the statutory maximum, or to".

(5) After subsection (4), there shall be inserted the following subsection—

"(4A) Any person who fails to comply with a requirement imposed on him under section 8A of this Act shall be guilty of an offence, and shall be liable—

(a) on summary conviction, to a fine not exceeding the statutory maximum or to imprisonment for a term not exceeding three months, or both;

(b) on conviction on indictment, to a fine, or to imprisonment for a term not exceeding two years, or both.".

(6) In subsection (5)(b) (offence of obstructing inspector)—

(a) at the beginning there shall be inserted the word "intentionally";

(b) for the words “the last preceding section” there shall be substituted the words “section twelve of this Act”; and

(c) after the word “provide” there shall be inserted the words “facilities or assistance or”.

(7) In subsection (5), in the words after paragraph (b), for the words after “offence” there shall be substituted the words “and shall be liable—

(i) on summary conviction, to a fine not exceeding the statutory maximum;

(ii) on conviction on indictment, to a fine.”

(8) In subsection (6) (pulling down, defacing etc, documents), for the words after “exceeding” there shall be substituted the words “level 2 on the standard scale.”.

(9) In subsection (7) (which restricts the persons who may authorise prosecutions in England and Wales), for the word “Minister” there shall be substituted the words “Secretary of State, the chief inspector”.

(10) After subsection (8) there shall be inserted the following subsection—

“(9) Where the commission by any person of an offence under this section is due to the act or default of some other person, that other person may be charged with and convicted of the offence by virtue of this subsection whether or not proceedings for the offence are taken against the first-mentioned person.”

Public access to certain information

15 After section 13 (offences) of the 1960 Act there shall be inserted the following section—

“13A Public access to local authority records relating to documents issued under this Act

“13A “13A Public access to local authority records relating to documents issued under this Act

(1) The chief inspector shall keep copies of—

(a) all applications made to him under any provision of this Act;

(b) all documents issued by him under any provision of this Act;

(c) all other documents sent by him to any local authority in pursuance of directions of the Secretary of State; and

(d) such records of convictions under section thirteen of this Act as may be prescribed in regulations;

and he shall make copies of those documents available to the public except to the extent that that would involve the disclosure of information relating to any relevant process or trade secret (within the meaning of subsection (3) of section thirteen of this Act) or would involve the disclosure of applications or certificates as respects which the Secretary of State has directed that knowledge should be restricted on grounds of national security.

(2) Each local authority shall keep and make available to the public copies of all documents sent to the authority under any provision of this Act unless directed by the chief inspector or, as the case may be, the Minister of

Agriculture, Fisheries and Food and the chief inspector, that all or any part of any such document is not to be available for inspection.

(3) Directions under the preceding subsection shall only be given for the purpose of preventing disclosure of relevant processes or trade secrets (within the meaning of subsection (3) of section thirteen of this Act) and may be given generally in respect of all, or any description of, documents or in respect of specific documents.

(4) The copies of documents required to be made available to the public by this section need not be kept in documentary form.

(5) The public shall have the right to inspect the copies of documents required to be made available under this section at all reasonable times and, on payment of a reasonable fee, to be provided with a copy of any such document."

Expenses and receipts

16 In section 16 of the 1960 Act (expenses and receipts)—

(a) in subsection (1)(a), for the words following "incurred by" there shall be substituted the words "the Secretary of State or the Minister of Agriculture, Fisheries and Food under this Act"; and

(b) in subsection (2), for the word "Minister" there shall be substituted the words "Secretary of State or the Minister of Agriculture, Fisheries and Food".

Meaning of "radioactive material" for purposes of 1960 Act

17 In section 18 of the 1960 Act (meaning of expression "radioactive material" in that Act) after subsection (3) there shall be inserted the following subsection—

"(3A) For the purposes of paragraph (b) of subsection (2) of this section, a substance shall not be treated as radioactive material if the level of radioactivity is less than such level as may be prescribed for substances of that description."

PART II

AMENDMENTS RELATING TO SCOTLAND AND NORTHERN IRELAND

Scotland

18 In section 20 of the 1960 Act (application of Act to Scotland)—

(a) for paragraphs (a) and (b) there shall be substituted the following paragraphs—

"(a) for any reference to the chief inspector there shall be substituted a reference to the chief inspector for Scotland, being the inspector so appointed by the Secretary of State for the purposes of this Act in relation to Scotland;

(b) any reference to the Minister of Agriculture, Fisheries and Food shall be omitted and anything required to be done in

England by both the chief inspector and that Minister shall be done in Scotland by the chief inspector for Scotland.";

(b) after paragraph (e) there shall be inserted the following paragraph—

"(f) in section 11, subsections (1) and (4) shall be omitted."

19 (1) In Schedule 1 to the 1960 Act (enactments, other than local enactments, to which section 9(1) applies)—

(a) paragraphs 9 and 11 shall be omitted;

(b) after paragraph 17 there shall be added the following paragraphs—

"17A Section 201 of the Local Government (Scotland) Act 1973.

17B Section 124 of the Civic Government (Scotland) Act 1982."

Northern Ireland

20 In section 21 of the 1960 Act (application of Act to Northern Ireland)—

(a) in subsection (2)—

(i) for paragraph (a) there shall be substituted the following paragraph—

"(a) except in section sixteen of this Act any reference to the Secretary of State shall be construed as a reference to the Department of the Environment for Northern Ireland, any reference to the Minister of Agriculture, Fisheries and Food shall be construed as a reference to the Department of Agriculture for Northern Ireland and any reference to the Treasury shall be construed as a reference to the Department of Finance and Personnel for Northern Ireland;";

(ii) at the end there shall be added the following paragraphs—

"(k) in section 11A(3) of this Act the reference to section 16 of the Environmental Protection Act 1990 shall be construed as a reference to section 10 of the Alkali & Works Regulation Act 1906;

(l) section 12(7B) of this Act shall be omitted;

(m) for section 12B(3) of this Act there shall be substituted—

"(3) Schedule 8 to the Health and Personal Social Services (Northern Ireland) Order 1972 (provisions as to inquiries) shall apply to inquiries in pursuance of subsection (2) above.";

(n) in section 15A of this Act the reference to each House of Parliament shall be construed as a reference to the Northern Ireland Assembly;

(o) any reference to the Crown shall be construed as including a reference to the Crown in right of Her Majesty's Government in Northern Ireland"; and

(b) subsection (4) shall be omitted.

SCHEDULE 6

Section 128.

THE NATURE CONSERVANCY COUNCILS FOR ENGLAND AND SCOTLAND AND THE COUNTRYSIDE COUNCIL FOR WALES: CONSTITUTION.

Preliminary

1 In this Part of this Schedule any reference to the council is a reference to each of the Councils established by section 128 of this Act.

Constitution and membership

2 The council shall be a body corporate.

3 (1) The council shall not be regarded as the servant or agent of the Crown, or as enjoying any status, immunity or privilege of the Crown; and the council's property shall not be regarded as property of, or property held on behalf of, the Crown.

(2) Sub-paragraph (1) above has effect subject to paragraph 18 below.

4 (1) The Secretary of State shall appoint one of the members of the council to be chairman of the council and may appoint a member to be deputy chairman.

(2) The chairman, deputy chairman and other members of the council shall hold and vacate office in accordance with the terms of their appointment.

(3) A member of the council may, by notice in writing addressed to the Secretary of State, resign his membership, and the chairman and deputy chairman of the council may by such a notice resign their office as such without resigning their membership.

5 A member of the council who ceases to be a member or ceases to be chairman or deputy chairman of the council shall be eligible for reappointment.

6 The Secretary of State may remove a member of the council from membership if he has—

(a) become bankrupt or made an arrangement with his creditors or, in Scotland, had his estate sequestrated or made a trust deed for behoof of his creditors or a composition contract; or

(b) been absent from meetings of the council for a period longer than six consecutive months without the permission of the council;

or if he is, in the opinion of the Secretary of State unable or unfit to discharge the functions of a member.

Remuneration and allowances for members of council

7 (1) The council shall—

(a) pay to their members such remuneration and allowances (if any); and

(b) as regards any member or former member in whose case the Secretary of State may so determine, pay such pension, allowance or gratuity to or in respect of him, or make such payments towards the provision of such pension, allowance or gratuity,

as the Secretary of State may with the approval of the Treasury determine.

(2) If a person ceases to be a member of the council, and it appears to the Secretary of State that there are special circumstances which make it right that he should receive

compensation, the Secretary of State may require the council to pay to that person a sum of such amount as the Secretary of State may with the approval of the Treasury determine.

Staff

8 (1) There shall be a chief officer of the council.

(2) The first appointment of a chief officer shall be made by the Secretary of State after consultation with the chairman of the council (if there is a person holding that office when the appointment is made); and the council shall, with the approval of the Secretary of State, make the subsequent appointments.

9 The council may appoint such number of other employees as they may, with the approval of the Secretary of State given with the consent of the Treasury, determine.

10 The council shall pay to the chief officer and their other employees such remuneration and allowances as the council may, with the approval of the Secretary of State given with the consent of the Treasury, determine.

11 The council shall, in the case of such of their employees or former employees as they may, with the approval of the Secretary of State given with the consent of the Treasury, determine—

(a) pay such pensions, allowances or gratuities to or in respect of those employees,

(b) make such payments towards provision of such pensions, allowances or gratuities, or

(c) provide and maintain such schemes (whether contributory or not) for the payment of such pensions, allowances or gratuities,

as they may, with the approval of the Secretary of State given with the consent of the Treasury, determine.

Proceedings

12 (1) The council may regulate their own procedure (including making provision in relation to quorum).

(2) The proceedings of the council and any committee of the council shall not be invalidated by any vacancy amongst their members or by any defect in the appointment of any such member.

Delegation of powers

13 (1) Anything authorised or required by or under any enactment to be done by the council may be done by any committee of theirs which, or by any member or employee of the council who, is authorised (generally or specially) for the purpose by the council.

(2) Nothing in sub-paragraph (1) above shall prevent the council from doing anything that a committee, member or employee has been authorised to do.

Committees

14 (1) The council may appoint persons who are not members of the council to be members of any committee established by the council (in addition to any members of the council).

(2) The council shall pay to a person so appointed such remuneration and allowances (if any) as the Secretary of State may with the approval of the Treasury determine.

(3) The council may regulate the procedure of any committee of theirs.

Documents

15 (1) This paragraph applies in England and Wales only.

(2) The application of the seal of the council shall be authenticated by the signature of any member or employee of the council who is authorised (generally or specially) for the purpose by the council.

(3) Any document purporting to be an instrument made or issued by the council and to be duly executed under the seal of the council, or to be signed or executed by a person authorised for the purpose by the council, shall be received in evidence and treated, without further proof, as being so made or issued unless the contrary is shown.

16 (1) Sub-paragraphs (2) and (3) below apply in Scotland only; and they do not apply where an enactment (including an enactment contained in a statutory instrument) provides otherwise.

(2) A document—

(a) is signed by the council if it is signed on their behalf by a member or by the chief officer or by a person authorised to sign the document on behalf of the council; and

(b) is subscribed by the council if it is subscribed on their behalf by being signed in accordance with the provisions of paragraph (a) above at the end of the last page of the document.

(3) A document shall be presumed, unless the contrary is shown, to have been subscribed in accordance with sub-paragraph (2) above if—

(a) it bears to have been subscribed on behalf of the council by a member or by the chief officer or by a person bearing to have been authorised to subscribe the document on behalf of the council; and

(b) it bears to have been signed by a person as a witness of the subscription of the member, chief officer or other person subscribing on behalf of the council or (if the subscription is not so witnessed) to have been sealed with the common seal of the council.

Public Records

17 In Schedule 1 to the Public Records Act 1958 (definition of public records), in Part II of the Table at the end of paragraph 3 (organisations whose records are public records) there shall be inserted in the appropriate places entries relating to the Countryside Council for Wales and the Nature Conservancy Council for England.

Land

18 (1) For the purposes of the application of any enactment or rule of law to land an interest in which belongs to the council, and which is managed as a nature reserve, the council shall be deemed to be a Government department; and any other land occupied by them shall be deemed, for the purpose of any rate on property, to be property occupied by or on behalf of the Crown for public purposes.

(2) In sub-paragraph (1) above "interest" and "land" have the meanings assigned to them by section 114 of the National Parks and Access to the Countryside Act 1949.

Reports, accounts etc.

19 The council shall—

(a) furnish the Secretary of State with such returns, accounts and other information with respect to their property and activities or proposed activities as he may from time to time require;

(b) afford to the Secretary of State facilities for the verification of information so furnished; and

(c) for the purpose of such verification, permit any person authorised in that behalf by the Secretary of State to inspect and make copies of the council's accounts, books, documents or papers and give that person such explanation of anything he is entitled to inspect as he may reasonably require.

20 (1) The council shall—

(a) as soon as possible after the 31st March following the date appointed under section 131(3) of this Act make to the Secretary of State a report on the exercise and performance of their functions down to that date, and

(b) make a similar report to him as to each period of twelve months thereafter as soon as possible after its end;

and a copy of each such report shall be laid before each House of Parliament by the Secretary of State.

(2) Without prejudice to the generality of sub-paragraph (1) above, the report of the Countryside Council for Wales for any year shall include a statement of the action taken by the Council to promote the enjoyment of the countryside by members of the public who are disabled.

21 (1) The council shall keep proper accounts and other records, and shall prepare for each financial year a statement of account in such form as the Secretary of State with the approval of the Treasury may direct and submit those statements of account to the Secretary of State at such time as he may with the approval of the Treasury direct.

(2) The Secretary of State shall, on or before 30th November in any year, transmit to the Comptroller and Auditor General the statements of account of the council for the financial year last ended.

(3) The Comptroller and Auditor General shall examine and certify the statements of account transmitted to him under this paragraph, and lay copies of them together with his report thereon before each House of Parliament.

(4) In this paragraph "financial year" means the period beginning with the day appointed under section 131(3) of this Act and ending with the 31st March following that date and each period of twelve months thereafter.

Superannuation Act 1965 (c. 74)

22 In paragraph 7 of section 39(1) of the Superannuation Act 1965 (public offices)—

(a) there shall be inserted in the appropriate place the following entry—

"The Countryside Council for Wales.";

(b) for the entry relating to the Nature Conservancy Council there shall be substituted the following entries—

"The Nature Conservancy Council for England.

The Nature Conservancy Council for Scotland."

Parliamentary Commissioner Act 1967 (c. 13)

23 In Schedule 2 to the Parliamentary Commissioner Act 1967 (departments and authorities subject to investigation)—

(a) after the entry for the Countryside Commission for Scotland there shall be inserted the following entry—

"Countryside Council for Wales.";

(b) for the entry relating to the Nature Conservancy Council there shall be substituted the following entries—

"Nature Conservancy Council for England.

Nature Conservancy Council for Scotland."

House of Commons Disqualification Act 1975 (c. 24)

24 In Part III of Schedule 1 to the House of Commons Disqualification Act 1975 (other disqualifying offices), for the entry relating to members of the Nature Conservancy Council in receipt of remuneration there shall be substituted—

"Any member of the Nature Conservancy Council for England, the Nature Conservancy Council for Scotland or the Countryside Council for Wales in receipt of remuneration."

Inheritance Tax Act 1984 (c. 51)

25 In Schedule 3 to the Inheritance Tax Act 1984 (gifts for national purposes), for the entry relating to the Nature Conservancy Council there shall be substituted the following entries—

"Nature Conservancy Council for England.

Nature Conservancy Council for Scotland.

Countryside Council for Wales."

SCHEDULE 7

Section 128.

THE JOINT NATURE CONSERVATION COMMITTEE

Preliminary

1 In this Schedule—

"chairman" means (except in paragraph 2(1) below) the chairman of the committee;

"the committee" means the Joint Nature Conservation Committee; and
"council" means a council established by section 128(1) of this Act.

Membership

2 (1) The committee shall consist of eleven voting members, namely—
(a) a chairman appointed by the Secretary of State;
(b) three members appointed by the Secretary of State;
(c) the chairman of each council and one other member of each council appointed by that council; and
(d) the chairman of the Countryside Commission;

and two non-voting members appointed by the Department of the Environment for Northern Ireland.

(2) The committee may appoint any voting member to be deputy chairman.

3 The chairman and the three members appointed by the Secretary of State shall be persons who are not members of any of the councils and shall hold and vacate office in accordance with the terms of their appointments.

4 (1) The three members appointed by the Secretary of State shall be persons appearing to the Secretary of State to have experience in or scientific knowledge of nature conservation; and the Secretary of State shall, in determining who to appoint, have regard to any recommendations made to him by the chairman.

(2) Before appointing such a member the Secretary of State shall consult the chairman and such persons having scientific knowledge of nature conservation as the Secretary of State considers appropriate.

Remuneration and allowances for members

5 (1) The councils shall—
(a) pay to the chairman such remuneration and allowances; and
(b) pay such pension, allowance or gratuity to or in respect of the chairman or make such payments towards the provision of such pension, allowance or gratuity;

as the Secretary of State may with the approval of the Treasury determine.

(2) If a person ceases to be chairman and it appears to the Secretary of State that there are special circumstances which make it right that he should receive compensation, the Secretary of State may require the councils to pay to that person a sum of such amount as the Secretary of State may with the approval of the Treasury determine.

6 The councils shall pay to the three members appointed by the Secretary of State, and to the non-voting members, such remuneration and allowances as the Secretary of State may with the approval of the Treasury determine.

Staff etc. and expenses

7 (1) The councils shall provide the committee with such staff, accommodation and other facilities, and such financial resources, as the councils, after consultation with the committee, consider appropriate for the proper discharge of the functions conferred by section 133(2) and (3) of this Act.

(2) The expenses of the committee shall be defrayed by the councils in such proportions as the councils may agree.

(3) In default of agreement between the councils as to any question arising under sub-paragraph (1) or (2) above the Secretary of State shall determine that question.

Proceedings

8 (1) The committee may regulate their own procedure (including making provision in relation to the quorum of voting members).

(2) The proceedings of the committee shall not be invalidated by any vacancy amongst their members or defect in the appointment of any member.

Delegation of functions

9 (1) Anything authorised or required to be done by the committee may be done by any member of the committee, by any council or by any employee of a council who is authorised (generally or specially) for the purpose by the committee.

(2) Nothing in sub-paragraph (1) above shall prevent the committee from doing anything that another person has been authorised to do.

Annual reports

10 (1) The committee shall—

(a) as soon as possible after 31st March following the date appointed under section 131(3) of this Act make to the Secretary of State a report on their activities down to that date; and

(b) make a similar report to him as to each period of twelve months thereafter as soon as possible after its end;

and a copy of each such report shall be laid before each House of Parliament by the Secretary of State.

(2) The committee shall, at the same time as they make a report under sub-paragraph (1) above, send a copy of it to each of the councils.

SCHEDULE 8

Section 130.

AMENDMENT OF ENACTMENTS RELATING TO COUNTRYSIDE MATTERS

National Parks and Access to the Countryside Act 1949 (c. 97)

1 (1) The National Parks and Access to the Countryside Act 1949 shall be amended as follows.

(2) For section 1 (the Countryside Commission) there shall be substituted the following section—

"1 The Countryside Commission and the Countryside Council for Wales

"1 **"1 The Countryside Commission and the Countryside Council for Wales**

(1) There shall be a Countryside Commission which shall exercise functions in relation to England for the purposes specified in subsection (2) below; and the Countryside Council for Wales (established by section 128 of the Environmental Protection Act 1990) shall exercise corresponding functions in relation to Wales for the corresponding purposes specified in section 130(2) of the Environmental Protection Act 1990.

(2) The purposes for which the functions of the Commission are exercisable are—

(a) the preservation and enhancement of natural beauty in England, both in the areas designated under this Act as National Parks or as areas of outstanding natural beauty and elsewhere;

(b) encouraging the provision or improvement, for persons resorting to National Parks, of facilities for the enjoyment thereof and for the enjoyment of the opportunities for open-air recreation and the study of nature afforded thereby."

(3) In section 3 (power of Minister to give directions), in subsection (1) after the word "Commission" in the first place it occurs there shall be inserted the words "or to the Council" and after that word in the second place it occurs there shall be inserted the words "or Council".

(4) Before section 5 (National Parks) there shall be inserted the following section—

"4A Application of Part II of this Act in Wales

"4A **"4A Application of Part II of this Act in Wales**

(1) The provisions of this Part of this Act shall, subject to the next following subsection, apply to land in Wales as they apply to land in England.

(2) Where a provision of this Part of this Act confers a function on the Countryside Commission as respects England (or areas of any description in England), the Countryside Council for Wales shall have the corresponding function as respects Wales (or areas of a similar description in Wales)."

(5) In sections 5(2) and 6(1) the words "and Wales" shall be omitted.

(6) Before section 51 (long-distance routes) there shall be inserted the following section—

"50A Application of Part IV of this Act in Wales

"50A **"50A Application of Part IV of this Act in Wales**

(1) The provisions of this Part of this Act shall, subject to the next following subsection, apply to land in Wales as they apply to land in England.

(2) Where a provision of this Part of this Act confers a function on the Countryside Commission as respects England (or land of any description in

England), the Countryside Council for Wales shall have the corresponding function as respects Wales (or land of a similar description in Wales)."

(7) In section 51(1) the words "or Wales" shall be omitted.

(8) In sections 62(1) and 64(5) (consultation requirements as to land in National Parks), after the word "Commission" there shall be inserted the words "(where the Park is in England) or the Council (where the Park is in Wales)".

(9) In section 65 (access orders), in subsection (5), after the word "Park" in both places in which it occurs, there shall be inserted the words "in England" and after that subsection there shall be inserted the following subsection—

"(5A) The preceding subsection shall apply in relation to National Parks in Wales, and the Council, as it applies in relation to National Parks in England, and the Commission."

(10) In section 85 (general advisory duties)—

(a) for the words "the duties of the Commission" there shall be substituted the words "their respective duties";

(b) after the word "Commission", in the second place in which it occurs, there shall be inserted the words "and the Council";

(c) in paragraph (b), after the word "Commission" there shall be inserted the words ", or, as the case may be, to the Minister and to the Council,"; and

(d) in paragraph (c), after the word "Commission" there shall be inserted the words "(as respects England) or to the Council (as respects Wales)".

(11) After section 86 (information services provided by Commission regarding National Parks) there shall be inserted the following section—

"86A Information services to be provided by Council

"86A "86A Information services to be provided by Council

The provisions of section eighty-six of this Act shall apply to the Council in relation to National Parks and other land in Wales as they apply to the Commission in relation to National Parks and other land in England."

(12) In section 87 (designation of areas of outstanding natural beauty)—

(a) in subsection (1), after the word "Commission" there shall be inserted the words ", or as the case may be, the Council,";

(b) after that subsection there shall be inserted the following subsection—

"(1A) The following provisions shall apply to the Council in relation to land in Wales as they apply to the Commission in relation to land in England."

(13) In section 88 (application of provisions of Part II to designated areas), after subsection (2) there shall be inserted the following subsection—

"(2A) The provisions of section 4A of this Act shall apply to the provisions mentioned in the preceding subsection for the purposes of their application to areas of outstanding natural beauty as the provisions of that section apply for the purposes of Part II of this Act."

(14) In section 90(4) (consultation before making certain byelaws) after the word "Commission" there shall be inserted the words "(as regards land in England) or the Council (as regards land in Wales)".

(15) In section 91(1) (consultation before making certain byelaws) after the word "Commission" there shall be inserted the words "(as regards land or waterways in England) or the Council (as regards land or waterways in Wales)".

(16) In section 114 (interpretation), after the definition of "area of outstanding natural beauty" there shall be inserted the following definitions—

""the Commission" means the Commission established by section one of this Act;

"the Council" means the Countryside Council for Wales;".

(17) In the first Schedule (procedure for certain orders), in paragraph 2(5), after the word "Commission" where it first appears there shall be inserted the words ", the Council" and after that word in the second place it appears there shall be inserted the word ", Council".

The Countryside Act 1968 (c. 41)

2 (1) The Countryside Act 1968 shall be amended as follows.

(2) In section 1 (additional general functions)—

(a) for subsection (1) there shall be substituted the following subsections—

"(1) The National Parks Commission shall in future be known as the "Countryside Commission" and shall exercise functions in relation to England.

(1A) The functions of the Countryside Commission (in this Act referred to as "the Commission") in England and the corresponding functions of the Countryside Council for Wales (in this Act referred to as "the Council") in Wales shall be enlarged in accordance with this Act.";

(b) in subsection (2)—

(i) after the word "recreation" there shall be inserted the words "and the study of nature"; and

(ii) at the end, there shall be inserted the words "; and the purposes for which the functions of the Council in Wales are to be exercised are the corresponding purposes specified in section 130(2) of the Environmental Protection Act 1990.";

(c) in subsection (3) for the word "shall" there shall be substituted the words "and the Council shall each".

(3) In section 2 (new functions)—

(a) in subsection (1), for the word "shall" where it first appears there shall be substituted the words "and the Council shall each" and after the word "Commission" in the second and third place it appears there shall be inserted the words "or Council";

(b) in subsections (2) and (3), after the word "Commission" where it first appears there shall be inserted the words "and the Council" and after that word in the second place it appears there shall be inserted the words "or Council";

(c) in subsection (4), after the word "Commission" where it first appears there shall be inserted the words "and the Council" and after that word in the second and third place it appears there shall be inserted the words "or Council";

(d) in subsection (5), after the word "Commission" where it first appears there shall be inserted the words "or to the Council" and after that word in the second place it appears there shall be inserted the words "or , as the case may be, the Council";

(e) in subsection (5)(b), after the word "Commission" in each place it appears there shall be inserted the words "or Council";

(f) in subsection (6) after the word "Commission" there shall be inserted the words "and the Council";

(g) in subsections (7), (8) and (9), after the word "Commission" where it first appears there shall be inserted the words "and the Council" and after that word in the second place it appears there shall be inserted the words "or Council".

(4) In section 4 (experimental projects or schemes)—

(a) in subsection (1), after the word "Commission" where it first appears there shall be inserted the words "and the Council" and after that word in the second place it appears there shall be inserted the words "or Council";

(b) in subsection (3) after the word "Commission" there shall be inserted the words "or, as the case may be, the Council";

(c) in subsection (4) after the word "Commission" there shall be inserted the words "or Council";

(d) in subsection (5) after the word "Commission" where it first appears there shall be inserted the words "or by the Council" and after that word in the second place it appears there shall be inserted the words "or Council";

(e) in subsection (6), after the word "Commission" where it first appears there shall be inserted the words "or of the Council" and after that word in the second place it appears there shall be inserted the words "or Council".

(5) In section 8 (sailing, boating and fishing in country parks), in subsection (5) after the word "Commission" there shall be inserted the words "(if the works are in England) or the Council (if the works are in Wales)".

(6) In section 12 (facilities in or near National Parks)—

(a) in subsection (1) after the word "Commission" where it first appears there shall be inserted the words "or, as the case may be, the Council" and after that word in the second place it appears there shall be inserted the words "or the Council";

(b) in subsection (5) after the word "Commission" there shall be inserted the words "(if the National Park is in England) or the Council (if the National Park is in Wales)".

(7) In section 13 (control of boats etc. in National Parks) in subsection (4), after the word "Commission" there shall be inserted the words "(if the National Park is in England) or the Council (if the National Park is in Wales)".

(8) In section 23 (provision of facilities by Forestry Commissioners), in subsection (5) for the word "shall" there shall be inserted the words "and the Countryside Council for Wales shall each".

(9) In section 38 (avoidance of pollution) after the words "the Commission" there shall be inserted the words ", the Council".

(10) In section 41 (byelaws etc.)—

(a) in subsection (2), for the word "may" there shall be substituted the words "and the Council may each";

(b) in subsection (5), after the word "Commission" there shall be inserted the words "(as respects a park or area in England) or the Council (as respects a park or area in Wales)";

(c) in subsection (8), for the words "were a local authority" there shall be substituted the words "and the Council were local authorities";

(d) in subsection (9), for the words "or the Commission" there shall be substituted the words ", the Commission or the Council".

(11) In section 45 (agreements with landowners), in subsection (1) after the word "Commission" there shall be inserted the words ", the Council".

(12) In section 46 (application of general provisions of 1949 Act), in subsection (2), at the end there shall be inserted "and any reference to the Nature Conservancy Council, so far as referring to the Countryside Council for Wales for purposes connected with their nature conservation functions (within the meaning of section 131 of the Environmental Protection Act 1990) shall include a reference to that Council for purposes connected with their countryside functions (whether conferred by this Act, the Act of 1949 or otherwise.)".

(13) In section 49 (interpretation), after the definition of "bridleway" there shall be inserted the following definitions—

""the Commission" means the Countryside Commission;

""the Council" means the Countryside Council for Wales;""

Local Government Act 1972 (c. 70)

3 In Part I of Schedule 17 to the Local Government Act 1972 (discharge of planning and countryside functions in National Parks), after paragraph 21A there shall be inserted the following paragraph—

"Construction of references to the Countryside Commission

21B In this Part of this Schedule, references to the Countryside Commission shall, in relation to a National Park in Wales, be construed as references to the Countryside Council for Wales."

Local Government Act 1974 (c. 7)

4 In section 7 of the Local Government Act 1974 (supplementary grants for expenditure on National Parks), in subsection (3) after the word "Commission" there shall be inserted the words "(as respects National Parks in England) and the Countryside Council for Wales (as respects National Parks in Wales)" and in section 9 of that Act (grants and loans by the Countryside Commission)—

(a) in subsection (1), for the word "may" there shall be substituted the words "and the Countryside Council for Wales may each" and after the word

"Commission" in the second place it appears there shall be inserted the words "or, as the case may be, the Council";

(b) in subsection (2), after the word "Commission" there shall be inserted the words "or the Countryside Council for Wales";

(c) in subsection (3), for the words "Countryside Commission's power" there shall be substituted the words "the power of the Countryside Commission and of the Countryside Council for Wales" and after the word "Commission" in the second place it appears there shall be inserted the words "or to the Council".

Highways Act 1980 (c. 66)

5 (1) The Highways Act 1980 shall be amended as follows.

(2) In section 105A (environmental assessment for highway projects) in subsection (6)(a), after the word "land" there shall be inserted the words "in England" and, at the end, there shall be inserted the words "or the Countryside Council for Wales, if it relates to land in Wales falling within that paragraph of that subsection".

(3) In section 120 (orders for extinguishment or diversion of public paths), in subsection (2)(c), at the end there shall be inserted the words "(if the National Park is in England) or the Countryside Council for Wales (if the National Park is in Wales)".

Wildlife and Countryside Act 1981 (c. 69)

6 (1) The Wildlife and Countryside Act 1981 shall be amended as follows.

(2) In section 34 (limestone pavement orders), in subsection (6) in the definition of "the Commission", the words "and Wales" shall be omitted.

(3) In section 43 (maps of National Parks showing certain areas of moor or heath), in subsection (1A) the words "by the Countryside Commission" shall be omitted and—

(a) in subsection (1B) for the word "shall" there shall be substituted the words "and the Countryside Council for Wales shall each" and for the word "may" there shall be substituted "the Commission and the Council may each";

(b) in subsection (1C), after the word "Commission" there shall be inserted the words "or, as the case may be, the Council".

(4) Section 45 (power to vary orders designating National Parks) shall be subsection (1) of that section and, in that subsection, after the word "Park" in the first place it appears there shall be inserted the words "in England"; and at the end there shall be inserted, as subsection (2) of that section, the following words—

"(2) Subsection (1) shall apply to the Countryside Council for Wales, in relation to any National Park in Wales, as it applies to the Countryside Commission in relation to any National Park in England."

(5) In section 47(2) (power of Secretary of State to give grants) after the word "Commission" there shall be inserted the words "or to the Countryside Council for Wales".

(6) In section 49 (extension of power to appoint wardens), in subsection (1)(b), after the word "authority" in the second place it appears there shall be inserted the words ", the Countryside Council for Wales." and, in subsection (4), after the word "Commission"

in both places it appears there shall be inserted the words "or the Countryside Council for Wales".

The Road Traffic Regulation Act 1984 (c. 27)

7 In section 22 of the Road Traffic Regulation Act 1984 (traffic regulation orders in special areas), in subsection (1)(a)(iv), after the word "Commission" there shall be inserted the words "or the Countryside Council for Wales" and, in subsection (4), for the words from "or" in the first place it appears to "may", in the second place it appears, there shall be substituted ", the Countryside Council for Wales and the Countryside Commission for Scotland may each".

The Water Act 1989 (c. 15)

8 In section 152 of the Water Act 1989 (restrictions on disposal of land) in subsection (5)(c)(i), after the word "Commission" there shall be inserted the words "(as respects land in England) or the Countryside Council for Wales (as respects land in Wales)"; and, in subsection (5)(d),after the word "Commission", where it first appears there shall be inserted the words "or the Countryside Council for Wales" and at the end there shall be inserted the words "or that Council".

SCHEDULE 9

Section 132.

AMENDMENT OF ENACTMENTS CONFERRING NATURE CONSERVANCY FUNCTIONS

National Parks and Access to the Countryside Act 1949 (c. 97)

1 (1) The National Parks and Access to the Countryside Act 1949 shall be amended as follows.

(2) After section 15 there shall be inserted the following section—

"15A Meaning of "Nature Conservancy Council"

"15A "15A Meaning of "Nature Conservancy Council"

In this Part of this Act references to "the Nature Conservancy Council" are references—

(a) in relation to land in England, to the Nature Conservancy Council for England;

(b) in relation to land in Scotland, to the Nature Conservancy Council for Scotland; and

(c) in relation to land in Wales, to the Countryside Council for Wales."

(3) In section 16(5) (agreements in Scotland for establishing nature reserves), in paragraph (c) for the words "Nature Conservancy Council" there shall be substituted " Nature Conservancy Council for Scotland".

(4) In section 103 (general provisions as to acquisition of land)—

(a) in subsection (1), after the words "the Nature Conservancy Council" there shall be inserted the words "(as defined in section 15A of this Act)"; and

(b) in subsection (2), for the words "the Nature Conservancy Council" in both places there shall be substituted the words "the Nature Conservancy Council for Scotland".

(5) In section 106 (supplementary provisions as to bye-laws), in subsection (1), after the words "the Nature Conservancy Council" there shall be inserted the words "(as defined in section 15A of this Act)".

Deer (Scotland) Act 1959 (c. 40)

2 In section 1 of the Deer (Scotland) Act 1959 (constitution of the Red Deer Commission), in subsection (4)(a) there shall be inserted at the end the words "for Scotland".

Deer Act 1963 (c. 36)

3 In section 11 of the Deer Act 1963 (power to grant licences), after subsection (2) there shall be inserted—

"(3) In this section "the Nature Conservancy Council" means in relation to the doing of an act in Wales, the Countryside Council for Wales and in relation to the doing of an act in England, the Nature Conservancy Council for England".

Countryside Act 1968 (c. 41)

4 (1) The Countryside Act 1968 shall be amended as follows.

(2) In section 15 (areas of special scientific interest)—

(a) in subsection (2), the words "in the national interest" shall be omitted and, after the words "any such land" there shall be inserted the words "(or of any adjacent land)"; and

(b) after subsection (6), there shall be inserted the following subsection—

"(6A) In this section references to "the Nature Conservancy Council" or "the Council" are references to the Nature Conservancy Council for England, the Nature Conservancy Council for Scotland or the Council, according as the land in question is in England, Scotland or Wales".

(3) In section 37 (protection for interests in countryside) for the words "Nature Conservancy Council" there shall be substituted the words ", the Council, the Nature Conservancy Council for England and the Nature Conservancy Council for Scotland".

Conservation of Seals Act 1970 (c. 30)

5 In section 10 of the Conservation of Seals Act 1970 (power to grant licences), after subsection (4) there shall be inserted the following subsection—

"(5) In this section a reference to "the Nature Conservancy Council" is a reference to the Nature Conservancy Council for England, the Nature Conservancy Council for Scotland or the Countryside Council for Wales, according as the area in question is in or is in waters adjacent to England, Scotland or Wales."

Badgers Act 1973 (c. 57)

6 (1) Section 9 of the Badgers Act 1973 (power to grant licences) shall be amended as follows.

(2) In subsection (2)(a), for the words "Nature Conservancy Council" there shall be substituted the words "Nature Conservancy Council for England, the Nature Conservancy Council for Scotland or the Countryside Council for Wales (according as the area specified in the licence is in England, Scotland or Wales)".

(3) In subsection (4)—

(a) for the words from "the Nature" to "functions" there shall be substituted the words "each of the following bodies, namely, the Nature Conservancy Council for England, the Nature Conservancy Council for Scotland and the Countryside Council for Wales as to the exercise in the respective areas of those Councils of the functions of those Ministers"; and

(b) after the word "Council" in the second place it appears, there shall be inserted the words "for the area specified in the licence".

Import of Live Fish (Scotland) Act 1978 (c. 35)

7 In section 1 of the Import of Live Fish (Scotland) Act 1978 (power to limit imports) in subsection (2), after the word "Council" there shall be inserted the words "for Scotland".

Import of Live Fish (England and Wales) Act 1980 (c. 27)

8 In section 1 of the Import of Live Fish (England and Wales) Act 1980 (power to limit imports), in subsection (2) after the word "Council" there shall be inserted the words "for England, the Countryside Council for Wales".

Highways Act 1980 (c. 66)

9 In section 105A of the Highways Act 1980 (environmental assessment of highway projects), for subsection (6)(c) there shall be substituted the following paragraph—

"(c) the Nature Conservancy Council for England or the Countryside Council for Wales, if it relates to land in England or, as the case may be, in Wales, falling within paragraph (c)."

Animal Health Act 1981 (c. 22)

10 (1) The Animal Health Act 1981 shall be amended as follows.

(2) In section 21 (destruction of wildlife on infection)—

(a) in subsection (3), after the word "Council" there shall be inserted the words "for the area to which it will apply";

(b) in subsection (9), after the definition of "animals" there shall be inserted the following definition—

""Nature Conservancy Council" means the Nature Conservancy Council for England, the Nature Conservancy Council for Scotland or the Countryside Council for Wales,".

(3) In section 22 (powers of entry for s.21), in subsection (7)(a) for the words from "the Nature Conservancy" to "1973", there shall be substituted the words "a Nature Conservancy Council under section 132 of the Environmental Protection Act 1990".

Wildlife and Countryside Act 1981 (c. 69)

11 (1) The Wildlife and Countryside Act 1981 shall be amended as follows.

(2) In section 10(5) (consultation with Council required before taking or killing a bat) after the word "Council" there shall be inserted the words "for the area in which the house is situated or, as the case may be, the act is to take place".

(3) In section 15(2) (endangered species) for the word "Council" there shall be substituted the word "Councils".

(4) In section 16 (power to grant licences)—

(a) in subsection (9)(a) and (9)(c), before the word "Nature" there shall be inserted the word "relevant";

(b) in subsection (10)(a), for the words "the Nature Conservancy Council" there shall be substituted the words "each of the Nature Conservancy Councils" and, after the word "exercise" there shall be inserted the words "in the area of that Council";

(c) in subsection (10)(b), before the word "Council" there shall be inserted the word "relevant Nature Conservancy"; and

(d) after subsection (10) there shall be inserted the following subsection—

"(11) For the purposes of this section a reference to a relevant Nature Conservancy Council is a reference to the Nature Conservancy Council for the area in which it is proposed to carry on the activity requiring a licence."

(5) In section 22(3) (power of Secretary of State to amend Schedules 5 or 8 to Act) for the words "to him by the Nature Conservancy Council" there shall be substituted the words "jointly to him by the Nature Conservancy Councils", and at the end of that subsection there shall be inserted the words—

"and the functions of the Nature Conservancy Councils under this subsection shall be special functions of the Councils for the purposes of section 133 of the Environmental Protection Act 1990".

(6) In section 24 (functions of Nature Conservancy Council)—

(a) in subsection (1), for the word "Council" there shall be substituted the words "Councils, acting jointly,", for the words "the passing of this Act" there shall be substituted the words "30th October 1991" and at the end there shall be inserted the words—

"and the functions of the Nature Conservancy Councils under this subsection shall be special functions of the Councils for the purposes of section 133 of the Environmental Protection Act 1990";

(b) in subsection (2), for the words from "the Council" to the end there shall be substituted the words "to that advice being given.";

(c) for subsection (3) there shall be substituted the following subsection—

"(3) The Secretary of State shall lay before each House of Parliament a copy of any advice so given and the statements accompanying it."; and

(d) in subsection (4), for the word "Council" there shall be substituted the words "Nature Conservancy Councils".

(7) In section 27 (interpretation of Part I)—

(a) in subsection (1), in the definition of authorised person, for the words "the Nature Conservancy Council" there shall be substituted the words "any of the Nature Conservancy Councils"; and

(b) after subsection (3) there shall be inserted the following subsection—

"(3A) Any reference in this Part to the Nature Conservancy Councils is a reference to the Nature Conservancy Council for England, the Nature Conservancy Council for Scotland and the Countryside Council for Wales."

(8) In Part II (nature conservation etc.), before section 28 there shall be inserted the following section—

"27A Construction of references to Nature Conservancy Council

"27A "27A Construction of references to Nature Conservancy Council

In this Part references to "the Nature Conservancy Council" are, unless the contrary intention appears, references—

(a) in relation to land in, or land covered by waters adjacent to, England, to the Nature Conservancy Council for England;

(b) in relation to land in, or land covered by waters adjacent to, Scotland, to the Nature Conservancy Council for Scotland; and

(c) in relation to land in, or land covered by waters adjacent to, Wales, to the Countryside Council for Wales;

and references to "the Council" shall be construed accordingly."

(9) In section 29 (special protection for certain areas of special scientific interest), in subsection (4)(a), for the words "commencement date" there shall be substituted the words "making of the order".

(10) In section 29 (special protection for certain areas of special scientific interest), in subsection (4)(a), after the word "Council" there shall be inserted the word "written".

(11) In section 29 (protection for areas of special scientific interest), in subsection (11), for the words "paragraph 17 of Schedule 3 to the Nature Conservancy Council Act 1973" there shall be substituted the words "paragraph 20 of Schedule 6 to the Environmental Protection Act 1990".

(12) In section 33 (Ministerial guidance) in subsection (1) for the word "Council" there shall be substituted the word "Councils".

(13) In section 52 (interpretation of Part II), in subsection (1) at the end there shall be inserted the following words—

"the Nature Conservancy Councils" means the Nature Conservancy Council for England, the Nature Conservancy Council for Scotland and the Countryside Council for Wales;

and references to "the Nature Conservancy Council" shall be construed in accordance with section 27A.

Roads (Scotland) Act 1984 (c. 54)

12 In section 20A of the Roads (Scotland) Act 1984 (environmental assessment of roads projects), in subsection (6)(c) after the word "Council" there shall be inserted the words "for Scotland".

Agriculture Act 1986 (c. 49)

13 In section 18 of the Agriculture Act 1986 (environmentally sensitive areas), in subsection (2)—

(a) in paragraph (a) after the word "Council" there shall be inserted the words "for England";

(b) in paragraph (b) for the words "Countryside Commission and the Nature Conservancy Council" there shall be substituted the words "Countryside Council for Wales";

(c) in paragraph (c) after the word "Council" there shall be inserted the words "for Scotland".

Channel Tunnel Act 1987 (c. 53)

14 In paragraph 5 of Schedule 2, and in paragraph 17 of Schedule 3, to the Channel Tunnel Act 1987, after the words "Nature Conservancy Council" there shall be inserted the words "for England".

Norfolk and Suffolk Broads Act 1988 (c. 4)

15 In the Norfolk and Suffolk Broads Act 1988, for each reference to the Nature Conservancy Council there shall be substituted a reference to the Nature Conservancy Council for England.

Electricity Act 1989 (c. 29)

16 In Schedule 9 to the Electricity Act 1989 (preservation of amenity)—

(a) in paragraph 2(2) for the words from "the Nature" to "Wales", where it first appears, there shall be substituted the words "and—

    (a) where the activities which he is authorised by his licence to carry on include activities in England, the Nature Conservancy Council for England and the Historic Buildings and Monuments Commission for England; and

    (b) where those activities include activities in Wales, the Countryside Council for Wales and"; and

(b) in paragraph 4(2), after the words "Conservancy Council" there shall be inserted the words "for Scotland".

Water Act 1989 (c. 15)

17 (1) The Water Act 1989 shall be amended as follows.

(2) In section 9 (environmental duties)—

(a) in subsection (1) after the words "Conservancy Council" there shall be inserted the words "for England or the Countryside Council for Wales" and after the word "land" where it first appears there shall be inserted the words "in England or (as the case may be) in Wales";

(b) in subsection (4), after the word "Council" there shall be inserted the words "in question".

(3) In section 10 (codes of practice), in subsection (4) after the words "Conservancy Council" there shall be inserted the words "for England, the Countryside Council for Wales".

(4) In section 152 (restriction on disposals of land), in subsection (5)(c)(i) after the word "interest" there shall be inserted the words "in England" and after the word "Council" there shall be inserted the words "for England".

SCHEDULE 10

Sections 135, 136 and 137.

TRANSFER SCHEMES AND STAFF OF EXISTING COUNCILS

PART I

TRANSFER SCHEMES: NATURE CONSERVANCY COUNCIL

Making and approval of schemes

1 (1) Before such date or dates as the Secretary of State may direct, the Nature Conservancy Council shall make, and submit to the Secretary of State for his approval, their transfer scheme or schemes under section 135 of this Act (in this Part of this Schedule referred to as a "transfer scheme").

(2) A transfer scheme shall not take effect unless approved by the Secretary of State, who may modify such a scheme before approving it.

(3) The Secretary of State may make a transfer scheme himself if—

(a) he decides not to approve a scheme which has been submitted to him before the due date (with or without modifications); or

(b) no scheme is submitted to him for approval before the due date;

but nothing in this sub-paragraph shall prevent the Secretary of State from approving any scheme which may be submitted to him after the due date.

(4) A scheme made by the Secretary of State shall be treated for all purposes as having been made by the Council and approved by him.

Modification of schemes

2 (1) If at any time after a transfer scheme has come into force the Secretary of State considers it appropriate to do so, having consulted any of the Councils established by section 128 of this Act (in this Schedule referred to as "the new Councils") which may be affected, he may by order provide that the scheme shall for all purposes be deemed to have come into force with such modifications as may be specified in the order.

(2) An order under sub-paragraph (1) above may make, with effect from the coming into force of the scheme, such provision as could have been made by the scheme and in connection with giving effect to that provision from that time may contain such supplemental, consequential and transitional provision as the Secretary of State considers appropriate.

Provision of information to Secretary of State

3 It shall be the duty of the Nature Conservancy Council and the new Councils to provide the Secretary of State with all such information and other assistance as he may reasonably require for the purposes of or in connection with the exercise of any power conferred on him by paragraphs 1 and 2 above.

Contents of schemes

4 A transfer scheme may—

(a) define the property, rights and liabilities to be allocated to a particular new Council by specifying or describing them or by referring to all the property, rights and liabilities comprised in a specified part of the undertaking of the Nature Conservancy Council (or partly in one way and partly in the other);

(b) create in favour of a new Council—

(i) an interest in or right over property transferred in accordance with the scheme (or any earlier scheme) to another new Council;

(ii) new rights and liabilities as between that Council and the others;

(c) provide that any rights or liabilities specified or described in the scheme shall, or shall to any extent, be enforceable either by or against each of the new Councils or by or against any two of the new Councils which are so specified;

(d) require a new Council to enter into written agreements with, or execute other instruments in favour of, another new Council;

and a scheme may make such supplemental, incidental and consequential provision as the Nature Conservancy Council considers appropriate (including provision as to the order in which transfers or transactions are to be regarded as having occurred).

5 For the avoidance of doubt property, rights and liabilities of the Nature Conservancy Council may be allocated to a new Council notwithstanding—

(a) that they would not, or would not without the consent or concurrence of another person, otherwise be capable of being transferred or assigned;

(b) that, in the case of foreign property, steps must be taken by the Council to secure its effective vesting under the relevant foreign law.

PART II

TRANSFER SCHEMES: THE COUNTRYSIDE COMMISSION

Making and approval of schemes

6 (1) Before such date or dates as the Secretary of State may direct, the Countryside Commission shall make, and submit to the Secretary of State for his approval, their

transfer scheme or schemes under section 136 of this Act (in this Part of this Schedule referred to as a "transfer scheme").

(2) A transfer scheme shall not take effect unless approved by the Secretary of State, who may modify such a scheme before approving it.

(3) The Secretary of State may make a transfer scheme himself if—

(a) he decides not to approve a scheme which has been submitted to him before the due date (with or without modifications); or

(b) no scheme is submitted to him for approval before the due date;

but nothing in this sub-paragraph shall prevent the Secretary of State from approving any scheme which may be submitted to him after the due date.

(4) A scheme made by the Secretary of State shall be treated for all purposes as having been made by the Countryside Commission and approved by him.

Modification of schemes

7 (1) If at any time after a transfer scheme has come into force the Secretary of State considers it appropriate to do so, having consulted the Countryside Council for Wales and the Countryside Commission, he may by order provide that the scheme shall for all purposes be deemed to have come into force with such modifications as may be specified in the order.

(2) An order under sub-paragraph (1) above may make, with effect from the coming into force of the scheme, such provision as could have been made by the scheme and in connection with giving effect to that provision from that time may contain such supplemental, consequential and transitional provision as the Secretary of State considers appropriate.

Provision of information to Secretary of State

8 It shall be the duty of the Countryside Council for Wales and the Countryside Commission to provide the Secretary of State with all such information and other assistance as he may reasonably require for the purposes of or in connection with the exercise of any power conferred on him by paragraphs 6 and 7 above.

Contents of schemes

9 (1) A transfer scheme may—

(a) define the property, rights and liabilities to be allocated to the Countryside Council for Wales by specifying or describing them or by referring to all the property, rights and liabilities comprised in a specified part of the undertaking of the Countryside Commission (or partly in one way and partly in the other);

(b) create in favour of the Countryside Commission an interest in or right over property transferred in accordance with the scheme (or any earlier scheme) to the Countryside Council for Wales;

(c) require the Countryside Council for Wales to enter into written agreements with, or execute other instruments in favour of, the Countryside Commission;

and a scheme may make such supplemental, incidental and consequential provision as the Countryside Commission consider appropriate (including provision as to the order in which transfers or transactions are to be regarded as having occurred).

(2) Paragraph 5 above shall apply to transfer schemes under section 136 of this Act.

PART III

EMPLOYMENT OF STAFF OF EXISTING BODIES

Proposals for staff of Nature Conservancy Council

10 Not later than such date or dates as the Secretary of State may determine, the Nature Conservancy Council shall prepare and submit to the Secretary of State for approval proposals that would secure that an offer is made by one of the new Councils to each person who will be entitled to receive an offer under section 137 of this Act.

11 (1) The Secretary of State may, after consultation with the new Councils—

(a) approve the proposals submitted to him under paragraph 10 above or modify the proposals before approving them;

(b) if he decides not to approve the proposals or if the Nature Conservancy Council fail to submit the proposals by the due date, make his own proposals;

and any proposals made by the Secretary of State shall be treated for all purposes as if they were made by the Council and approved by him.

(2) It shall be the duty of the Nature Conservancy Council and the new Councils to provide the Secretary of State with all such information and other assistance as he may reasonably require for the purposes of or in connection with the exercise of any power conferred on him by this paragraph.

Proposals for certain staff of the Countryside Commission

12 Not later than such date or dates as the Secretary of State may determine, the Countryside Commission shall prepare and submit to the Secretary of State for approval proposals as to which of their employees are to receive offers of employment from the Countryside Council for Wales under section 137 of this Act.

13 (1) The Secretary of State may, after consultation with the Countryside Council for Wales—

(a) approve the proposals submitted to him under paragraph 12 above or modify the proposals before approving them;

(b) if he decides not to approve the proposals or if the Countryside Commission fail to submit the proposals by the due date, make his own proposals;

and any proposals made by the Secretary of State shall be treated for all purposes as if they were made by the Commission and approved by him.

(2) It shall be the duty of the Countryside Commission and the Countryside Council for Wales to provide the Secretary of State with all such information and other assistance as he may reasonably require for the purposes of or in connection with the exercise of any power conferred on him by this paragraph.

Offers of employment

14 (1) Each new Council shall, before such date as the Secretary of State may direct, make offers of employment in accordance with this paragraph to those persons allocated to that Council by the proposals under paragraph 10 above as approved by the Secretary of State.

(2) The Countryside Council for Wales shall, before such date as the Secretary of State may direct, make offers of employment in accordance with this paragraph to those persons who are the subject of proposals under paragraph 12 above as approved by the Secretary of State.

(3) The terms of employment to be offered shall be such that they are, taken as a whole, not less favourable to the person to whom the offer is made than the terms on which he is employed on the date on which the offer is made.

(4) An offer under this paragraph shall not be revocable during the period of 3 months commencing with the date on which it is made.

Continuity of employment, redundancy etc.

15 Where a person becomes an employee of a new Council in consequence of an offer made under paragraph 14(1) or (2) above, then, for the purposes of the Employment Protection (Consolidation) Act 1978, his period of employment with the Nature Conservancy Council, or as the case may be, the Countryside Commission shall count as a period of employment by the new Council and the change of employment shall not break the continuity of the period of employment.

16 Where an offer is made to a person in pursuance of paragraph 14(1) or (2) above, none of the redundancy procedures applicable to such a person shall apply to him; and where that person ceases to be employed by the Nature Conservancy Council or, as the case may be, the Countryside Commission—

(a) on becoming employed by a new Council, or

(b) having unreasonably refused an offer,

Part VI of the Employment Protection (Consolidation) Act 1978 shall not apply to him and he shall not be treated for the purposes of any superannuation or other pension scheme as having been retired on redundancy.

Disputes

17 (1) Any dispute as to whether an offer under paragraph 14(1) or (2) above complies with sub-paragraph (3) of that paragraph shall be referred to and determined by an industrial tribunal.

(2) An industrial tribunal shall not consider a complaint referred to it under sub-paragraph (1) above unless the complaint is presented to the tribunal before the end of the period of 3 months beginning with the date of the offer or, where the tribunal is satisfied that it was not reasonably practicable for that to be done, within such further period as the tribunal considers reasonable.

(3) Subject to sub-paragraph (4) below, there shall be no appeal from the decision of an industrial tribunal under this paragraph.

(4) An appeal to the Employment Appeal Tribunal may be made only on a point of law arising from a decision of, or in proceedings before, an industrial tribunal under this paragraph.

SCHEDULE 11

Section 139.

Transitional Provisions and Savings for Part VII

Part I

Countryside Functions

Preliminary

1 In this Part of this Schedule—

"the appointed day" means the day appointed under section 130(4) of this Act;

"the Commission" means the Countryside Commission;

"the Council" means the Countryside Council for Wales;

"relevant", in relation to anything done by or in relation to the Commission before the appointed day, means anything which, if it were to be done on or after the appointed day, would be done by or in relation to the Council or, as the case may be, by or in relation to both the Commission (so far as concerning England) and the Council (so far as concerning Wales).

Continuity of exercise of functions

2 (1) Any relevant thing done by or in relation to the Commission before the appointed day shall, so far as is required for continuing its effect on and after that date, have effect as if done by or in relation to the Council or, as the case may be, by or in relation to both the Council and the Commission.

(2) Any relevant thing which, immediately before the appointed day, is in the process of being done by or in relation to the Commission may be continued by or in relation to the Council or, as the case may be, by or in relation to both the Council and the Commission.

Construction of references to the Countryside Commission

3 (1) This paragraph applies to any provision of any agreement, or of any instrument or other document, subsisting immediately before the appointed day which refers (in whatever terms) to the Commission and does so (or is to be construed as doing so) in relation to, or to things being done in or in connection with, Wales.

(2) Any provision to which this paragraph applies shall, subject to sub-paragraphs (3) and (4) below, have effect on and after the appointed day with the substitution for, or the inclusion in, any reference to the Commission of a reference to the Council, according as the reference concerns Wales only or concerns both England and Wales.

(3) Any provision to which this paragraph applies which refers in general terms to members of or to persons employed by or agents of the Commission shall have effect on and after the appointed day with the substitution for, or the inclusion in, any such reference of a reference to members of or persons employed by or agents of the Council, according as the reference concerns Wales only or concerns both England and Wales.

(4) Any provision to which this paragraph applies which refers to a member or employee of the Commission shall have effect on and after the appointed day with the substitution for, or the inclusion in, any such reference of—

(a) a reference to such person as the Council may appoint, or

(b) in default of appointment, to the member or employee of the Council who corresponds as nearly as may be to the member or employee in question,

according as the reference concerns Wales only or concerns both England and Wales.

4 (1) This paragraph applies to any provision of a local Act passed, or subordinate legislation made, before the appointed day which refers (in whatever terms) to the Commission and relates to, or to things being done in or in connection with, Wales.

(2) The Secretary of State may by order make such consequential modifications of any provision to which this paragraph applies as appear to him to be necessary or expedient.

(3) Subject to any exercise of the power conferred by sub-paragraph (2) above, any provision to which this paragraph applies shall have effect on and after the appointed day with the substitution for, or inclusion in, any reference to the Commission of a reference to the Council, according as the reference concerns Wales only or concerns both England and Wales.

Existing areas of outstanding natural beauty and long distance routes

5 (1) This paragraph applies to—

(a) any area of land which immediately before the appointed day is an area of outstanding natural beauty designated under section 87 of the 1949 Act of which part is in England and part is in Wales (referred to as "the two parts" of such an area); and

(b) any long distance route under Part IV of that Act of which some parts are in England and other parts in Wales.

(2) On and after the appointed day the two parts of an area to which this paragraph applies shall be treated as if each were a distinct area of outstanding natural beauty; and accordingly, so far as may be necessary for the purpose of applying paragraphs 2 and 3 above, anything done by or in relation to the Commission in relation to both parts of that area shall be treated as having been done in relation to the part in Wales by or in relation to the Council.

(3) On and after the appointed day any route to which this paragraph applies shall not cease, by virtue of this Part of this Act to be a single route for the purposes of Part IV of the 1949 Act; but any function which before that day is exercisable by or in relation to the Commission shall, on and after that day be exercisable by or in relation to the Commission (so far as concerns parts of the route in England) and by or in relation to the Council (so far as concerns parts of the route in Wales).

(4) On or after the appointed day the Commission and the Council shall each exercise any function of theirs in relation to an area or route to which this paragraph applies only after consultation with the other; and the Commission and the Council may make arrangements for discharging any of their functions in relation to such an area or route jointly.

PART II

NATURE CONSERVATION FUNCTIONS

Preliminary

6 In this Part of this Schedule—

"appointed day" means the date appointed under section 131(3) of this Act;

"appropriate new council" shall be construed in accordance with paragraph 7 below; and

"new council" means a council established by section 128(1) of this Act.

7 (1) In this Part of this Schedule a reference to "the appropriate new council" is, in relation to or to things done in connection with property, rights or liabilities of the Nature Conservancy Council which are transferred by section 135(2) of this Act to a new council, a reference to that new council.

(2) Subject to sub-paragraph (1) above, a reference in this Part of this Schedule to "the appropriate new council" is, in relation to anything else done before the appointed day by or in relation to the Nature Conservancy Council in the exercise of or in connection with any function of theirs (other than a function corresponding to a special function of the new councils)—

(a) a reference to the new council by whom the nature conservation function corresponding to that function is exercisable on and after that date; or

(b) where the thing done relates to a matter affecting the area of more than one new council, a reference to each new council by whom the nature conservation function corresponding to that function is exercisable on and after that date;

and in relation to anything done in the exercise of or in connection with any function of the Nature Conservancy Council corresponding to a special function of the new councils a reference to "the appropriate new council" is a reference to the joint committee or, where directions under section 133(5) of this Act have been given, the new council by whom the corresponding special function is dischargeable (on behalf of the new councils) on and after that day.

(3) Any question arising under this paragraph as to which new council is the appropriate new council in relation to any particular function of the Nature Conservancy Council may be determined by a direction given by the Secretary of State.

Continuity of exercise of functions

8 (1) Anything done (or deemed by any enactment to have been done) by or in relation to the Nature Conservancy Council before the appointed day shall, so far as is required

for continuing its effect on and after that date, have effect as if done by or in relation to the appropriate new council.

(2) Anything which immediately before the appointed day is in the process of being done by or in relation to the Nature Conservancy Council may be continued by or in relation to the appropriate new council as if it had been done by or in relation to that council.

Construction of references to the Nature Conservancy Council

9 (1) This paragraph applies to any agreement, any instrument and any other document subsisting immediately before the appointed day which refers (in whatever terms) to the Nature Conservancy Council, other than a scheme provided by that Council under paragraph 12 of Schedule 3 to the Nature Conservancy Council Act 1973.

(2) Any agreement, instrument or other document to which this paragraph applies shall have effect on and after the appointed day with the substitution—

(a) for any reference to the Nature Conservancy Council of a reference to the appropriate new council;

(b) for any reference in general terms to members of or to persons employed by or agents of the Nature Conservancy Council of a reference to members of or persons employed by or agents of the appropriate new council; and

(c) for any reference to a member or officer of the Nature Conservancy Council of a reference to such person as the appropriate new council may appoint or, in default of appointment, to the member or employee of that council who corresponds as nearly as may be to the member or officer in question.

10 (1) This paragraph applies to any provision of a local Act passed, or subordinate legislation made, before the appointed day which refers (in whatever terms) to the Nature Conservancy Council.

(2) The Secretary of State may by order make such consequential modifications of any provision to which this paragraph applies as appear to him to be necessary or expedient.

(3) Subject to any exercise of the power conferred by sub-paragraph (2) above, any provision to which this paragraph applies shall have effect on and after the appointed day with the substitution for each reference to the Nature Conservancy Council of a reference to such one or more of the new councils as may be appropriate, according as the provision relates to, or to things being done in or in connection with, England, Scotland or Wales.

Pensions for Nature Conservancy Council staff

11 (1) The repeal by this Act of paragraph 12 of Schedule 3 to the Nature Conservancy Council Act 1973 shall not affect the operation on and after the appointed day of any scheme provided by the Nature Conservancy Council for the payment to or in respect of its officers of pensions, allowances or gratuities.

(2) Any such scheme shall have effect on and after the appointed day with the substitution for any reference to the Nature Conservancy Council of a reference to the Secretary of State.

Existing nature reserves and areas of special scientific interest

12 (1) This paragraph applies to any land which, immediately before the appointed day is—

(a) a nature reserve (within the meaning of Part III of the 1949 Act) which is managed by, or under an agreement entered into with, the Nature Conservancy Council or which is the subject of a declaration under section 35 of the 1981 Act; or

(b) an area of special scientific interest which has been notified by the Nature Conservancy Council under section 28(1) of the 1981 Act or is treated by section 28(13) of that Act as having been notified under section 28(1)(a) of that Act or is an area to which an order under section 29(1) of that Act relates;

and of which part is in England and part is in Wales or, as the case may be, part is in England and part is in Scotland (referred to as "the two parts" of such a reserve or area).

(2) On and after the appointed day, the two parts of any reserve or area to which this paragraph applies shall be treated as if each were a distinct nature reserve or area of special scientific interest; and accordingly, so far as may be necessary for the purpose of applying paragraphs 8 and 9 above, anything done by or in relation to the Nature Conservancy Council affecting both parts of that reserve or area shall be treated as having been done by or in relation to each of the two parts separately.

(3) On and after the appointed day the new council exercising functions as respects either part of a reserve or area to which this paragraph applies shall exercise those functions only after consultation with the new council exercising functions as respects the other part; and those councils may make arrangements for discharging any of those functions jointly.

PART III

SUPPLEMENTARY

13 Paragraphs 3, 4, 5, 8, 9, 10 and 12 above are without prejudice to any provision made by or under this Part of this Act in relation to any particular functions, property, rights or liabilities; and, in particular, nothing in this Schedule applies in relation to contracts of employment made by the Countryside Commission or the Nature Conservancy Council.

14 The Secretary of State may, in relation to any particular functions of the Countryside Commission or the Nature Conservancy Council, by order exclude, or modify or supplement any provision of this Schedule or make such other transitional provision as he may think necessary or expedient.

15 In this Schedule "the 1949 Act" means the National Parks and Access to the Countryside Act 1949 and "the 1981 Act" means the Wildlife and Countryside Act 1981.

SCHEDULE 12

Sections 140 and 142.

INJURIOUS OR HAZARDOUS SUBSTANCES: ADVISORY COMMITTEE

1 The Secretary of State shall appoint the members of the committee, and shall appoint one of those members to be chairman.

2 The committee shall include persons who appear to the Secretary of State to be representative of—

(a) persons engaged in carrying on industrial or commercial undertakings;

(b) persons having scientific knowledge of matters concerning pollution of the environment;

(c) bodies concerned with the protection or improvement of the environment; and

(d) bodies concerned with the protection of persons using substances or articles subject to regulation under section 140 or 142 of this Act.

3 The Secretary of State may make provision by regulations with respect to the terms on which members of the committee are to hold and vacate office, including the terms on which any person appointed as chairman is to hold and vacate office as chairman.

4 The Secretary of State shall provide the committee with such services and other facilities as appear to him to be necessary or expedient for the proper performance of the committee's functions.

5 The Secretary of State may pay to the members of the committee such remuneration (if any) and such allowances as may be determined by the Secretary of State with the consent of the Treasury.

SCHEDULE 13

Section 144.

AMENDMENTS OF HAZARDOUS SUBSTANCES LEGISLATION

PART I

ENGLAND AND WALES

1 The Planning (Hazardous Substances) Act 1990 shall be amended as provided in this Part of this Schedule.

2 (1) Section 2 (appropriate Minister to be hazardous substances authority for land used or to be used by statutory undertakers) shall be omitted.

(2) In section 7(3), for the words from "means" to "with" in the third place it occurs there shall be substituted the words "means consultations with the Health and Safety Executive and with".

(3) In section 10(2), for the words from the beginning to "3" there shall be substituted the words "A hazardous substances authority".

(4) In section 28(1)—

(a) in paragraph (a), for the words following the word "consent" there shall be substituted the words "made to that authority;

(aa) to applications under section 17(1) made to that authority;"; and

(b) after paragraph (d), there shall be inserted the following words—

"; and every such register shall also contain such information as may be prescribed as to the manner in which applications for hazardous substances consent have been dealt with."

(5) In section 29, in subsection (3) and (4), for the words "appropriate body" there shall be substituted the words "Health and Safety Executive".

(6) In section 38(5) for the words "1 to 3" there shall be substituted "1, 3".

(7) In section 39(1), in the definition of "hazardous substances authority", for the word "to", in the second place it occurs, there shall be inserted the word "and".

3 In section 7(1)(a) (applications for consent), after the word "applications" there shall be inserted the words "under this Act".

4 In section 11 (deemed hazardous substances consent in transitional cases)—

(a) in subsection (2) for the words "immediately before the relevant date" there shall be substituted the words "while it was so present"; and

(b) in subsection (7), in paragraph (a), at the beginning there shall be inserted the words "to the condition that" and, for paragraphs (b) and (c), there shall be substituted the words ", and

(b) to such other conditions (if any) as are prescribed for the purposes of this section and are applicable in the case of that consent."

5 In section 12 (deemed consent: government authorisation), at the end there shall be added the following subsection—

"(6) A government department or the Secretary of State shall, as respects any hazardous substances consent deemed to be granted by virtue of directions under this section, send to the hazardous substances authority concerned any such information as appears to be required by them for the purposes of a register under section 28."

6 In section 13 (applications for hazardous substances consent in place of subsisting consent subject to conditions), subsection (7) shall be omitted.

7 In section 22 (validity of decisions as to applications), in subsection (4), for the words "1971 Act" there shall be substituted the words "principal Act".

8 In section 25(1)(c) (provisions of principal Act capable of application to hazardous substances contravention notices), after "184," there shall be inserted "186,".

9 Before section 27 there shall be inserted the following section—

"26A Fees for consent applications

"26A "26A Fees for consent applications

(1) Provision may be made by regulations for the payment of a fee of the prescribed amount to a hazardous substances authority in respect of an application for, or for the continuation of, hazardous substances consent.

(2) Regulations under this section may provide for the payment to the Secretary of State of a fee of the prescribed amount in respect of any application which is, by virtue of regulations under section 25, deemed to have been made for hazardous substances consent.

(3) Regulations under this section may provide—

(a) for the transfer of prescribed fees received by a hazardous substances authority in respect of any application which is referred to the Secretary of State under section 20;

(b) for the remission or refunding of a prescribed fee (in whole or in part) in prescribed circumstances or in pursuance of a direction given by the Secretary of State;

and the regulations may make different provision for different areas or for different cases or descriptions of cases."

10 In section 303(6) of the Town and Country Planning Act 1990 (meaning of "Planning Acts" for purposes of fees chargeable under that section), at the end there shall be inserted the words "or the Planning (Hazardous Substances) Act 1990.")

PART II

SCOTLAND

11 (1) The Town and Country Planning (Scotland) Act 1972 shall be amended as provided in this paragraph.

(2) Section 56B (appropriate Minister to be planning authority in respect of hazardous substances in relation to land used or to be used by statutory undertakers) shall be omitted.

(3) In section 56D(1)(a) (applications for consent), after the word "applications" there shall be inserted the words "under this Act".

(4) In section 56D(5) for the words from "means" to "with" in the third place it occurs there shall be substituted the words "means consultations with the Health and Safety Executive and with".

(5) After section 56D there shall be inserted the following section—

"56DA Fees

"56DA "56DA Fees

(1) The Secretary of State may by regulations make provision for fees of the prescribed amount in respect of applications for, or for the continuation of, hazardous substances consent—

(a) made to an urban development corporation under section 56A(2) above to be paid to the corporation;

(b) referred to him under section 32 above as having effect by virtue of section 56F below to be paid to him;

(c) deemed to have been made to him under section 85(7) below by virtue of regulations made under section 97B(10) below to be paid to him.

(2) Regulations made under this section may provide for—

(a) the transfer to the Secretary of State of any fee received by a planning authority in respect of an application referred to in paragraph (b) or (c) of subsection (1) above;

(b) the remission or refunding of a prescribed fee (in whole or in part) in prescribed circumstances or in pursuance of a direction given by him;

and the regulations may make different provision for different areas or for different cases or descriptions of cases."

(6) In section 56E(5) for the words "a planning authority other than the appropriate Minister" there shall be substituted the word "they".

(7) In section 56G (deemed consent: government authorisation), at the end there shall be added the following subsection—

"(5) A government department or the Secretary of State shall, as respects any hazardous substances consent deemed to be granted by virtue of directions under this section, send to the planning authority concerned any such information as appears to be required by them for the purposes of a register under section 56N."

(8) In section 56H (applications for hazardous substances consent in place of subsisting consent subject to conditions) subsection (5) shall be omitted.

(9) In section 56N(1)—

(a) in paragraph (a), for the words following the word "consent" there shall be substituted the words "made to that authority;

(aa) to applications under section 56K(2) above made to that authority;" and

(b) after paragraph (d), there shall be inserted the following words—

", and every such register shall also contain such information as may be prescribed as to the manner in which applications for hazardous substances consent have been dealt with."

(10) In section 56O, in subsections (2) and (3), for the words "appropriate body" there shall be substituted the words "Health and Safety Executive".

(11) In section 97B(10)(c) (hazardous substances contravention notices), after "89A" there shall be inserted "and 166".

12 (1) Section 38 of the Housing and Planning Act 1986 (transitional provisions) shall be amended as provided in this paragraph.

(2) In subsection (4), for the words "immediately before the commencement date" there shall be substituted the words "while it was so present".

(3) In subsection (9)—

(a) for the words "subject to the conditions that— (a)" there shall be substituted the words "subject to—

(a) the condition that";

(b) for paragraphs (b) and (c) there shall be substituted—

"(b) such other conditions (if any) as are prescribed, by statutory instrument subject to annulment in pursuance of a resolution of either House of Parliament, for the purposes of this section and are applicable in the case of that consent".

13 In section 87 of the Local Government, Planning and Land Act 1980 (fees for planning applications etc.), at the end there shall be inserted the following subsection—

"(9) Without prejudice to the generality of subsection (1) above, the reference in that subsection to an application for any consent includes, in relation to a planning authority in Scotland, an application under section 56K(2) of the Town and Country Planning (Scotland) Act 1972 for the continuation of hazardous substances consent."

SCHEDULE 14

Section 148.

AMENDMENTS OF THE PREVENTION OF OIL POLLUTION ACT 1971

1 The Prevention of Oil Pollution Act 1971 shall be amended as follows.

2 In section 19 (prosecutions), after subsection (4), there shall be inserted the following subsection—

"(4A) Any document required or authorised, by virtue of any statutory provision, to be served on a foreign company for the purposes of the institution of, or otherwise in connection with, proceedings for an offence under section 2(2A) of this Act alleged to have been committed by the company as the owner of a vessel shall be treated as duly served on that company if the document is served on the master of the vessel; and any person authorised to serve any document for the purposes of the institution of, or otherwise in connection with, proceedings for an offence under this Act (whether or not in pursuance of the foregoing provisions of this subsection) shall, for that purpose, have the right to go on board the vessel in question.

(4B) In subsection (4A) of this section a "foreign company" means a company or body which is not one to whom any of the following provisions applies—

(a) sections 695 and 725 of the Companies Act 1985;

(b) Articles 645 and 673 of the Companies (Northern Ireland) Order 1986,

so as to authorise the service of the document in question under any of those provisions."

3 After that section there shall be inserted the following section—

"19A Power to detain vessels

"19A "19A Power to detain vessels

(1) Where a harbour master has reason to believe that the master or owner of a vessel has committed an offence under section 2(2A) of this Act by the discharge from the vessel of oil, or a mixture containing oil, into the waters of the harbour, the harbour master may detain the vessel.

(2) Subsections (1) and (2) of section 692 of the Merchant Shipping Act 1894 (enforcing detention of ship) shall apply in relation to a vessel detained under subsection (1) of this section as they apply in relation to a ship detained under that Act but as if—

(a) in subsection (1) (penalties where ship proceeds to sea while subject to detention)—

(i) for the words from "any commissioned officer" to "and if" there were substituted the word "and"; and

(ii) for the reference to competent authority there were substituted a reference to the harbour authority; and

(b) in subsection (2) (penalties where a ship so proceeds to sea when any officer authorised to detain the ship is on board), for any reference to any officer authorised to detain the ship, or any surveyor or officer of the Secretary of State or any officer of Customs and Excise there were substituted a reference to the harbour master or any person acting on his behalf.

(3) Where a harbour master detains a ship other than a United Kingdom ship (within the meaning of section 21(2) of the Merchant Shipping Act 1979) under this section he shall immediately notify the Secretary of State who shall then inform the consul or diplomatic representative of the State whose flag the ship is entitled to fly or the appropriate maritime authorities of that State.

(4) A harbour master who exercises the power conferred by subsection (1) of this section shall immediately release the vessel—

(a) if no proceedings for the offence in question are instituted within the period of 7 days beginning with the day on which the vessel is detained;

(b) if such proceedings, having been instituted within that period, are concluded without the master or owner being convicted;

(c) if either—

(i) the sum of £55,000 is paid to the harbour authority by way of security, or

(ii) security which, in the opinion of the harbour authority, is satisfactory and is for an amount not less than £55,000 is given to the harbour authority,

by or on behalf of the master or owner; or

(d) where the master or owner is convicted of the offence, if any costs or expenses ordered to be paid by him, and any fine imposed on him, have been paid.

(5) The harbour authority shall repay any sum paid in pursuance of subsection (4)(c) of this section or release any security so given—

(a) if no proceedings for the offence in question are instituted within the period of 7 days beginning with the day on which the sum is paid; or

(b) if such proceedings, having been instituted within that period, are concluded without the master or owner being convicted.

(6) Where a sum has been paid, or security has been given, by any person in pursuance of subsection (4)(c) of this section and the master or owner is convicted of the offence in question, the sum so paid or the amount made available under the security shall be applied as follows—

(a) first in payment of any costs or expenses ordered by the court to be paid by the master or owner; and

(b) next in payment of any fine imposed by the court;

and any balance shall be repaid to the first mentioned person.

(7) Any reference in this section to a harbour master or a harbour authority shall, where the harbour in question consists of or includes the whole or any part of a dockyard port within the meaning of the Dockyard Ports Regulation Act 1865, be construed as including a reference to the Queen's harbour master for the port.

(8) For the purposes of this section in its application to England and Wales and, subject to section 30(4A) of this Act, in its application to Northern Ireland—

(a) proceedings for an offence are instituted—

(i) when a justice of the peace issues a summons or warrant under section 1 of the Magistrates' Courts Act 1980 in respect of the offence,

(ii) when a person is charged with the offence after being taken into custody without a warrant,

(iii) when a bill of indictment is preferred by virtue of section 2(2)(b) of the Administration of Justice (Miscellaneous Provisions) Act 1933;

and where the application of this paragraph would result in there being more than one time for the institution of proceedings, they shall be taken to have been instituted at the earliest of those times; and

(b) proceedings for an offence are concluded without the master or owner being convicted on the occurrence of one of the following events—

(i) the discontinuance of the proceedings;

(ii) the acquittal of the master or owner;

(iii) the quashing of the master or owner's conviction for the offence;

(iv) the grant of Her Majesty's pardon in respect of the master or owner's conviction for the offence.

(9) For the purposes of this section in its application to Scotland—

(a) proceedings for an offence are instituted—

(i) on the granting by the sheriff of a warrant in respect of the offence on presentation of a petition under section 12 of the Criminal Procedure (Scotland) Act 1975;

(ii) when, in the absence of a warrant or citation, the master or owner is first brought before a court competent to deal with the case;

(iii) when, in a case where he is liberated upon a written undertaking in terms of section 18(2)(a), 294(2)(a) or 295(1)(a) of the Criminal Procedure (Scotland) Act 1975, the master or owner appears at the specified court at the specified time;

(iv) when, in a case mentioned in paragraph (iii) above where the master or owner fails to appear at the specified court at the specified time, the court grants warrant for his apprehension;

(v) when summary proceedings are commenced in terms of section 331(3) of the Criminal Procedure (Scotland) Act 1975; and

(b) proceedings for an offence are concluded without the master or owner being convicted on the occurrence of one of the following events—

(i) the court makes a finding of not guilty or not proven against the master or owner in respect of the offence;

(ii) the proceedings are expressly abandoned (other than *pro loco et tempore*) by the prosecutor or are deserted simpliciter;

(iii) the conviction is quashed;

(iv) the accused receives Her Majesty's pardon in respect of the conviction.

(10) This section shall not apply in relation to any vessel of Her Majesty's navy or to any Government ship (within the meaning of section 80 of the Merchant Shipping Act 1906)."

4 In section 20(1) (power of court to direct amount of unpaid fine to be levied by distress or poinding and sale of vessel) after the words "is not paid" there shall be inserted the words ", or any costs or expenses ordered to be paid by him are not paid,".

5 In section 24(2) (application of Act to Government ships), for the words "and subsection (4) of section 16" there shall be substituted the words ", subsection (4) of section 16 and subsection (10) of section 19A".

6 In section 25(1) (power to extend provisions of Act to Isle of Man, Channel Islands etc), after the words "other than section 3" there shall be inserted the words "or 19A".

7 In section 30 (provisions as to Northern Ireland), after subsection (4), there shall be inserted the following subsection—

"(4A) In its application to proceedings in Northern Ireland, subsection (8)(a) of section 19A of this Act shall have effect as if—

(a) in sub-paragraph (i), for the references to section 1 of the Magistrates' Courts Act 1980 there were substituted a reference to

Article 20 of the Magistrates' Courts (Northern Ireland) Order 1981; and

(b) for sub-paragraph (iii) there were substituted—

"(iii) when an indictment is presented under section 2(2)(c), (e) or (f) of the Grand Jury (Abolition) Act (Northern Ireland) 1969;"."

SCHEDULE 15

Section 162.

Consequential and Minor Amendments of Enactments

Statutory nuisances: Scotland

1 In section 3 of the Public Health (Scotland) Act 1897 at the end there shall be added the following paragraph—

"The word "ratepayer" means a person who either is liable to pay any of the community charges or community water charges imposed under the Abolition of Domestic Rates Etc. (Scotland) Act 1987 (or would be so liable but for any enactment or anything provided or done under any enactment) or is a non-domestic ratepayer.".

Exclusion of Alkali Works Act for prescribed processes

2 In the Alkali, &c. Works Regulation Act 1906 there shall be inserted, after section 2, the following section—

"2A Relation to Environmental Protection Act 1990, Part I

"2A "2A Relation to Environmental Protection Act 1990, Part I

(1) The preceding provisions of this Part of this Act shall not apply to any process which is a prescribed process as from the date which is the determination date for that process.

(2) The "determination date" for a prescribed process is—

(a) in the case of a process for which an authorisation is granted, the date on which the enforcing authority grants it, whether in pursuance of the application or, on an appeal, of a direction to grant it;

(b) in the case of a process for which an authorisation is refused, the date of the refusal or, on an appeal, of the affirmation of the refusal.

(3) In this section "authorisation", "enforcing authority" and "prescribed process" have the meaning given in section 1 of the Environmental Protection Act 1990 and the reference to an appeal is a reference to an appeal under section 15 of that Act.".

and, immediately before section 25, as section 24A, a section in the same terms as the section 2A inserted after section 2.

Stray dogs

3 (1) The following provisions of the Dogs Act 1906 shall be amended as follows.

(2) The amendments made to section 3 by section 39(2) of the Local Government Act 1988 and section 128(1)(a) of the Civic Government (Scotland) Act 1982 shall cease to have effect.

(3) In section 4—

(a) subsection (1) shall be omitted;

(b) in subsection (2), for the words "so taken to a police station" there shall be substituted the words "taken to a police station in pursuance of section 150(1) of the Environmental Protection Act 1990";

(c) in subsection (2)(a), for the words from "his name and address" to "other" there shall be substituted the words "this fact and shall furnish his name and address and the police officer shall, having complied with the procedure (if any) prescribed under subsection (5) below, allow the finder to remove the dog";

(d) in subsection (3), for the words from "fails" to "section" there shall be substituted the words "removes the dog but fails to keep it for at least one month,"; and

(e) after subsection (3) or, as respects Scotland, subsection (4) there shall be inserted as subsection (4) or subsection (5) the following subsection—

> "( ) The Secretary of State may, by regulations made by statutory instrument, prescribe the procedure to be followed under subsection (2)(a) above and any instrument containing regulations under this subsection shall be subject to annulment in pursuance of a resolution of either House of Parliament."

Statutory nuisances

4 (1) The following provisions of the Public Health Act 1936 (matters deemed statutory nuisances) shall be amended as follows.

(2) In section 141, for the words "Part III of this Act" there shall be substituted the words "Part III of the Environmental Protection Act 1990".

(3) in section 259(1), for the words "Part III of this Act" there shall be substituted the words "Part III of the Environmental Protection Act 1990".

(4) In section 268—

(a) in subsection (1), for the words "Parts III" there shall be substituted the words "Part III of the Environmental Protection Act 1990 and Parts";

(b) in subsection (2), for the words "the said Part III" there shall be substituted the words "Part III of the Environmental Protection Act 1990"; and

(c) in subsection (3), for the words "Part III of this Act" there shall be substituted the words "Part III of the Environmental Protection Act 1990".

5 (1) Section 151 of the Mines and Quarries Act 1954 (matters deemed statutory nuisances) shall be amended as follows.

(2) In subsection (2), for the words "Part III of the Public Health Act 1936" there shall be substituted the words "Part III of the Environmental Protection Act 1990".

(3) In subsection (3), for the words "Part III of the Public Health Act 1936" there shall be substituted the words "Part III of the Environmental Protection Act 1990".

(4) In subsection (5), for the words "Part III of the Public Health Act 1936" there shall be substituted the words "Part III of the Environmental Protection Act 1990".

Exclusion of Clean Air Act 1956 for prescribed processes

6 In the Clean Air Act 1956 there shall be inserted, immediately before section 17, the following section—

"16A Relation to Environmental Protection Act 1990, Part I

"16A "16A Relation to Environmental Protection Act 1990, Part I

(1) The preceding provisions of this Act shall not apply to any process which is a prescribed process as from the date which is the determination date for that process.

(2) The "determination date" for a prescribed process is—

(a) in the case of a process for which an authorisation is granted, the date on which the enforcing authority grants it, whether in pursuance of the application or, on an appeal, of a direction to grant it;

(b) in the case of a process for which an authorisation is refused, the date of the refusal or, on an appeal, of the affirmation of the refusal.

(3) In this section "authorisation", "enforcing authority" and "prescribed process" have the meaning given in section 1 of the Environmental Protection Act 1990 and the reference to an appeal is a reference to an appeal under section 15 of that Act."

Statutory nuisances

7 (1) The following provisions of the Clean Air Act 1956 (references to statutory nuisances) shall be amended as follows.

(2) In section 18(2) and (5) for the words "section ninety-two of the Public Health Act 1936" there shall be substituted the words "the provisions of Part III of the Environmental Protection Act 1990".

(3) In section 21(1)—

(a) for the words "or the Clean Air Act 1968" there shall be substituted the words ", the Clean Air Act 1968 or the Environmental Protection Act 1990"; and

(b) in paragraph (a), at the end, there shall be inserted the words "and Part III of the Environmental Protection Act 1990,"

8 The Radioactive Substances Act 1960 shall be amended by the insertion in Part I of Schedule 1 (exclusion of other controls) at the end, of the following paragraph—

"9 Part III of the Environmental Protection Act 1990."

9 In section 1(1)(g) of the Hovercraft Act 1986 (power to exclude noise nuisance proceedings), after the word "1974" there shall be inserted the words "or Part III of the Environmental Protection Act 1990."

Goods vehicle operators' licences: pollution offences

10 (1) The following provisions of of the Transport Act 1968 shall be amended as follows.

(2) In section 69 (revocation, suspension etc of goods vehicle operators' licence on grounds of convictions, etc)—

(a) in subsection (1)(b)(i), for the words "paragraphs (a) to (fff)" there shall be substituted the words "paragraphs (a) to (ffff)". and

(b) in subsection (4), after paragraph (fff) there shall be inserted the following paragraph—

"(ffff) a conviction of the holder of the licence or a servant or agent of his under—

(i) section 3 of the Control of Pollution Act 1974;

(ii) section 2 of the Refuse Disposal (Amenity) Act 1978;

(iii) section 1 of the Control of Pollution (Amendment) Act 1989, and

(iv) section 33 of the Environmental Protection Act 1990."

(3) In section 108(1) (statutory nuisance proceedings in relation to waterways), for the words "said Act of 1936" there shall be substituted the words "Environmental Protection Act 1990".

National Park Wardens

11 In section 42 of the Countryside Act 1968 (National Park Wardens), in subsection (4)(a), for the words "section 1 of the Litter Act 1983" there shall be substituted the words "section 87 of the Environmental Protection Act 1990".

Exclusion of Clean Air Act 1968 for prescribed processes

12 In the Clean Air Act 1968 there shall be inserted, after section 11, the following section—

"11A Relation to Environmental Protection Act 1990, Part I

"11A "11A Relation to Environmental Protection Act 1990, Part I

(1) The preceding provisions of this Act shall not apply to any process which is a prescribed process as from the date which is the determination date for that process.

(2) The "determination date" for a prescribed process is—

(a) in the case of a process for which an authorisation is granted, the date on which the enforcing authority grants it, whether in pursuance of the application or, on an appeal, of a direction to grant it;

(b) in the case of a process for which an authorisation is refused the date of the refusal or, on an appeal, of the affirmation of the refusal.

(3) In this section "authorisation", "enforcing authority" and "prescribed process" have the meaning given in section 1 of the Environmental

Protection Act 1990 and the reference to an appeal is a reference to an appeal under section 15 of that Act."

Sale of electricity: Scotland

13 In section 170A(3) of the Local Government (Scotland) Act 1973 (restriction on sale of electricity by local authority) after the word "prescribed," there shall be inserted the words "or in cases where it is produced from waste,".

Workplace emissions into the air

14 Section 5 of the Health and Safety at Work etc. Act 1974 (general duty in relation to harmful emissions into the air from prescribed premises) shall be amended by the insertion—

(a) in subsection (1), at the beginning, of the words "Subject to subsection (5) below,"; and

(b) after subsection (4), of the following subsections—

"(5) The foregoing provisions of this section shall not apply in relation to any process which is a prescribed process as from the date which is the determination date for that process.

(6) For the purposes of subsection (6) above, the "determination date" for a prescribed process is—

(a) in the case of a process for which an authorisation is granted, the date on which the enforcing authority grants it, whether in pursuance of the application or, on an appeal, of a direction to grant it;

(b) in the case of a process for which an authorisation is refused, the date of the refusal or, on an appeal, of the affirmation of the refusal.

(7) In subsections (5) and (6) above "authorisation", "enforcing authority" and "prescribed process" have the meaning given in section 1 of the Environmental Protection Act 1990 and the reference to an appeal is a reference to an appeal under section 15 of that Act."

Water, noise and atmospheric pollution

15 (1) The following provisions of the Control of Pollution Act 1974 shall be amended as follows.

(2) In section 30D, after the words "and 1965" there shall be inserted the words "and of the Environmental Protection Act 1990".

(3) In section 61(9), at the end, there shall be inserted the words "(in relation to Scotland) or section 82 of the Environmental Protection Act 1990 (in relation to England and Wales)".

(4) In section 65(8), at the end, there shall be inserted the words "(in relation to Scotland) or section 82 of the Environmental Protection Act 1990 (in relation to England and Wales)".

(5) In section 74(2), after paragraph (b), there shall be inserted the following "; or

(c) under section 80(4) of the Environmental Protection Act 1990,".

(6) In section 76(4)(a), after the words "part of a" there shall be inserted the words "process subject to Part I of the Environmental Protection Act 1990 or".

(7) In section 78(1), after the words "unless the" there shall be inserted the words "burning is part of a process subject to Part I of the Environmental Protection Act 1990 or the".

(8) In section 79(4), after the words "emissions from any" there shall be inserted the words "process subject to Part I of the Environmental Protection Act 1990 or".

(9) In section 80(3), after the words "relates to a" there shall be inserted the words "process subject to Part I of the Environmental Protection Act 1990 or a".

16 (1) The Control of Pollution Act 1974 shall be further amended as follows.

(2) In section 31 (control of pollution of rivers etc.) in subsection (2)(b) at the end there shall be inserted—

"(v) an authorisation granted under Part I of the Environmental Protection Act 1990 for a prescribed process designated for central control; or

(vi) a waste management licence granted under Part II of the Environmental Protection Act 1990; or"

(3) In section 32 (control of discharges into rivers etc.) in subsection (4) after paragraph (b) there shall be inserted "or

(c) is authorised by an authorisation granted under Part I of the Environmental Protection Act 1990 for a prescribed process designated for central control,".

Exclusion of Part II of Control of Pollution Act 1974 for radioactive substances: Scotland

17 For subsection (6) of section 56 of the Control of Pollution Act 1974 (interpretation of Part II) there shall be substituted the following subsection—

"(6) Except as provided by regulations made under this subsection, nothing in this Part of this Act applies to radioactive waste within the meaning of the Radioactive Substances Act 1960; but regulations may—

(a) provide for prescribed provisions of this Part of this Act to have effect with such modifications as the Secretary of State considers appropriate for the purposes of dealing with such radioactive waste;

(b) make such modifications of the Radioactive Substances Act 1960 and any other Act as the Secretary of State considers appropriate in connection with regulations made under paragraph (a) above."

Statutory nuisances

18 In Section 33(2) of the Land Drainage Act 1976 (restriction on deposit of spoil), for the words "Part III of the Public Health Act 1936" there shall be substituted the words "Part III of the Environmental Protection Act 1990".

Refuse Disposal: Scotland

19 (1) Section 1 of the Refuse Disposal (Amenity) Act 1978 (provision by waste disposal authorities of places etc. for disposal of refuse) shall be amended in relation to Scotland as follows.

(2) In subsection (1) at the end there shall be inserted the words "and to dispose of refuse so deposited".

(3) In subsection (6) for the words from "mandamus" to the end of the subsection there shall be substituted the words "by proceedings under section 45 of the Court of Session Act 1988".

(4) In subsection (7) the definition of "local authority" and the word "and" which follows it shall be omitted.

Street cleansing: Scotland

20 In section 25 of the Local Government and Planning (Scotland) Act 1982, for subsection (3) there shall be substituted—

"(3) In subsection (2) above "cleansing" means such cleansing as appears to the islands or as the case may be district council to be necessary in the interests of public health or safety or of the amenities of their area but does not include operations for the removal of snow or ice and "relevant land" means any land, in the open air, to which members of the public have access and which is not comprehended in a public road within the meaning of the Roads (Scotland) Act 1984.".

Byelaws relating to straw or stubble burning

21 Section 43 of the Criminal Justice Act 1982 (creation by byelaws of offences relating to burning of straw or stubble) shall cease to have effect.

Functions assignable to London port health authority

22 In section 7(4) of the Public Health (Control of Disease) Act 1984 (enactments functions under which are assignable to London port health authority), after the paragraph (k) inserted by paragraph 23 of Schedule 6 to the Building Act 1984, there shall be inserted the following paragraphs—

"(l) Part I of the Environmental Protection Act 1990;

(m) Part III of the Environmental Protection Act 1990;".

Street cleaning, etc: restriction of traffic

23 (1) Section 14 of the Road Traffic Regulation Act 1984 (temporary prohibition or restriction of traffic) shall be amended as follows.

(2) In section 14, after subsection (3) there shall be inserted the following subsection—

"(3A) Subject to the following provisions of this section and to sections 15 and 16 of this Act, a highway or roads authority may also make an order under subsection (1) or issue a notice under subsection (3) above where the authority is satisfied or (as the case may be) where it appears to the authority that traffic on the highway or road should be restricted or prohibited for the purpose of enabling the duty imposed by subsection (1)(a) or (2) of section 89 of the Environmental Protection Act 1990 (litter clearing and cleaning) to be discharged."

Statutory nuisance

24 In section 76(1)(b) and (4)(a) of the Building Act 1984, for the words "sections 93 to 96 of the Public Health Act 1936" there shall be substituted the words "section 80 of the Environmental Protection Act 1990".

Registers of deposits etc. at sea: Northern Ireland Assembly control of regulations

25 In section 25(3) of the Food and Environment Protection Act 1985, after paragraph (a)(ii) there shall be inserted the following sub-paragraph—

"(iii) in section 14(8), for the words from "and any such power" onwards there shall be substituted the words "and any such regulations shall be subject to negative resolution within the meaning of section 41(6) of the Interpretation Act (Northern Ireland) 1954; and"".

Constitution of authorities for waste disposal

26 In section 10 of the Local Government Act 1985 (joint arrangements for waste disposal functions), in subsection (4), for the words "Part I of the Control of Pollution Act 1974" there shall be substituted the words "Part II of the Environmental Protection Act 1990".

Meaning of household waste: competition

27 In Schedule 1 to the Local Government Act 1988 (competition: collection of household waste), paragraph 1 shall be amended as follows—

(a) in sub-paragraph (1), the words "In the application of this Part to England and Wales," shall be omitted;
(b) in sub-paragraph (2)(a), for the words "section 12 of the Control of Pollution Act 1974" there shall be substituted the words "section 45 of the Environmental Protection Act 1990";
(c) in sub-paragraph (3), for the words "section 30(4) of the Control of Pollution Act 1974" there shall be substituted the words "section 75(8) of the Environmental Protection Act 1990"; and
(d) sub-paragraph (4) shall be omitted.

Exclusion of Water Act 1989 controls of exercise of trade effluent functions in case of prescribed processes

28 (1) Section 74 of the Water Act 1989 (control by Secretary of State of exercise of trade effluent functions in certain cases) shall be amended as follows.

(2) In subsection (1), after the word "shall" there shall be inserted the words "subject to subsection (3) below".

(3) After subsection (2), there shall be inserted the following subsections—

"(3) The provisions of Schedule 9 shall not apply in relation to any trade effluent produced or to be produced in any process which is a prescribed process designated for central control as from the date which is the determination date for that process.

(4) The "determination date" for a prescribed process is—

(a) in the case of a process for which an authorisation is granted, the date on which the enforcing authority grants it, whether in pursuance of the application or, on an appeal, of a direction to grant it;

(b) in the case of a process for which an authorisation is refused, the date of the refusal or, on an appeal, of the affirmation of the refusal.

(5) In this section, "authorisation", "enforcing authority" and "prescribed process" have the meaning given in section 1 of the Environmental Protection Act 1990 and the references to designation for central control and an appeal are references respectively to designation under section 4 and an appeal under section 15 of that Act."

Exclusion of Part III of Water Act 1989 for discharges from prescribed processes

29 (1) Section 108 of the Water Act 1989 (no pollution offence where discharge authorised) shall be amended as follows.

(2) In subsection (1)—

(a) after paragraph (a), there shall be inserted the following paragraph—

"(aa) an authorisation for a prescribed process designated for central control granted under Part I of the Environmental Protection Act 1990;";

(b) in paragraph (b), at the beginning, there shall be inserted the words "a waste management licence or".

(3) In subsection (9) the word "and" shall be omitted and at the end, there shall be inserted the words "; "waste management licence" means such a licence granted under Part II of the Environmental Protection Act 1990.

Contents of registers of National Rivers Authority

30 In section 117(1) of the Water Act 1989 (registers for purposes of pollution control) at the end, there shall be inserted the following paragraph—

"(f) any matter about which particulars are required to be kept in any register under section 20 of the Environmental Protection Act 1990 (particulars about authorisations for prescribed processes, etc.) by the chief inspector under Part I of that Act.".

Carriers of controlled waste

31 (1) The Control of Pollution (Amendment) Act 1989 shall be amended as follows.

(2) In the following provisions, for the words "disposal authority" and "disposal authorities" there shall be substituted the words "regulation authority" and "regulation authorities" respectively, that is to say, in sections 1(4)(a), 2(1), 2(b) and (e), (3)(a) and (e) and (4)(a), (b) and (c), 3(1), (2) and (6), 4(1), (3), (4), (5) and (8)

(b) and (c), 5(1) and (4)(a), 6(1), (2), (3), (5), (6), (7)(a) and (c), (8) and (9) and 7(1), (2), (3)(a) and (8).

(3) In section 6(1) (offences justifying seizure of vehicles), in paragraph (a)(i)—

(a) after "1974" there shall be inserted the words "or section 33 of the Environmental Protection Act 1990"; and

(b) after the word "unlicensed" there shall be inserted the words "deposit, treatment or".

(4) In section 7 (enforcement)—

(a) in subsection (1), for the words from "91" to "information)" there shall be substituted the words "68(3), (4) and (5), 69, 70 and 71 of the Environmental Protection Act 1990 (powers of entry, of dealing with imminent pollution and to obtain information)";

(b) in subsection (2), paragraph (b) shall be omitted; and

(c) in subsection (8), for the words "97 of the Control of Pollution Act 1974" there shall be substituted the words "72 of the Environmental Protection Act 1990".

(5) In section 9(1)—

(a) in the definition of "controlled waste"—

(i) for the words ", subject to subsection (2) below," there shall be substituted the words ", at any time,"; and

(ii) for the words "in Part I of the Control of Pollution Act 1974" there shall be substituted the words "for the purposes of Part II of the Environmental Protection Act 1990",

(b) the definition of "disposal authority" shall be omitted; and

(c) after the definition of "prescribed" there shall be inserted the following definition—

""""regulation authority" means a waste regulation authority for the purposes of Part II of the Environmental Protection Act 1990;"

(6) Section 9(2) shall be omitted.

SCHEDULE 16

REPEALS

PART I

ENACTMENTS RELATING TO PROCESSES

Chapter	*Short title*	*Extent of repeal*
1906 c. 14.	Alkali, &c. Works Regulation Act 1906.	The whole Act so far as unrepealed.
1956 c. 52.	Clean Air Act 1956.	Section 17(4).

Note: The repeal of the Alkali, &c. Works Regulation Act 1906 does not extend to Northern Ireland.

Chapter	*Short title*	*Extent of repeal*
		In section 29(1), in the proviso, paragraph (a).
		In section 31(1), the words from "(other" to "1906)".
		Schedule 2.
1968 c. 62.	Clean Air Act 1968.	Section 11.
1972 c. 70.	Local Government Act 1972.	In section 180(3), paragraph (b).
1973 c. 65.	Local Government (Scotland) Act 1973.	In section 142(2), paragraph (b).
1974 c. 37.	Health and Safety at Work etc. Act 1974.	Section 1(1)(d) and the word "and" preceding it.
		Section 5.
1974 c. 40.	Control of Pollution Act 1974.	In section 76(4), the words "or work subject to the Alkali Act".
		In section 78(1), the words "or work subject to the Alkali Act".
		In section 79(4), the words "or work subject to the Alkali Act".
		In section 80(3), the words "or work subject to the Alkali Act".
		In section 84(1), the definition of "a work subject to the Alkali Act".
		In section 103(1)(a), the words "Alkali Act or the".
		In section 105(1), the definition of "the Alkali Act".
1990 c. 43.	Environmental Protection Act 1990.	In section 79(10), the words following "Part I".

Note: The repeal of the Alkali, &c. Works Regulation Act 1906 does not extend to Northern Ireland.

PART II

ENACTMENTS RELATING TO WASTE ON LAND

Chapter	*Short title*	*Extent of repeal*
1974 c. 40.	Control of Pollution Act 1974.	Sections 1 to 21.
		Sections 27 to 30.
1978 c. 3.	Refuse Disposal (Amenity) Act 1978.	Sections 1.
1982 c. 45.	Civic Government (Scotland) Act 1982.	Sections 124 and 125 and in section 126, subsections (1) and (3).
1988 c. 9.	Local Government Act 1988.	In Schedule 1, in paragraph 1, in sub-paragraph (1) the words "in the application of this Part to England and Wales," and sub-paragraph (4).
1989 c. 14.	Control of Pollution (Amendment) Act 1989.	In section 7(2), paragraph (b) and the word "and" preceding it.
		In section 9, in subsection (1), the definition of "disposal authority" and subsection (2).
1989 c. 15.	Water Act 1989.	In Schedule 25, in paragraph 48, sub-paragraphs (1) to (6).
1989 c. 29.	Electricity Act 1989.	In Schedule 16, paragraph 18.
1990 c. 43.	Environmental Protection Act 1990.	In section 34(3)(b), the words following "below".
		Section 36(8).

Note: The repeal in the Refuse Disposal (Amenity) Act 1978 does not extend to Scotland.

PART III

ENACTMENTS RELATING TO STATUTORY NUISANCES

Chapter	*Short title*	*Extent of repeal*
1936 c. 49.	Public Health Act 1936.	Sections 91 to 100.
		Sections 107 and 108.
		Sections 109 and 110.

Note: The repeals in the Clean Air Act 1956, the Control of Pollution Act 1974 and the Control of Smoke Pollution Act 1989 do not extend to Scotland.

Chapter	*Short title*	*Extent of repeal*
		In section 267(4), "III"
1956 c. 52.	Clean Air Act 1956.	Section 16.
		In section 30(1), the words from "or a nuisance" to "existed".
1960 c. 34.	Radioactive Substances Act 1960.	In Schedule 1— (a) In paragraph 3, the words "and ninety-two"; (b) in paragraph 3, the words "subsection (2) of section one hundred and eight"; and (c) in paragraph 8, the words "and sixteen".
1961 c. 64.	Public Health Act 1961.	Section 72.
1963 c. 33.	London Government Act 1963.	In Schedule 11, in Part I, paragraph 20.
1963 c. 41.	Offices, Shops and Railway Premises Act 1963.	Section 76(3).
1969 c. 25.	Public Health (Recurring Nuisances) Act 1969.	The whole Act.
1972 c. 70.	Local Government Act 1972.	In section 180(3), paragraph (j).
		In Schedule 14— (a) in paragraph 4, the words "107(1) and (2), 108"; (b) paragraph 11; and (c) paragraph 12.
1974 c. 40.	Control of Pollution Act 1974.	In section 57, paragraph (a).
		Sections 58 and 59.
		In section 69, in subsection (1), paragraph (a) and, in paragraph (c), the words "section 59(2) or", and in subsection (3) the words "section 59(6) or" and paragraph (i).
		In Schedule 2, paragraphs 11 and 12.

Note: The repeals in the Clean Air Act 1956, the Control of Pollution Act 1974 and the Control of Smoke Pollution Act 1989 do not extend to Scotland.

Chapter	*Short title*	*Extent of repeal*
1982 c. 30.	Local Government (Miscellaneous Provisions) Act 1982.	Section 26(1) and (2).
1989 c. 17.	Control of Smoke Pollution Act 1989.	Section 1.
1990 c. 8.	Town and Country Planning Act 1990.	In Schedule 17, paragraph 1.

Note: The repeals in the Clean Air Act 1956, the Control of Pollution Act 1974 and the Control of Smoke Pollution Act 1989 do not extend to Scotland.

PART IV

ENACTMENTS RELATING TO LITTER

Chapter	*Short title*	*Extent of repeal*
1974 c. 40.	Control of Pollution Act 1974.	Section 22(1) and (2).
1982 c. 43	Local Government and Planning (Scotland) Act 1982.	Section 25(1).
1983 c. 35.	Litter Act 1983.	Section 1 and 2.
		Section 12(1).
1986 c. ii.	Berkshire Act 1986.	Section 13.
1987 c. xi.	Exeter City Council Act 1987.	Section 24.
1988 c. viii.	City of Westminster Act 1988.	The whole Act.
1990 c. vii.	London Local Authorities Act 1990.	Section 43.

PART V

ENACTMENTS RELATING TO RADIOACTIVE SUBSTANCES

Chapter	*Short title*	*Extent of repeal*
1960 c. 34.	Radioactive Substances Act 1960.	Section 2(1).
		In section 4, subsection (1) and in subsection (2) the word "further".
		Section 7(3)(a).
		Section 8(1)(a).

Chapter	*Short title*	*Extent of repeal*
		In section 12, subsection (1), in subsection (2)(b) the words “of waste” and, at the end “and”, and in subsection (3)(b) the words “subsection (1) or”.
		In section 19(1) the definition of “the Minister”.
		Section 21(4).
		In Schedule 1, paragraphs 9 and 11.

Part VI

Enactments Relating to Nature Conservation and Countryside Matters

Chapter	*Short title*	*Extent of repeal*
1968 c. 41.	Countryside Act 1968.	In section 15(2), the words “in the national interest”.
		Section 19.
		In section 46(2), the words “and (2)”
1973 c. 54.	Nature Conservancy Council Act 1973.	In section 1, subsections (1), (2) and (4) to (8).
		Sections 2 and 4.
		In Schedule 1, paragraphs 6, 10 and 12.
		In Schedule 3, Parts I and II.
1981 c. 69.	Wildlife and Countryside Act 1981.	In section 34(6) the words “and Wales”.
		Section 38.
		In section 43(1A) the words “by the Countryside Commission”.
		In Schedule 13, paragraph 5.

Part VII

Enactments Relating to Hazardous Substances

Chapter	Short title	Extent of repeal
1972 c. 52.	Town and Country Planning (Scotland) Act 1972.	In section 56A(1), the words "and to section 56B below".
		Section 56B.
		In section 56E(2)(e) and 56K(5)(b), the words "or Health and Safety Commission".
		In section 56F(1), the words "and (3)".
		Section 56F(3).
		Section 56H(5).
		In section 56J(5), the words from "other" to "applies".
		In section 56M(3), the words "Subject to subsection (4) below,".
		Section 56M(4).
		In section 56N, in subsection (1)(b), the words from "or" to "would be" and subsection (2).
		In section 56O, the definition of "the appropriate body" and the word "and" immediately following.
1986 c. 63.	Housing and Planning Act 1986.	In Part II of Schedule 7, in paragraph 8 the word "56B,".
1989 c. 29.	Electricity Act 1989.	In Schedule 17, paragraph 37(1)(b).
1990 c. 10.	Planning (Hazardous Substances) Act 1990.	In section 1, the words "2 or".
		Section 2.
		Section 3(6).
		In section 9(2)(e) and 18(2)(b), the words "or Health and Safety Commission".
		In section 11(7), the words "to the conditions that".

Chapter	Short title	Extent of repeal
		Section 13(7).
		In section 15(1), the words from "other" to "applies)".
		Section 20(6).
		Section 21(7).
		Section 27(4).
		In section 28(1), the words "authority who are a" and the words "by virtue of section 1 or 3".
		In section 28(1)(b), the words "or but for section 2 would be".
		Section 28(2).
		In section 29(6), the definition of "the appropriate body" and the word "and" immediately following that definition.
		In section 30(1), the words "by virtue of section 1 or 3".
		Section 33.
		In section 38(2), the words "(being a local planning authority)".
		In section 39(2), the entries for "the 1971 Act", "the appropriate Minister" and "operational land".
		In section 39(4), the words "2," and "and his undertaking a statutory undertaking".
		In section 39(5), the word "2,", in the first place it occurs and the words following "undertaker" in the second place it occurs.
		In section 39(6), the words "and their undertakings statutory undertakings".
		Section 39(7) and (8).

Chapter	Short title	Extent of repeal
1990 c. 11.	Planning (Consequential Provisions) Act 1990.	In Schedule 2, paragraph 82(2).

PART VIII

ENACTMENTS RELATING TO DEPOSITS AT SEA

Chapter	Short title	Extent of repeal
1985 c. 48.	Food and Environment Protection Act 1985.	Section 5(c), (d) and (e)(iii). Section 6(1)(a)(iii). Schedule 4.

PART IX

MISCELLANEOUS ENACTMENTS

Chapter	Short title	Extent of repeal
1906 c. 32.	Dogs Act 1906.	Section 4(1).
1974 c. 40.	Control of Pollution Act 1974.	Section 100.
1982 c. 45.	Civic Government (Scotland) Act 1982.	Section 128(1).
1982 c. 48.	Criminal Justice Act 1982.	Section 43.
1988 c. 9.	Local Government Act 1988.	Section 39(2) and (4).
1988 c. 33.	Criminal Justice Act 1988.	Section 58.

Adapted and published by GRANGIS under the OGL Licence 3.0.

www.nationalarchives.gov.uk/doc/open-government-licence/version/3/

GRANGIS - UK PUBLISHING 2022.
Thank you for taking the time to leave us a review regarding this version

★★★★★

For further inquiries, contact us at:
www.grangis.com / contact@grangis.com

www.ingramcontent.com/pod-product-compliance
Lightning Source LLC
LaVergne TN
LVHW060211210926
848481LV00008B/2693